Your Star Sign

Your Star Sign

Per Henrik Gullfoss
Author of The Complete Book of Spiritual Astrology

Chicago, Illinois

First Edition.
Second Printing, 2023.

Paperback ISBN: 978-1-959883-13-5
Library of Congress Control Number: 2023934709

Cover design by Wycke Malliway.
Typesetting by Gianna Rini.
Edited by Becca Fleming.
Illustrations provided courtesy of the author.

Published by:
Crossed Crow Books, LLC
6934 N Glenwood Ave, Suite C
Chicago, IL 60626
www.crossedcrowbooks.com

Printed in the United States of America.

Contents

Aries

Taurus

Gemini

Cancer

Leo

Virgo

Libra

Scorpio

Sagittarius

Capricorn

Aquarius

Pisces

A Note from the Author

Hello,

This book will be your guide on an amazing journey through the astrological signs.

Being born in one particular star sign shows that you have special needs and ways to express and experience yourself and the world.

This book will teach you how to cooperate with yourself and help you find a powerful and deep contact with your inner being and individual preferences.

You will find methods for creating greater balance and harmony in your life and in co-creation with those around you.

In the same way as the Sun gives life and warmth to all the planets in the solar system, your star sign is your inner Sun that gives life and warmth to you. The vision of this book is to show you how to bask in the warmth and light of your inner Sun.

Astrology divides life into twelve major segments. This book will take each star sign on a journey through these areas of life and show you exactly what you need to know to get the best from yourself and others in every aspect of life.

Life is an exciting adventure. My hope and belief is that this book will be a contribution to making your life joyful, colorful, and magical.

Warmth and love,

Per Henrik Gullfoss

Aries

March 21st—April 19th

Element: Fire
Quality: Cardinal
Ruling Planet: Mars

How to Present Yourself

The Aries often seems strong and secure. Others might believe that Aries knows who they are and what they want and believe that is why Aries is so clear, bold, and direct. But when experienced from the inside, reality is different. Aries functions like a warrior, and it is the immature warrior that has to show off their bravery, guts, and independence all the time. The mature warrior does not have any need to display their strength and security—on the contrary, they seem meek and humble. When the Aries knows their own strength and worth, they have no need to show off. If Aries is insecure and does not feel their power and strength, that's when they find it important to project strength, security, and power to others. An insecure warrior feels safe when others are a bit intimidated and wouldn't dare pick a fight. The truth is that the more insecure an Aries is, the more they will try to make you believe that they are steady, secure, and strong. Another reason for their need to prove themselves is that they need to test themselves against others to understand who they truly are. They can be just as astonished by their own behavior and actions as the rest of us. For Aries, much of life revolves around trying out new things and experiencing unknown situations, not so much to test out the unknown but to test out their own reactions to the new and the unknown.

"*Aha…*" the Aries thinks. "*So that is how I handled that situation. That really tells me something about who I am.*" Do not misunderstand; Aries does not have a weak sense of ego or a lack of identity. On the contrary, they have a very strong sense of identity but are a tad insecure about the consistency of said identity. In a way, Aries likes to be an eternal, curious youngster who looks at the world with amazed eyes. No other sign gets as lost if they try to behave like a responsible, serious, and boring adult all the time. The natural process of acting first and thinking later is embedded in the Aries temperament. Without this spontaneity and the ability to break patterns and do the unexpected, they will become either passive and unhappy or largely mechanical robots. A healthy Aries will know that they need and enjoy being presented with challenges. They need to go along for the ride and be a person that enjoys the adventure of life. They also need others to give them the space necessary to be a bit unpredictable, quarrelsome, and charming in an adorable, innocent, childish way. Aries is born with the grace of innocence. If they use it as a weapon or as a tool for manipulation, that innocence becomes polluted and changes into a river of toxic waste that destroys the purity and clarity of life.

As an Aries, you thrive when you present yourself as openly, directly, and honestly as possible. Hidden games and agendas are not your strong suit, anyway. You will always end up getting caught and unmasked if you try to accomplish things via sleight of hand and trickery, so you might as well show the truth about yourself from the start. That means showing your honest and straightforward side and not sugarcoating your words but calling things by their proper name. If you, like a force of nature, occasionally cross the boundaries of others and step on their toes, just smile your innocent smile and tell the truth—which is that it was an accident, not your intention. You just didn't pay attention to the fact that their toes were in the exact spot where you put down your foot.

How to Get the Best from Your Talents and Resources

You love seeing your energies manifest in reality and as something you can touch and feel. As an Aries, you can have long periods of inactivity and rest, but once you start an activity, you can go for a very long time, not stopping until the job is done.

Aries is stubborn and enduring. They are not very into multitasking and can easily become confused if they have to do more than one thing at a time. This sign can become a little fixated and single-minded about their way of doing things and can suffer from trying to forge ahead, whatever the consequences, instead of using their imagination to see other paths they could follow. They have a tendency to repeat the same procedure again and again. When everything is functioning well, they have a great ability to use their talents to manifest valuable results. But no other sign can so stubbornly refuse to change and try to headbutt their way through obstacles. I believe that it has to have been an Aries who first said that "success is 5 percent inspiration and 95 percent perspiration." Aries has a combination of speed and thoroughness that yields either great results or great disasters.

Often, the Aries likes to start at the beginning or on the bottom and work their way up to the top as fast as they can. They want results and can sometimes get into trouble if they have to do things and use talents that are too abstract. They want to put theories and philosophies into action. In many cases, they find and understand their own talents and value after they have created some tangible result through an effort of pure will. It is by *doing* that Aries realizes what *being* is. The result tells them how the process really was. All this energy and go-ahead spirit gives them a tendency to prioritize quantity over quality. They feel that getting a result is the goal and do not always evaluate the quality of that result.

In the area of pleasure, the Aries also has a tendency to value quantity of satisfaction over quality. Their solutions to challenges and problems can be a bit too simplistic. They can become one-dimensional and naive, lacking the substance that is needed to address a given situation. At other times, their naive simplicity is a sign of genius. The Aries likes things that have lasting value and does not need things to be new and shiny. Since Aries, in one way or another, must reinvent themselves all the time, they will find much joy in old things and traditions. There is a danger—as in everything, for an Aries—of overdoing it. They might become too fixated and stuck. They can take a long time to change directions, but when the change finally comes, it is often very sudden and unexpected. They are good at pushing things forward and making things happen. They are going for results and really enjoy seeing ideas and impulses become reality. The quality of the product is of course connected with the quality of the impulses and the willingness to be thorough. The most important lesson for an Aries to learn is how to differentiate between good and bad ideas.

As an Aries, you are driving your own destiny and enjoy sitting in the hot seat. You want to be productive and engulfed in activity. What's essential is knowing why you do what you do so that you don't take action just so your energy goes somewhere. You need to do things that are really connected with your fundamental values and understanding of what is compassionate toward humans and other living beings on this planet.

Communication and Immediate Surroundings

Aries enjoys the moment, likes to establish contact, and can talk to anyone easily and directly. They can be good at listening, but only when they are truly focused and not busy with talking. They enjoy having a multitude of ideas and connections at the same time. They are curious, full of questions, and want to know and find the answers. They are easily engaged but can be difficult to reach when they are occupied with something. When they are not interested, they can be very silent and show their lack of interest in a demonstrative manner. But once their interest grows, the gears in their brain start turning, and they start talking, it can be difficult to stop them. Their mouth sometimes spews out all the thoughts that go through their mind in rapid succession. Such a wild river of thoughts and ideas might easily be a bit overwhelming for others who feel as if they are drowning in words.

Aries is not an expert at reading signals from others when they are engulfed in their own world of ideas, concepts, and possibilities. Because of this difficulty with seeing the connection between the spoken word and emotions, they can seem quite insensitive, create difficult situations, and hurt the feelings of others without intending to. There is a catch here though because, in the beginning, they do not take what others say personally at all—they are just words. But when an Aries begins to take things personally, they become *very* personal, and easily feels hurt and misunderstood. They may also become like soft, fuzzy kittens—so sensitive and comforting. Aries can be seen as the fearless warrior who fights relentlessly for ideals, thoughts, and justice, or Aries can be the lawyer who just likes the battle and knows how it feels from both sides. The battle is not personal, but any Aries will try to win with all the tools and weapons at their disposal. But be aware: the moment that an Aries warrior feels you are after them personally, the scene changes. They become sad and feel misunderstood. They wonder why you don't like them and want to hurt them so much. They react by showing even more of the armor that makes you believe they can't be hurt by anybody, or else they really stop caring about anything at all. The really mature ones just stop playing at war while the game is still good.

An Aries needs activity and for things to happen. They enjoy seeing new people and generally thrive when they have speed and direction in their daily life. They want a lot of stimulation—but not so much depth and intimacy. They enjoy having some space and do not need to have close friends by at all times. They enjoy light, easy, and superficial relationships because they are simple and more filled with joy and laughter than serious "let us talk about all our emotional problems" relationships. An Aries is not very good at keeping secrets unless they themselves really understand that it's important. An Aries is headstrong and does what they personally think is right or wrong. The shadow side of this self-confidence is that most of the time, they think that they know what is right and wrong for others, too. They need to learn that others have just as much right to choose and to follow their own minds and emotions. The Aries likes words and people who are clever with them. Sometimes, they get seduced by fine words and their own ideas that seem so brilliant inside their mind. Many of them are also good with words themselves. Their greatest challenge is using the right number of words. They can easily end up using too few, such as when something difficult needs to be said, or too many, such as when they are caught up in the flow of their own ideas. The better an Aries masters the noble art of using words in an appropriate number and manner, the easier it will be for them to make friends and feel good. It is beautiful for them to discover that all they need to do to get to the place of understanding what they so long for is to learn to speak and listen in the right way.

Home and Family

An Aries is very connected to their home and family—both the family that they come from and the family they create themselves. Family serves as their roots and the foundation that they need to build their house of love upon. They are emotionally dependent on having someone to share things with and somewhere to belong. It is of essential importance for them to feel that they belong to a human family that they can feel safe and relaxed with. They are sentimental regarding the past and have difficulty letting go of old ties and outlived emotions.

The Aries feels so singular that it is absolutely necessary for them to feel a sense of connection and belonging to a greater whole, such as their family or groups of old friends. Since they are always exploring and discovering themselves and the world, there has to be someplace that they can call home and use as a base for their actions. In truth, their need to be cared for and to belong is just as strong as their need for individual freedom and adventure. In many ways, Aries is the sign that has the most difficulties with growing up and understanding what it really means to be an adult. They have strong ties to childhood, especially to their mother. The Aries often looks for somebody to mother them, which goes for women as well as men. But they revolt against smothering and demand the freedom to explore the world like a little kid. If this is done properly, the Aries will learn not to be smothered by their partner's compassion but rather develop into a mature being that can have deep and significant relationships with other individuals.

Remember that behind the daredevil surface, there resides a great heart that really does have compassion and the ability to care and give. They are extremely loyal to their nearest and dearest and would gladly sacrifice anything for their family, even if they do like to demonstrate their independence from their partner. An Aries in a lasting and loving relationship is much more dependable than they like to give the impression of being. In fact, they often are so vulnerable and emotional that they have to play hardball to avoid being confronted with their own sensitivity. The Aries is rough with people in general but sensitive and soft toward those they really love. Promise not to tell anyone, but when it comes down to it, those born under the sign of Aries are some of the most considerate, thoughtful, and kind people to exist...once they have opened their hearts and dared to let you in. You may think that their homes are too small and have too many things inside, but maybe there is something of the caveman left in this sign. They enjoy the feeling of being enclosed by caves, and since they have a tendency to cling to the past and not throw anything away easily, they enjoy the feeling of stuffiness in their homes.

Creativity and Leisure

This sign simply loves to play. They want to do everything that is exciting and preferably a bit dangerous. They love feeling the flow of adrenaline rushing through their body and never tire of the kicks, big or small, that give them such a wonderful sensation of being alive. Since they want to feel the pulse of life so intensely, normal life might become a trifle boring. Many born in this sign go to extremes just to feel alive. They are not easily bored; they just don't have any patience for boredom. They just have to get something to happen. As the famous writer Henrik Ibsen once said, "Peace is not the best, to want something is!"

For Aries, the most important thing in life is not doing something specific but having something going on. These creatures are very engulfed in themselves and their own needs when it comes to having fun. You cannot have fun on the behalf of others. They know a lot about this compassionate, "being there for others" stuff, but as far as having fun, that is something they have to manage themselves. And they really do feel that life ought to be fun—all of the time. In this respect, they have something important to show and teach the rest of the zodiac. They love attention, the spotlight, and noisy applause. Well…at least as long as they are amateurs; as professionals, they can get in big trouble with stage fright. This comes from the fact that they set very high standards for their own performances. The directness and spontaneity of the amateur are easier for an Aries to manage than a well-rehearsed performance that has to be repeated. They are so eloquent, and when they are in the mood and flow, they can be extremely entertaining and funny. They love making other people laugh and very much enjoy the feeling of sowing the sparks of life and laughter all around. Sometimes it is like they are set afire and can burn a little too hot and heavy for those standing close by. If you want to put out that fire, you can just call them stupid and childish, and say that you find them ridiculous in an unentertaining way. They will react like they have been fatally wounded—or they will become twice as noisy just to spite you and prove that they can be just as stupid as they want.

As a non-Aries, you should remember that it is actually the times when they seem most invulnerable (and a bit manic) that they are most easily hurt, exposed, and left feeling stupid. Few signs can become as sour or brooding as this sign. They like vacations that are full of energy and activities—beneath the pillows, if nowhere else. They just love flirting; they are energized when others find them attractive and love to dramatize and show their feelings with grand gestures. They do not always have to go all the way, but they love the energy and the electricity that can flow between people who are sexually awakened by each other. They are a bit like crows who like everything shiny, everything that radiates energy and light. They love to play with the playful and love to tease the serious. One of the greatest gifts an Aries can give is to share their naive spontaneity and enthusiasm with you. In fact, you may think they can be a bit too much and take up too much space. But fear not, the smaller you try to make them, the more space they will take up… but the more you allow them to shine and open up, the more space you will have. In fact, there will be more space for you than you had by yourself.

Health, Order, and the Necessary

The transition from party time and fun to seriousness and routine happens in the blink of an eye. It is like someone suddenly flipped a switch and everything changed. Since this happens so abruptly and suddenly for Aries, the rest of the zodiac can have difficulty with the sudden change and feel like they have been left behind in an alternate universe. In daily life, Aries is a perfectionist and can obsess over details, forgetting the big picture. Sometimes they see the goal and forget what happens on the road. Other times, they become so preoccupied with something that they forget where they were headed.

One of the most important skills for Aries to learn is to know *what* should be done and *when*. There is a time to forget self-analysis and criticism and just go for it. There is a time for details, for being acutely aware that great projects can be destroyed when small things are overlooked. At certain moments, the most important thing is to be aware of your own shortcomings and see what you need to do to develop further. At others, it is more important to believe in the possibility of miracles and throw yourself into the unknown like a daredevil. Generally speaking, the Aries needs to be thorough and check every detail in the planning stage of any undertaking. They will always get the best results when they are well prepared. This is often the most boring but still very necessary part of work for Aries: planning, preparing, and applying common sense down to the smallest grain of salt. We can see Aries as a high jumper, because when you first start the actual jump, you need to relax, totally forget your brain, and trust your instincts. If you try jumping with your head, it doesn't work very well. They can benefit enormously from training and preparation. The Boy Scouts' motto "Be prepared" is fitting for any Aries, but as they throw themselves over the edge of the cliff, they have to be able to grasp the situation in the blink of an eye and trust that they will know what to do without having to stop and analyze everything.

An Aries will create difficulties health-wise if they are discordant in their expression and actions. They can be incredibly healthy…that is until they suddenly become ill. It is important for them to be aware of their symptoms so that they can make the necessary corrections before they hit a wall. Because of their intensity, small disturbances can easily become great problems, so it is important to be aware without making every small disturbance into an overwhelming problem. Aries enjoys having what they feel is order and structure in their surroundings and a rhythm of living. Since stuff happens very quickly, it is good to know where things are when they are needed in a hurry. They are good at adapting to circumstances and can be excellent employees. They are also very good as inspirational leaders. Their difficulty lies in playing different roles at the same time. They thrive when they have clear rules and know their exact position in the game and hierarchy. When they are completely safe in their position—whether as goalkeepers, attackers, or defense players—their guts, enthusiasm, and creative intelligence will serve them best. It is so good for them to feel absolutely secure in their position and their relationships with coworkers and the system. Then, they can just relax and do what they are best at—having fun and enjoying both life and the moment in a way that is of great benefit to themselves and everybody around them.

One-on-One Relationships

Aries is on the lookout to find someone they can attain balance with. They need a partner and other close relationships with people who display the qualities they personally seem to lack. Often, this leads to finding partners who are so different from them that the relationship becomes close to impossible to maintain. In some sense that is okay for Aries, because their most important mission in life is not finding peace. It might swing the other way around as well, meaning that they may find a partner who is very similar to them. In reality, this might be an even more problematic relationship than the two odd ones together. Such a relationship can easily turn into twice the same challenges and lack of harmony. To solve this problem, Aries has to go for both dynamics at the same time. They have to seek out partners who are similar and different at the same time. They have to be able to play the same game on the same field but in ways that are just different enough to make things interesting. Be sure that if an Aries lacks a partner, they are hunting for one.

They are independent and need a lot of freedom, but they are also very much in need of a mirror to use to discover themselves. They need someone who can tell them what they see and what they do and verbalize what they perceive. Aries easily falls in love and goes for it 100 percent every time. They wish and intend for any relationship to last for life and do not easily leave a partner. As a rule, they are loyal, faithful, and romantic souls. Their partner may, on the other hand, start to wonder what the relationship is about or what they really are doing there. Aries is not always the best at showing others that they care in the long run. They can easily take things for granted as time goes on. They might even have problems with seeing the needs and reality of the other person. They will benefit from working with themselves to understand that a relationship requires more than just being around each other—that it takes a lot of work to get closer and deeper into each other's hearts and realities.

Sharing their inner world at deeper and deeper levels is almost always a challenge for an Aries. The immature Aries just wants a partner to give them balance and the necessary support so they can go on to open themselves up more freely. The partner becomes a support system for them instead of a real partner to share with. It is important for Aries to give the relationship enough room and attention to grow and unfold. They also need to know that quarreling with their partner is okay because they will be friends again. Aries needs to work on finding that sense of equanimity. If equality is missing, the relationship will be an eternal struggle for power and control. The Aries needs a partner that can handle it when they change from strong and powerful to childish and naive in a matter of seconds. They adore partners that are beautiful, sophisticated, and socially successful. There is always something wild and raw in Aries that looks for the smooth and civilized in others. Through being honed and refined by their partner, the Aries learns about the true depth and beauty that are created in the meeting between human souls. When they open the door to this world of love, they gain access to a new and endlessly rewarding realm of true love and compassion.

Beneath the Surface—Sex and Taboos

This sign just loves to break taboos. They enjoy letting the primitive and instinctive take them to new territories as they explore unknown terrain. In this area, Aries is truly fearless. They march directly toward the dark taboos that other people try to avoid or look away from. If an Aries wants to stay ignorant about the hidden and dark sides of themselves, however, they will project those qualities onto another person and talk about how dreadful that person is. An Aries is incapable of keeping things down and out of sight for long periods of time, but they can easily believe that their own garbage belongs to others. One indicator of this is how often they get into conflicts with other people whom they perceive as untrustworthy. The more often they go to war with others, the more they dump their shit on them.

As an Aries, you are both effective and ruthless when war is being waged. If things get dirty, you are prepared to use all the dirty tricks in the book—and even invent some new ones. There is just one thing that interests Aries when the battle is on, and that is *winning*.

This sign does what it does with intensity and totality. They can be incredibly lazy or destructive if they are predisposed to those qualities, or they can carry out a great and thorough cleaning of their inner world if that's where they decide their focus lives. They prefer activity, high voltage, movement, and new experiences. They are not so well suited to sitting silently and pondering life or just digging into their inner emotions without acting out. For most Rams, the animal to which the Aries zodiac is assigned, *being* without *doing* is an anomaly. They want adventure, and if battle and fighting are necessary steps on that golden road to a happy ending, they are more than willing to keep walking. If this means that they have to battle their inner demons, they do so as intensely and with just as much focus as they fight their outer enemies. Some of them do discover that the r battles are more fantastic, unpredictable, and enjoyable than outer quarreling. They find such an inspiring and endless richness in the inner world and know that it is a far greater and more courageous task to fight inner demons than to be the tough one in the outer world.

Their sexuality follows the same pattern. It can be wild and animalistic, totally blocked off and almost armored, or a deep and intimate search for melding. What their sexuality never looks like is lukewarm and halfhearted. This sign doesn't do lukewarm. They can be moralistic and focused on what is immoral, or they can be very busy tearing down fences and breaking taboos—without much in between. They are erotically stimulated by a partner that fully displays their lust. They like people who are direct and clearly show what they want and enjoy. That silly game with acting uninterested when you actually are is of no interest to an Aries. If you want intimacy or sexuality with an Aries, show your lust. They are seldom shocked or scared. They feel rejected if you take too much time to linger and don't get to the point fast enough.

Know that the time window is limited with an Aries. You have to act in the moment and not wait for a second or third chance. The train has probably left the station without you if you did not catch it as it passed by. And remember, Aries is capable of depth and longtime commitments to their heart and those that they love—commitments that go far beyond what most people would believe from watching what they show on the surface. This sign is willing to go all the way, so be prepared for a long ride if you really are getting under their skin.

Education, Adventure, and Life Philosophy

An Aries likes the feeling of being educated and knowing their business backward and forward. Usually, they are enthusiastic about their chosen path in life and have clear and defined goals. Often, they are treading a path connected to something that has to do with morals and justice or something connected to faraway places and different life philosophies than the ones they learned in the community where they grew up. In certain periods of their life, they seem to be very anarchistic, and it seems like they are doing whatever they think is right at the moment. In other periods of their lives, they are very into law and order and think that everybody has to abide by the same rules. They can be very eager when creating rules and standards or very busy with taking care that others follow the rules. Likewise, they can be very irritated by those same rules and become busy breaking them.

One thing that all Rams will learn through their professional life is how the rules work. What happens when you follow them blindly and what happens when you break them? This is some of the wisdom taught to all people with this sign throughout their lives. An Aries seldom runs around trying to do ten things at a time. They most often give themselves a target and follow the road to the end. When they have finished one project, the time is ripe for another and another. We could say that their basic nature, as far as projects and philosophies go, is not polygamy but rather serial monogamy. The Aries wants to really know, learn from, and understand the topic they are into. It is not just about knowledge and getting results, but also about learning and gaining wisdom and insight.

More than anything else, Aries loves to move toward the unknown and explore new horizons. They seek the beautiful and the great. If someone wants to be the hero riding into the sunset on a white horse, it is Aries. They love to experience the world of myths and that which is greater than the small world of daily grievances. They are hunters for the true meaning and the real content that lies behind the outer appearance. But often, they just want the happy-go-lucky version of depth on the heroic journey. If they have to work shoveling dirt in the stables, that can be fun for a while, but not as a vocation. They often really want to avoid the pitfalls in their inner areas in the search for wisdom. In some sense, they want wisdom without paying the price that is often extracted through pain. Most of them love traveling but are often stopped from doing so because they have to do so many other important things. In many ways, Aries has just a single enemy: themselves. When they fall, it is because they trip over their own legs and tumble down. Every Aries has to learn the noble art of choosing and sticking to what they have chosen. Because of this, it is important for them to learn patience. If you grab the first and best thing that comes along and then are stuck with it for the rest of your life, it might get a bit boring and annoying. And Aries has to remember that it is not luxury or success that is their prime goal, but the fight and the wisdom acquired along the road. As long as life has meaning and what they do is significant, they can just as well be poor and live simple lives. If they do not follow their own truth, they can be rich and successful but still really unhappy and dissatisfied.

As an Aries, you have to let go of the reins every now and then, and just observe what kind of sunset and mountains your white horse brings you to. The essence of your wisdom and education is to learn to trust your instincts. Life unfolds in great, enriching, and unpredictable ways when you let go of all the planning and just allow yourself to accept and follow that which unfolds.

Goals, Profession, and Career

Mostly, people with an Aries star sign are very ambitious, methodical, and systematic as far as their career goes. They leave as little as possible to lady luck and hold all their cards in a tight grip. They are hardworking, prepare themselves thoroughly for each task at hand,

and have their eyes set on their goal from the minute they begin the race. They can be very enduring and are known to have and accomplish their five-year plans. They might change and reconsider as they are on that path, but only if their goal is discovered to be an illusion or if the methods they have been deploying turn out to be inadequate. Another possibility that can persuade an Aries to change directions is when they have reached their partial goals and the result does not live up to their expectations.

As leaders, they are very responsible. They make it clear to everybody where the power is and that they are willing to use it when needed. At the same time, they work harder than most of their employees in order to show that they really deserve to have the position they have. Sometimes, they can take a bit too much responsibility and try to control everything, instead of knowing how to delegate both work and responsibility. This comes from the fact that they often believe that they are the only one who really knows how to do it right and that if they want something done to their full satisfaction, they have to do it themselves. In this area, they are almost always well prepared, and little is left to chance or spontaneity. They are methodical and often follow well-known prescriptions for success. They have more originality in their goals than in their methods. An Aries boss is often a bit old-fashioned and can become insecure if things change too quickly. They enjoy having clear chains of command and knowing exactly what goes on in every link of the chain.

Aries is best suited for hierarchical structures where everybody has their defined place and task. They easily become confused and uncertain if things are undefined and there are hazy lines around who has responsibility for what. They are not the best at social games but thrive when hard work and honesty are what matter. They need a job where they can rise up and where effort is rewarded. They enjoy rising in the hierarchy and want to be respected and admired for their work. Beneath their devil-may-care attitude, they have a heart that swells with pride when they get praise and appreciation. They need demanding and challenging work where they have to stretch their abilities and use their resources to the fullest. They enjoy being overachievers—which is more sympathetic than being a person who does something unimportant or uninteresting. They perform best under pressure and need to be self-reliant and independent in their profession.

The ability to make your own decisions and evaluations is one of the things that makes an Aries a good boss. As an Aries, in your professional life, you are very capable of putting aside your personal interests and doing what is best for everyone. It is important that you respect the rights others have to evaluate and decide what to do just as much as you demand the right to do so yourself. Without cooperation, you may find these aspects to be at best problematic, and at worst, impossible. As mentioned, you will thrive in a place where you can rely on your own decisions and instincts—or at least a place where the chain of command and individual responsibility is well and clearly defined.

Friends, Future, and Ideals

This sign can attract a strange bunch of friends. They like people that have special qualities, but one of each quality is enough. Because of this, it is quite common for this sign to have friends that do not get along well together. It can work out very nicely if the divergence between all these people enables them to open each other's minds and lives to new and interesting ideas and areas. An Aries might have one or two very close friends, but they enjoy having a whole bunch of friends where each serves a special purpose. The friends they have are in many ways a reflection of all the contrasts and diverging interests they have in their own life. An Aries can also be completely satisfied with having and serving a special purpose for their friends. Like being a drinking mate for one and a fishing/shopping mate for another.

Aries is a very tolerant sign as far as the private areas of life go. If an Aries judges people, it is not because of who they are, but because of what they do. Aries will give everybody a fair chance, regardless of nationality, sexuality, or belief. But if a person has proven unworthy of the trust, the friendship is finished, regardless of nationality, sexuality, or belief.

An intolerant and discriminating Aries is equally intolerant of and discriminatory toward everybody. When they have formed a conviction and a negative opinion about a person, social group, or anything else, it goes deep and will be hard to get rid of. One strange fact is that when an Aries has changed a belief or opinion, they hardly remember that there was a time they thought something different. In a sense, they live in the moment and believe that what they think and hold as true in the present is what they always have and always will hold as true.

On the other hand, this sign is a natural optimist as far as the future goes. They believe that everything can change and that everything will be better at some point in the future. They enjoy having plans and visions. If they are not totally engulfed in their own minds or in the work they are doing at the moment, they are naturally inclined toward idealism. But common sense and fixation on what works and the logical next step may easily block their idealism from being put into action. They really do want to create and live in a better world but have problems understanding how that theory might become reality. They are not easily led into believing that dreams are real or that it is common sense to bet all your money on the nicest horse. Instead, they feel that the right thing to do is to use any existing opportunities to the fullest, and thus explore the roads that are open to travel. Creating a better world has to wait a while, and they often accept that it is their secondary—not their primary—goal in life. (The primary being to *live* in the moment.)

Action might be very sensible, but Aries loves to talk about all the possibilities that exist in the world and how it really should be organized. In theory, they enjoy riding that white horse to grand possibilities and utopia. Often, they feel that they are on a quest for justice and that they are in opposition to the system and enjoy fighting for the downtrodden. In reality, they are just going for their piece of the pie like most others. A more mature version of this sign sees the glitches and accepts the weakness of the system, while at the same time, they do their best to improve it. They accept their own shortcomings and take a more honest look at the role they themselves play in the grand scheme of things. In a way, they combine their common sense and acceptance of the situation with their idealism and vision of making the world a better place for us all. In this case, the Aries does not think that something is wrong with the world and just howls and complains to the Moon with the rest of the pack. They see a lovely world that can be even better and fairer and more fantastic than it already is.

Seeking and the Spiritual

In the universe of an Aries, anything is possible. The probable truth and reality are one thing, and the possible is another. When they move into the realm of spirituality, they become just as fascinated and engulfed by that as by anything else. A spiritual Aries has to work hard just to keep one foot on the ground. When the doors to the inner world are open, they are wide open. Since the dimension of spirit is so vast and unlimited, they can have some "small" problems with separating one universe from another. The ability to believe is unlimited for an Aries. When they are connected to the physical outer world, they believe in an individual's ability to create their own reality and they believe in the laws and rules that are applied to the physical world. As they move their beliefs into the spiritual, these limits disappear. An Aries needs structure and clear-cut frameworks to be able to orient themselves and get things done. At the same time, they know that the structure is something they have created to make the world more surveyable. They can view their own life as something happening within a sandbox, but the moment they leave the sandbox, they must learn to use and trust tools other than logic and knowledge. They must trust their intuition, which is quite strong when used and very absent when not. They have problems with doing more than one thing at a time. When the intuition switch is on, the logic switch is off, and vice versa. Logic and common sense often pick a fight with the intuition and inner guidance of an Aries. It is an important task for this sign to learn to listen to both at the same time.

In the depth of their inner world, Aries knows that love is the force that penetrates and is the origin of everything. They also know that they are visiting Earth to learn how this love functions and to learn what happens when it is not working as it should. This is simple for an Aries. The difficult task is understanding how to get this source of love to function properly when it is channeled through an individual ego identity. Understanding this is the spiritual road and task for their souls of this life. All the rest are just pieces in the puzzle; this is the big picture. They need to experience many different sides of life to solve this puzzle, and their intensity is just a tool used to dig deep enough to catch the one true realization that is sought by all born in this sign. How does love function in this world? How can one love both that which is new and unknown and that which is old and known?

As an Aries, you have a great longing to learn how you can surrender to the force of pure love without losing yourself. How can you be true to thine own self, enjoy being so, and explore the world...and at the same time be a channel for love and let that love flow without guilt or shame? Your road to love goes through three steps.

To find yourself...the discovery.
To reveal yourself...the freedom.
To give yourself as a gift...the love.

Taurus

April 20th—May 20st

Element: Earth
Quality: Fixed
Ruling Planet: Venus

How to Present Yourself

Taureans like to be seen as reliable and trustworthy. They want to come off as harmonious, creative, and energetic. While some people believe that a Taurus's outward calmness stems from passivity and lack of initiative, it actually comes from the fact that they are good at hiding what is really happening beneath the surface. Only people who are closest to a Taurus are invited to swim in the whirlpools that are gushing through their inner emotional world. This sign puts great care and importance into being seen as a valuable person of high quality. They like to look good and to have a pleasing appearance. They want to seem natural, so they try to enlarge and expose their natural talents and beauty. Normally, this sign is not too fixated on outer beauty but rather is occupied with the outer form that allows true inner beauty to shine through. Taureans look best clad in simplicity.

They like to be seen as productive doers. They want to be that person you really want to be seen with, that person you invite to things so you can show others just how valuable they are to you. Taureans will be very insulted if you hint at the possibility that they are not going to fulfill their promises. They might be slow to give concrete promises, but once that promise is made, Taureans will move Heaven and Earth to fulfill them. They so want to be reliable and trustworthy. They can be seen as stubborn (and often are). This comes partly from their sense of reliability. If they have said "yes," then they are stuck with the "yes." Of course, the same goes in the case of "no." This sign might seem a little slow but remember that they often just are slow starters. Once they are up to speed, they keep on going faster and sometimes reach an amazing velocity. They might be called the semitrailers of the zodiac. They are heavy and gain speed slowly and do, of course, need a longer time than most in order to slow down and stop as well. So, you see, when they are at maximum speed, they just roll on, and it is definitely not advisable to try to stop a Taurean that is moving down the highway at full speed. All toreadors know this. Taurus does not really want to harm anyone, they just don't want to be stopped. Apart from that, they are mostly kind, good-tempered, and friendly— until someone waves the red cloth, of course. So be careful not to be a hindrance on the road, even for the kindest of Taureans. They have so much power and weight invested in their movement that it can be very difficult for them to avoid hitting you.

This sign does not like to be pushed or stressed. They want to take their time but enjoy arriving too early rather than too late. Taureans like to talk about things that are real for them but enjoy doing things together with others even more. Every so often, however, the Taurean really wants to just be left alone. When they are interested in you, they will show it clearly and strongly. They don't play games and act like they're not interested when they actually are. They do not even know how that game is played. If you are a hindrance, you might easily feel like that irritating flea they want to squash. As a Taurean, you will make the best impression on others by just being yourself, which in this respect is the only thing you are really good at. You are, however, "allowed" to underline your natural talents and advantages without exaggerating.

How to Get the Best from Your Talents and Resources

This sign is loaded with talents and the need to use many of them. Taureans like to explore new areas and prefer doing things that grant some kind of mental freedom. It can be difficult for Taureans to choose since they often want to have both of everything. They are pulled in many directions and are curious to discover what they are really good at. Exploring their many talents is a life theme for this sign. Even if they seem stuck, it is just because they explore all alternatives thoroughly and they never cease to amaze themselves with their own diversity and curiosity. If you believe they have a one-track mind, you have to look closer. Hidden beneath that steady surface they are planning and exploring a multitude of realities and possibilities. Their mind is constantly working on developing new thoughts, concepts, and ideas that will expand their opportunities—especially their opportunities for using and earning money by manifesting their talents into reality. Every Taurean wants to use their talents and capacities to the fullest, and this ability to exploit their own resources down to the last bit might be their greatest talent. Taureans are creative and productive and want to do things in their own way and by their own methods. At the same time, they are very adaptive to outer circumstances that create the framework they have to work within if they want to use their talents. They are good at getting the best out of every situation.

Their values are, in that respect, often flexible and change as the situation is changing. They have what is called an "adaptive value system." They understand that they have to go with the flow of possibilities and are practical idealists at their best. At their worst, they are ruthless opportunists. In some sense, they adopt the values that give them the most opportunities for doing and getting what they want to do and have.

Why is growth so important for this sign? Because without it, they become so terribly stuck and bored. They really have an ongoing need for something or somebody to explore—or for somebody to explore something new with. Since their value system is in so many ways flexible, they need to have other people around to help them understand and adjust to social standards. Sometimes they become unethical without seeing or knowing it themselves. In that respect, they are in need of moral guidance and input from the world.

As a Taurean, you need to be aware of the fact that both your needs and your values change as the years pass by. What was right, nice, and ethical when you were six is not necessarily that when you are sixty. On the other hand, you are never too old to change or get a fresh start. One of your strengths is your youthful drive, which tells you that it is never too late. As a Taurus, you know that you are never too old to do anything and you are genuinely surprised to discover the fact that you, at some point, will become too old and fragile to perform as you did in your youth. But most of the time you are right: you are never too old.

Communication and Immediate Surroundings

This sign likes intimate conversations. Closeness, depth, and soul contact are conversational fodder for Taureans. They enjoy tears and talking about feelings, needs, and the inner realm of life. This goes for both men and women born in Taurus. They enjoy when they are needed and can show compassion through their words. This sign does not fear physical closeness. They enjoy touching and often do so—they just can't help themselves sometimes. Touch is an important part of how they express and orient themself in the world. Often it is easier for them to talk with their hands than with their words. Feelings are more easily expressed this way than through a bunch of words. It is nice to remember that they enjoy intimacy, even if they, at times, talk very little about what they feel.

When they are relaxed, they easily express their love and intimacy in daily life—unless, of course, they have hidden inside a shell. If Taureans feel rejected and unappreciated, they might become the most closed off and emotionally inaccessible of all beings.

As a Taurus, you are vulnerable to the words of others, and your ability to communicate and express your inner world is very dependent on your feelings in the here and now. Sometimes you have an almost endless capacity for talking about feelings and all that is important—and sometimes it is very hard and painful to express anything at all. Taureans may have problems in conversations where the words are just words, and an emotional exchange is absent. They enjoy having a deeper, more emotional exchange, which gives them a feeling of safety and security. It is like they have to know that you feel well and enjoy their company to feel safe themselves. When this contact is absent, Taurus might become very practical and matter-of-fact or distant and cold. When Taureans speak and listen, they are more tuned in to the feelings being emitted than the content of the words being used. Often, they are considered to be good listeners. This can cause a lot of misunderstandings because, as mentioned, they often haven't heard the words at all. They might know everything about your emotional state and how you feel but have missed the intellectual content and the meaning of the words you have spoken completely.

If you are frustrated, angry, or irritated when you talk to a Taurean but are angry at the subject of discussion instead of the Taurean, they will still feel hurt, confused, and sad. They have a tendency to take the feelings you radiate while you talk very personally. And remember, what a Taurus says to you is always personal and loaded with feelings and thoughts that are meant specifically for you. They can feel rejected if you do not catch the real intentions and feelings behind their words. With all these opportunities for misunderstandings, it is not strange that Taureans often choose to keep their mouth closed. This is a pity since they can be experts in deep and personal exchange when they have mastered their own sensitivity and understand how emotional they are. For them, it is a given that what they tell you is personal and not supposed to be spread to others. They do not even ask you not to tell it to anyone—you are supposed to understand that implicitly, and if you "violate" their trust, they just stop giving it.

It is a good thing for this sign to be surrounded by people they know and are familiar with in their daily life and doings. They like big changes, but not too many small ones. On the other hand, they will often keep you at a certain distance from their heart unless they specifically choose to open the door. They want to be the master of who and when they love.

As a Taurean, you need to learn that real intimacy and communication go both ways. It is not enough that you feel safe and know everything about the feelings of others, you need to share your innermost feelings, longings, and fears with them as well. You have to learn to not just be the caretaker and receiver but to show and share yourself as naked and vulnerable as you really are.

Home and Family

If there is a sign that created the saying "my home is my castle," it is Taurus. They simply love to be the reigning monarch in their own home. They want to be the main person inside the fort and crave full freedom to be who they are and do whatever they want in their own home. They do not like any kind of limitations on what they are supposed to do or not to do in their own space. They do not want to feel like they are subordinate to anybody, be it their spouse, their children, or their dog—don't mess with the chief! As they develop, they can learn to find solutions that are based on equal rights and worth, but never subordinate—never. On the other hand, they enjoy being admired by their spouse, children, dogs, and whoever comes by. They often feel that there is one person who has real responsibility for the family, and that is them. They are responsible for taking care of it and making sure that it survives and gets through tough times. In this respect, they easily fall into the role of the cliff of Gibraltar. They feel they are the rock and foundation of their little kingdom, and they are partly correct. No one can build kingdoms and foundations that last for eternity as well as Taureans can.

In their heart, a Taurus believes that in the end, the only being they can trust 100 percent is themself. Sometimes, they have a tendency to believe that the same goes for others—that they (the Taurus) are the only person others really can trust. So, they have to carry the worlds of others on their shoulders like the Greek hero Atlas. What they need to understand is that everybody must learn to trust themselves and that everybody can take real and deep responsibility if the need arises. It is important for this sign to avoid making others addicted to them and helpless without them. It is also important for every Taurean to train in the noble art of learning to trust life in general and others specifically. The true service this sign gives their closest ones is helping them become just as independent and self-sovereign as the Taurean can be when they take responsibility for themself instead of others.

One of the reasons Taureans are so occupied with safety is the belief that they have to provide all of it by themselves. They do not easily trust that anyone else can give them that. They often strive for inner safety by trying to control and master everything in the outside world. The real trick for this sign is to start with acquiring an inner feeling of safety. As that is achieved, they can begin to breathe more easily and let go of the need to control their outer circumstances.

Taurus learns by doing things from scratch. They learn about inner life and what true feelings and safety are by taking full responsibility for their own feelings and needs.

It is not through recognition or fame that Taureans find their true self and inner sanctuary, it is through their own acknowledgment and the experience of their inner identity and trust. Being respected by their loved ones means so much; being respected by the general public means nothing. Taureans must learn to trust their own inner authority. They need to know that deep down they respect themselves for what they are and what they do. They need to have this absolute trust that they will do what is true and right for them, whatever the conditions and circumstances. They will not find the right path through life by looking at the possibilities that exist outside. They have to look inside and then do what provides them with the most self-respect. When they have found this basis of respect and trust in themselves, they can easily carry the world on their shoulders without getting tired.

Creativity and Leisure

Taureans are specific when it comes to holidays and what they want to do for fun and joy. Many things that others find stimulating and interesting; they find boring. Some of them prefer to have as little leisure time as possible, since time off means time to think about what they really want to do in life, and this could even turn into some sort of self-analysis. It is so much simpler to just do what one enjoys without thinking too much about it. On the other hand, this sign is at least as occupied with doing things perfectly when they do things for fun as when they do things for work. In fact, they are even more critical of things they do just for fun. Professionally, they are satisfied if the product is good enough and meets the necessary standards. Being creative and doing things just for fun is much more demanding and dangerous. When you really express yourself, you have to be sure that you get a good result, because what you create tells the world about your individual values and quality. Beneath their calm surfaces, Taureans are really striving for recognition and admiration. Most of them are very creative, but they have to confront their fear of not being good enough. They evaluate themselves so strictly that they, at times, become unable to open up and reveal their creativity. As children, they might have some problems with understanding the difference between play and reality. Taureans just hate losing. They are benevolent when they win but are often really sore losers.

This desire to be admired and seen as competent often makes Taureans very proficient at their hobbies. They often begin doing things as an amateur and end up working in that area as a professional. Their real education comes through life, not through school. A happy Taurus is a Taurus that combines their love of being excellent and doing what they really love with their love for earning money. On the playful side, Taureans do enjoy flirting and love the innocence of flirtation, but most of them avoid taking the risk of getting rejected. They are not so good when it comes to dirty tricks and sordid stuff. They play cleanly and can be stupid and charmingly naive. If you want to get closer to a person of this kind, the best way is to be simple, honest, and tell the truth. Lies make them cast you off. They only accept lies from people who are very close to them and for reasons they can understand (like not wanting to hurt the ones they love). When Taureans must do necessary chores in their spare time, they often work like they get paid for every drop of sweat. This comes from the fact that they want to finish as quickly as possible so they can enjoy doing nothing for the rest of the day. The same goes for the way they approach other people and pleasures: either fully focused and totally involved, or bored and visibly uninterested. Small distractions and things out of order can totally destroy the pleasure of a Taurus. If there are too many *ifs* and *maybes*, they often get bored and lose their lust before the fun even gets started. Trouble and criticism make them run in the other direction, so if you want a Taurus to perform, it's better to use the carrot than the stick. If the fun of doing something has disappeared, why should they bother doing it at all? Well, if they get paid, that's another story. But fun is for fun… and that is final.

Many Taureans meet so much resistance and carry so much responsibility in their professional lives that they try to avoid everything that seems unpleasant in all the other areas of life. As a Taurus, it is important that you learn to accept some discomfort and resistance, including when you do things just for fun. Let other people know that just as you like to finish your work undisturbed when you decide you want to be alone, you want to stay alone until you make the decision to get up and get going.

Health, Order, and the Necessary

Taureans have a rather superficial relationship with health and neatness. If it looks nice and clean on the surface, it is okay with them. They do not fear illness or messy stuff, even if they prefer beauty, harmony, and order. Other people worry more about the health of Taureans than they do themselves. Taurus is more occupied with having a good time than being overly healthy. Often, you will hear them say that "to do what you really enjoy is what keeps you healthy and fresh." As we know, this is not always the case, but Taureans often have a really good time on the road to bodily decay. Most of them would rather have fun and pay the price than never have fun and stay healthy.

The most important reason for their eventual health problems is their tendency to enjoy luxury and laziness. They really enjoy the good life and often need some motivation—like money or a post-activity reward—if they are going to do something they find boring and unpleasant. On the other hand, the visual is important for them, and they enjoy beauty. They might even consider staying healthy because they want to look beautiful. In this area, they are more influenced by vanity than common sense. Taureans can be really bothered by shrill voices and other kinds of disruptive noises that disturb the peace. Many of them prefer either silence or listening to music as they work. Many of them are listening more to the tone of your voice when you talk than to the words you say. The result is that they very often know exactly how you feel but do not really know anything about what you think.

Germs and other things that are invisible to the naked eye do not bother them at all. Most of the time, they do not believe in what cannot be seen or touched, and germs are no exception to the rule. Most Taureans are hardy people and can take a lot of the stuff that makes others sick. But sometimes they forget that they have a limit and push themselves over the edge or expose themselves to far too many unhealthy things. Do not let yourself be fooled into believing them if they try to be tough and say that beauty is of no importance to them. They can live with the crude and primitive, but that doesn't mean they do not enjoy the exquisite. They can enjoy eating a lot of simple food but do also have a fine palate and know how to enjoy all kinds of different flavors. In fact, they enjoy enjoying things and like to taste a lot of everything. What they do not enjoy is having to end the game when they are having so much fun. They want the pleasure to never stop and often fall victim to the dangers and hazards of some prolonged enjoyment such as overeating.

They know how to get their life in order when they want to impress or satisfy someone. By themselves, they do not really care, but when they learn that their success and work can give real pleasure to others, they often find it worth the trouble to do the work. They are occupied with being inferior to no one and at least equal to everybody. They do not like conflicts or trouble, especially not at their workplace or when they are doing something important. In fact, they have very romantic notions about work and their workplace. They do a lot of things to make others happy and easily believe that they are liked and loved for the work they do. They can be blind to professional jealousy and the real intentions of their bosses and coworkers. In many ways, Taureans are naive and honest, and can easily be exploited and taken advantage of by more crafty beings. At times, they have problems with doing things that serve their own interest. They easily become so occupied with being loved and liked by others that they forget what they really love and like to do. A Taurus that has true balance will create and share beauty and harmony with their fellow human beings and at their workplace—not because they try to do it, but because they are filled with it.

One-on-One Relationships

Relationships are a deep and challenging matter for this sign. They long for a relationship that is magical, intense, and passionate, but they also strive for easygoing, cozy stuff.

Relationships are the arena in which Taureans meet the aspects of themselves that they are otherwise too friendly and civilized to experience. The partner to this star sign will always be a remarkably good mirror to the Taurean's shadow side. This might come from the fact that the partner wakes up unknown parts of the Taurean's psyche or because Taureans project the parts of themselves they do not acknowledge onto their partners. This can be seen as something terrible or as fortunate and positive. These relationships give them the chance to become more conscious and to bring up resources and qualities that so far have not been seen or utilized. But, of course, they can also be a living hell where the partner is seen as the devil and the source of all problems for the Taurus. A partner can inspire this sign to let go of old patterns, change, and become better on a deep level.

Close relationships are of great importance for this sign because otherwise they easily stagnate in their old patterns and habits. Taurus is often emotionally dependent on their partner and has difficulty with letting go and breaking off connections where they have invested so much of themselves. They tend to linger on, even when a relationship has become stagnant or destructive. This is because they know that if they tear up the roots of the relationship and leave, there is no way back. Leaving is a one-time thing for this sign.

A Taurus has a tendency to get involved with people who have a strong and intense emotional life. It seems that this intensity makes it possible for Taurus to gain access to their own deeper feelings, which otherwise are hidden beneath their calm exterior. Another facet is that this intensity might be overwhelming for the Taurus because it disrupts the peace and harmony they search for. They can also easily feel that their partner is trying to own them and often attract the jealous type. Some of them become very jealous because the prospect of losing someone whom they are closely and emotionally connected with is very scary. One sign that their love is deep and true is if they are willing to accept that someone has wounded them badly, but they still want to go on with the relationship. As much as possible, they prefer to avoid hurting or being hurt by others. Another sign of deep love from a Taurus is if, after hurting someone deeply, they are willing to stay with them and take the blame and experience the pain that they feel instead of running away. One of the most painful and difficult things Taurus can experience is being responsible for hurting, disappointing, or wounding the ones they love.

If you are a Taurean, it is important that you do not sacrifice your own needs and wishes to avoid hurting your partner. You really do need to have the faith and strength to believe that your partner's love is strong enough to withstand and hold that which you really are. As you learn that you are worth loving—with all your shortcomings, hidden sides, vices, lusts, and unpleasant thoughts—you will truly learn to open your own heart and soul and give of them fully. For you, love is to completely accept another human being. When a relationship is so intimate and deep that you no longer have any demands, conditions, or terms, you can relax completely, because you can fully trust and surrender to the power of love.

Beneath the Surface—Sex and Taboos

Taurus loves taboos. This sign enjoys trying what is forbidden. Where others need a reason to say yes, Taureans need a reason to say no. Well, at least when it comes to the possibilities of the sensual pleasures that life has to offer. Taureans also find power exciting. They do not necessarily enjoy obvious power where everything is visible, but rather appreciate the hidden power that controls money and resources. Many beings born in this sign enjoy this game, and they also enjoy having secret connections, powerful friends, and influence. As mentioned, they feel more comfortable with secret, hidden knowledge and power than the power that others can see and learn about. In this sign, there is a constant longing for more, which can be seen as greed—or just the search for new experiences. This inner hunger often makes them go on long after they are otherwise satisfied and fulfilled. This hunger can be about food, money, honor, fame, wisdom, or spiritual experiences.

In many ways, there are no taboos for this sign. On the surface, there might seem to be a lot of them, but most Taureans think that what people do not see or know about is none of their business. Their respect for taboos is mostly connected to not getting caught. In fact, their values are extremely flexible, and so are their ethics. It all boils down to what works! Therefore, what they want or don't want to do is not connected to taboos or others' views of the situation. In fact, it comes down to what they really want to do, whom they want to be, and their very personal ethics.

This sign often has a unique relationship to sexuality. At times, they might have a strong sexual drive; at other times, they may not be interested at all. For Taureans, sexuality is a sensual experience and something to do for fun. Whom they are having sex with is not so important, but the sex itself has to feel like it is filled with body and soul. The physical and spiritual are much more important than the egos involved. And often, to them, sex is not so different from a good meal: you need to have a good reason for declining it. In some ways, sex is far from the most intimate thing a Taurus can be involved in. For them, showing their deepest feelings, their vulnerability, and their economic status is far more intimate. The most intimate thing this sign can do is to trust you enough to give you the ability to hurt and reject them. Sex is just the spice, and why be faithful to one kind of spice? The kinds of sexual relationships they do have are founded on their personal ideas about right and wrong and the depth of their emotional life, although most Taureans stay faithful because they are loyal and do not want to hurt the feelings of others. Another very important reason for staying faithful is their fear of losing their security—but that loyalty very seldom comes from a lack of physical interest in others. Faithfulness is a choice for this sign.

The dangerous taboos for this sign are hidden deep within the Taurean psyche. Those taboos are connected with telling others what they really think, believe, and want. Taking a chance on showing their naive, childish, immature, and absolutely trusting side is very dangerous for them. For a Taurus, telling other people what they truly want or long for—from the bottom of their heart—and then taking the risk of not getting it is terrifying. They enjoy showing others their good sides and successes but letting people see their shortcomings and failures is downright scary. Sharing their deepest personal hope, longings, and visions with another person is something a Taurus only does with people they trust and are willing to let into the most secret chambers of their hearts.

Education, Adventure, and Life Philosophy

This sign likes to have a goal for their actions. They want to get results, learn from their travels and wanderings, and use what they have learned to create something valuable. They can have a very highly developed life philosophy, but it will always be founded on what works in this world. For them, play is not just play, nor adventures just adventures. Play and adventures are part of their education, the building of their character, and the great plan for their own existence. They can see life like climbing a mountain, and when they finally reach the summit, they will have reached fulfillment. Life might have *some* striving in it, as it often does when a person wants to fulfill something…like their destiny. They like to finish what they are doing before they go on to the next step. Even unpleasant things have to be finished before they can let go, and once the job is done, of course, the result has to be applied in a useful way.

The danger with all this striving for usefulness is that they might risk ending up in a situation where an education they did not want has landed them a job they aren't interested in, leading them to live a life they do not really want. It is like climbing a mountain just because it is there and not knowing why or what you are going to do on the top. They are known to work toward new horizons in a systematic and persistent way. When there's a result that they are satisfied with after having done the job, then they can rest, since they are really tired after climbing up that long, steep hill. They are not overly stressed or hurried and do not crave much fun on the road, but beneath this relaxed slowness, they really want to find something to do that gives them deep meaning and satisfaction. In a state of exhaustion, they can relax and feel that they deserve to rest and enjoy the luxury of just being and enjoying life. Having worked hard gives satisfaction in itself—it just isn't that satisfying to take the elevator up and cruise back down.

Confronting challenges and getting pressured to use their talents and resources are necessary for opening the sensory apparatus and developing the skills of this sign. They need to sense and experience everything themselves before they can understand and appreciate it. The wisdom and insight they eventually gain have to be embedded in the cells of their body and brain in order to be something other than a superficial idea. Real understanding for a Taurus is not about mental things but about deep bodily acknowledgment. They know with their guts and heart and hands, not with their brain alone. But the inner adventure of a Taurus always has to be played on the outer stage. Just living in the world of fantasy is nothing for them. They can't fulfill themselves through romantic dreams and fantasies. They do not even want to escape the real world, they want to transform it into something better. They want to build the castles of their dreams with flesh and blood. They are easily seduced by the outer world, but at the same time, they are deeply touched in their inner world by the outer. In this way, the outer world becomes the adventure, and the adventure becomes reality.

It is important for this sign to not become stuck in a fixed outer dream of their inner reality. They need to develop their ability to go deeper and deeper into nature and the magic and mystery of physical reality if they do not want to become stuck in a world that is dull, inflexible, and unchanging. They can be tremendously enriched by understanding that the world of their senses serves as the doors and keys to the magical dimensions that belong to realms other than the one that most of us call reality. When this sign does become spiritual and takes magic into their heart, it is because magic and the spiritual are absolute and real for them. They do not believe in belief; they believe in knowing the truth of their own heart and experiences of the outer, as well as the inner.

Goals, Profession, and Career

This sign might seem to be conventional and dull in their choices of professions and careers, but they do inevitably make their own twists and turns in everything. They can seem to follow the beaten path, while in fact they seldom do—they are just very good at pretending to be normal. If they happened to have a completely normal job and only completely normal interests, they would become so obsessed with it that they would go far beyond the limits of what is thought of as usual. In some ways, they are so normal and sane that it takes them into completely unexpected and insane places in life. Often, Taureans feel like they are the only sane person in a world that seems to be a planetary asylum. They can be extremely interested in adjusting and try to erase their own identity to feel at one with the group or the cause. On the other hand, they often go in the opposite direction and do everything by themselves and on their own terms. It is a bit of an either-or. They have this strange combination of being fixated and dull, while at the same time open-minded and ahead of their time. They want to develop, enhance, and create new systems and connections. Most Taureans need to learn how to really cooperate the hard way and they can only get this cooperation to work if they are connected to a group of individualists.

When they have become fixated and stale, it is next to impossible to make them move or change their opinions. If they are headed for the cliff and do not want to listen to advice, just let them go. Sometimes, the only way a Taurus can learn is to experience the catastrophe and total loss of safety and footing. They often believe that they have the best plans in the world. They easily think that they have the best solutions not only for themselves, but for everyone else, too, and that is maybe the greatest arrogance of this sign.

Their visions and dreams can often be beautiful and practical at the same time, but they have to learn to stop and listen, both to others and to the world at large. Despite being such a practical and down-to-earth sign, they can be tremendously naive when comes to what is possible to create here and now. Reality is not just about what is theoretically possible within this reality of time and space—it is also about emotional reality and seeing people. In this area, Taureans are known to be blind and have a hard time understanding the darkness and ugliness that sometimes is found inside people. They need to learn to see people as they truly are, not as they can be at their best, and must learn to cooperate with people as they are. Many Taureans find it difficult to accept and understand the true nature of other humans and become stuck in theoretical systems where they work hard and sensibly but do not really thrive or get ahead. They are clever but easily held captive by loyalty, good intentions, and faith in the goodness of others.

As mentioned, this sign is a practical realist but emotionally naive and easy to fool. To find their true path through life, they need to go their own way and find their own truth and direction. They have to take a chance and explore the unknown if they are ever going to get to know themselves and use their capabilities in a satisfying manner. They can be good at founding new enterprises, as they often have great visions and the ability to work hard to make them a reality. If a Taurus has a clear and defined goal, their determination and endurance will give them a great chance of reaching the goal they have set for themselves. Often, they build up such speed and power that, although they are slow beginners, they surpass their goal by far. Because they have such momentum, once they reach their goal, it takes a long time for them to apply the brakes and slow down.

Friends, Future, and Ideals

In the eyes of Taurus, the universe looks like a cornucopia, filled with endless possibilities and opportunities. In their dreams, they can imagine any possible abundance. This can make them greedy and unable to stop grasping for more and it can lead to a quagmire of disappointment and hopelessness. The logic is simple: if life has so much joy, abundance, and love to offer, why can't they get it all? But there is a problem with both how to achieve all these possibilities and how to find enough time for them. The Taurean knows that they can only be in one place at a time. This longing to fill themselves with all the things and experiences available results in our Taurean friends, through lack of limits, having severe physical or psychological problems. Either because they are trying to stuff themselves with too much money or food or because they have driven themselves so hard that they are burned out. In some sense, Taurus tries to conquer the future by taking it into their system—they may literally try to fill themself with the world. They have this drive to realize all their needs and longings as manifestations in the outer world. Harmless daydreaming is not an option for this sign. They can be without dreams…or else they want to build their dreams in flesh and blood. Taureans may have problems with their perspective on time. In some sense, they do not believe in the future. They are focused on the big, hairy now, and that which exists in the now fills their horizon. What is not manifested in the now is just some hazy illusion outside their experience. Since they know that everything is possible, it is difficult to understand that something isn't possible just now. This is a difficult concept for Taurus to understand. If they are ever going to get the rich and fulfilling life they desire, they must find the balance between reality and the possibility of creating something that does not yet exist. They may just as easily end up as disappointed and severely limited realists as disappointed dreamers. They can even manage to be both at the same time. This sign benefits greatly from getting into contact with their inner longing for physical paradise and then realizing that their destiny is to slowly work toward manifesting it in outer reality. They are not here to bring Heaven to Earth, but to move Earth closer to Heaven. They are here to start with reality and bring what is in closer alignment with what can be. Reality is expanded through practical dreaming. Understanding the difference is important: they are not here to escape to some heavenly paradise, but to make what exists in the inner more visible in the outer. If paradise were served on a silver platter, Taureans would probably not notice it, or maybe just find it boring. They feel joy and bliss when they manage to stretch and move toward paradise. The bliss comes when they are creators of their own fulfillment. It is not just the state they are after, but the feeling of being creators and the value of creating beauty…for both themselves and others.

Most Taureans have problems seeing the difference between egoism and altruism. They feel in their hearts that what is good and beautiful for them is also good and beautiful for others—and vice versa. Taureans easily love all life and humans, including their enemies. This ability to love is one of their most important qualities and gives them an edge in the work of aligning physical existence with paradise. If you want to be friends with a Taurean, know that you can't have them to yourself. You have to share—but that doesn't mean that you are less loved. Know that if you have a friend of this sign, they are loyal and enduring beyond imagination.

Seeking and the Spiritual

It is said that those who seek will find. As far as Taurus goes, this is very true. They possess some kind of spiritual wisdom, yet at the same time, it seems absent. Taureans have a natural understanding of inner dreams and sensations. They have easy access to the magic of nature and the miracle that is Earth, life, and the physical. On the other hand, they have difficulty accepting that which is beyond their senses. They are not convinced by, and often not even interested in, theoretical thoughts and concepts around the spiritual. Like everything else, spirituality must be lived, practical, and "sensible" for it to matter to a Taurus. This sign is not a great believer. They have a tendency to disbelieve until they have a personal experience that makes the spiritual a manifested inner reality.

As noted, if Taureans do not seek, they will not find. Spirituality does not fall out of the sky for them. They have to go and get it themselves, like most things they want in life. Taurus might be seen as the sign most strongly attached to reality as it is experienced in the moment. If they want to expand their understanding and experience, they have to take a chance and move outside the known. This can be scary and difficult for a Taurus. How do you find something when you don't know what it is or where to look? To seek the spiritual is a game of pure chance for this sign. They have to move into unknown terrain and be prepared to gain nothing. In fact, they have to live with the possibility that they are moving into a realm that does not exist and that it is just a wild fantasy that exists only in their imagination. There is absolutely no guarantee of either success or reward. The force driving them must be a longing to understand and to expand reality, as well as a deep *knowing* that more exists in this universe than meets the eye. Taureans have easier access to the fertile and sensual Earth goddesses than the flaming Sun gods of our times. On the other hand, their experience of the sacred and spiritual in nature is so self-evident that they often naturally sense it as divine. But a flower, a tree, and a rock being in some sense magical and holy is not evidence of the existence of gods or a greater spiritual reality. They have to get into contact with their own burning and passionate spirituality to begin to fathom, acknowledge, and integrate their spiritual heritage and belonging.

For this sign, the road to spiritual unity is always an individual one. By integrating spiritual individuality in themselves, they can begin to fathom the collective force of love that unites us all. In some sense, this sign is spiritually rewarded for their effort and willingness. They are paid for the work they do—as mentioned, seek and the reward is that you will find something. As a Taurus, know that there is no way to undo the steps you have taken. This is one of the reasons why Taurus may be careful with moving forward on the spiritual road. Once they have accepted spiritual reality or some aspect of it, it is no longer a belief but rather the living truth that exists inside them. Once they have found it, they must accept the consequence of their findings. They do need to live in daily life and the physical world in accordance with their spiritual understanding. They are lousy Sunday believers. Either they know about the spiritual every second of every day, or they do not. They are unable to put away what they have found. When it is part of their being, it has to be lived, and that is the true spirituality of a Taurus...it is who they are that matters, not what they say or think or preach about. Spirituality is a practical reality that must be manifested through their being—just like all other practical realities.

Gemini

May 21st—June 20th

Element: Air
Quality: Mutable
Ruling Planet: Mercury

How to Present Yourself

Gemini, the Twins, want to show the world that they are "dancers." They love the lightness and game of thoughts, words, and all kinds of exchanges of ideas. They want you to see their happy and joyful side. They want you to laugh and to be so mesmerized by their play that they can covertly look deeper and see behind your outer appearance. In this way, they can learn who you really are behind the mask—without giving away their own deeper self.

It is easy to believe that a Gemini is nothing but this superficial, airheaded child, but be aware: they also have a totally different aspect to their personality. If you pass the tests and endure the wait, you will be shown the other sides in bits and pieces. They test you because they do not want to let everyone see their deeper side which can be as dark and scary as the visible one is light and bright. Gemini likes to solve things with their agile minds, and when the truth is spoken, they are often a bit scared by, and quite insecure about, their own sensitive and vulnerable depths. They love to act like children. The reason is that they are a bit insecure around grown-up or adult stuff. What does it really mean to be a grown-up? Is life not supposed to be fun? And this responsibility thing, what does it mean to be responsible? Does it mean to have the answers and stop asking questions? Well, then Gemini is only moderately interested in growing up because their whole fun is based on asking questions and trying to find the answers. On the other hand, Gemini does love to play at being a grown-up. They change roles as others change clothes—and by the way, they also change clothes more rapidly and more often than most other beings in the zodiac.

They have a special knack for adapting to circumstances and the mental capacities of their surroundings. We could call them mental chameleons and they enjoy the shapeshifting that makes it possible for them to talk to everybody about everything. They are curious in things such as the difference between green and blue fighting fish. This ability to find everything interesting makes them well-liked and people often feel that they are easy to get to know. But be aware: Gemini often learns a lot about you while you, in fact, learn next to nothing about their inner workings. You know that you are getting beyond the layers and establishing true contact with these dancers when they start to talk to you about their emotions. You are even more trusted and close when they show you their true feelings. By themselves, Gemini does not recognize the need for all this sentimental mumbo-jumbo. They just want to be seen as mentally alert, smart, and someone to have interesting conversations and experiences with. Gemini likes to spread information and joy to their fellow human beings; that is at their heart.

As a Gemini, it is important that you learn to say what *you* really think instead of wanting to entertain others all the time. Your ability to communicate then becomes a real vessel for true communication instead of a mask you hide behind. It is fun to surf the waves, but take care that you do not become afraid of swimming deeper or finding out what keeps the boat afloat. By nature, you are a naive optimist and you shall live as that, but you also have a great need to withdraw and get untangled every now and then. Then you will have the time and ability to explore who you really are and listen to your heart. Often, the radio of the mind is so busy that it drowns out the voice of the heart. As long as you are tuned into the frequency of your heart, it is appropriate for you, as a Gemini, to express yourself through laughter and lightness.

How to Get the Best from Your Talents and Resources

Being talented and smart is a sensitive and touchy area for Geminis. They do not see talents as something they have, but as something they are. Because of this, they might be afraid to show their abilities openly to others. In fact, they are quite shy in their own showy way. It is easier for them to care about and nurture the talents of others than to really care for themselves. They are scared shitless by the possibility of being rejected and criticized when they use their own talents. Words are often an impersonal game for them. Geminis aren't hurt if somebody disagrees with them, but if they do something and you mention that you think what they have done is bad or lacking, they become personally wounded. This sign must be quite brave and has to feel safe in order to show the world their creations.

It may seem strange to some, but the values of a Gemini are linked to their ability to create safety, love, and care. This is the case even if they use their mouth to do it. This sign needs emotional stability to develop their talents. This may also seem strange but just think about it. Since they, in many ways, are unstable, stability is what they need to grow and expand. Often, they love to know a little bit about everything. Really diving into the depths of knowledge takes time—they seldom dig deeply, but rather accidentally sink into the depths from the weight of their amassed knowledge. They will vacillate between phases of low self-esteem and feeling like they are the geniuses of the world.

Geminis have a strange relationship to speed and consumption. One aspect of a Gemini has great velocity and consumes the things around them as fast as lightning. This side of them can be wasteful and sifts through a lot of things just for the fun of it. The other part of them is quite restricted and cautious. What they relate to through the mind falls into category one; what they relate to through the heart goes into the second. If a Gemini seems to be careless around money, it is because they do not connect money with emotional safety or lasting values. The more stingy and economically careful Geminis have an emotional relationship with money that makes them feel safe and valuable.

Gemini isn't very good at doing things alone or in silence and needs company and emotional bonding to be at their best. They crave support and can be fabulous at supporting their friends and loved ones. It is important for this sign to have friends that can support and protect them when they go into the vulnerable and unstable areas of their inner landscape. Developing the mental realm is piece of cake for Gemini—but the emotional scenery is something totally different and much more troublesome. This contrast easily manifests as one set of theoretical values, ideas, and opinions that are in conflict with Gemini's emotional and practical needs and reactions. Often, they feel torn and insecure because they experience themselves as unable to live up to the standard of their own ideals and expectations. If they want to develop an inner sense of security and maturity, they have to take the trouble to learn how theory can be implemented as praxis. They will benefit greatly from taking responsibility for their own actions, including responsibility for their own finances. It is not good for Geminis to be dependent on others for prolonged periods. They need to learn to be their own grown-ups, ones who can allow their inner child to play around.

Communication and Immediate Surroundings

Geminis love being constantly on the move, understanding each of their environments, and being familiar with everything and everyone around them—at the same time, they must know that things are moving and changing. They do not find pleasure in standing still. As children, they often got extra attention just because they were so cute, charming, or witty. That gave them a feeling of being interesting and special. They love attention and praise and are adaptable, seeming to float through conversations, but be aware: they do listen, and they take you more seriously than it seems. They do not show it, but they are easily offended and quite vulnerable to your opinions about them. In fact, they never forget if you have said something that really insulted or debased them.

Gemini likes to feel significant to the people in their social environment. In fact, they are quite proud, and if they feel unappreciated, they just vanish. They love talking a lot and give their total attention to whomever they are speaking with—either by listening as if your words are the most important thing they have ever heard or by speaking with the same intensity. They are fun to be with because they give those they are with that same feeling of being special and important. Yes, they even know how to make you feel lucky that you are getting so much attention from somebody as special and knowledgeable as they are. As a Gemini, you need to be aware of what can happen when you change the direction of your light. In this situation, a person who is used to standing in your spotlight might feel terribly overlooked, forgotten, forsaken, and abandoned. This is one of the reasons why Geminis can hurt and confuse people around them without knowing what the heck is going on. They really need to get a grip on how and why other people react emotionally and learn that verbal reactions and words do not necessarily tell the truth about a person's emotions.

Geminis are brilliant at praising others and talking about good, fun stuff, but they have to study hard in the school of life to learn to talk about difficult things. In many ways, they are good mirrors:

they respect people who respect themselves and are skeptical of people who are skeptical of themselves. In some ways, they seem like they float on the surface, but in fact, they reflect that which shines through from a deeper place within others. Geminis seem to adore strength, success, and power in others, but in fact, they just admire those who have the guts to be who they really are. This quality is something Geminis look for in themselves, and because of that, seek it out in others—who always are a mirror for this sign. For them, the saying "show me your friends and I can tell you who you are" is quite true. All the same, they do need to be careful. Since Geminis have so many contrasts and differing opinions spinning around inside themselves, they can put a little too much confidence in the solidity of others.

Gemini does not always tell the truth but is very good at talking to children and older people. They do not consider it a lie to withhold what they think or feel about a situation or person. They tend to avoid the trouble that telling the truth can create. On the other hand, they are very good at building self-esteem and a sense of possibility and optimism in others...at least, until reality comes rolling in like an unstoppable train. They are proficient at finding the right theoretical solutions—but practical reality and real life are another thing.

As a Gemini, you benefit from both seeing how good you are at making others feel good and knowing how important it is to face the unpleasant sides of life. Do not avoid challenges or problems for too long. They just grow and become larger and hairier. And remember: the most important thing is not that other people like you, nor that they like themselves, but that you respect yourself.

Home and Family

Geminis can be very fussy as parents. They enjoy having clean and organized homes and want their children to be nice, cute, and well-behaved. These ideals sometimes collapse in the face of reality, and the fact is that their homes and children might become quite chaotic at times. They are known for worrying about family matters like no one else. They can become both overly careful and overly protective. As mentioned, their need for order and sensible control in this area is so great that they often try too hard and create a situation of chaotic helplessness instead. As parents, they almost always question themselves and search for something they should have done better. As a matter of fact, they want to be perfect parents, and anything less feels inadequate.

The truth behind the scenes is that they are insecure and feel too immature for the job. Their demands are so huge that they get exhausted just from thinking about all they should have done. When you are exhausted from just thinking about all the chaos you should have tamed, there is little energy left to actually do the work needed to create the perfect order that exists inside your mind. Well, the only way to go in this area, for a Gemini, is to either be one of the few totally flawless superhumans that are said to exist on Earth or accept that life is always an adventure into the unknown—this also goes for parenting and family life.

Geminis like to have many friends but a small and tight-knit family. Family is very special to them, and the bonds of loyalty and belonging are strong and valuable. Often, this sign is depended on by the family. They can end up as the little helper that takes care of everybody else, like the child living with their own parents and caring for them in the twilight years of their lives. They feel great responsibility for their family and can be overly worried when something is wrong. Just the thought of something going wrong can unsettle them and make them very nervous. The dual nature of the Twins is, as always, clearly demonstrated. They want to be free and independent from family ties, but also crave the closeness and intimacy that those family ties offer. They are not as good at standing on their own two feet as they pretend to be. It is like their independence needs deep anchoring in a system where everything is stable, organized, and safe. When the family system is safe and sound, they can be very free and independent, because they have the knowledge of this deep belonging. Very often, the only people who know about the heaviness, anxiety, and worry that burden the seemingly easygoing butterfly of a Gemini are close family members.

Gemini often has a multitude of interests they cultivate at home. They like to learn new skills and enjoy being occupied, entertained, and free to pursue their interests. A Gemini that becomes passive and indolent in the home is an unhappy Gemini. By nature, their activities and interests are diversified and thinly spread across many areas. They can have difficulty concentrating on one subject for an extended period but enjoy doing a multitude of tasks at the same time. Most Geminis love the atmosphere of old times and antique objects, but at the same time, enjoy the newest and hottest thing. Consequently, their homes are often a strange mixture of sentimentality and futurism. They do not easily throw things away, so they collect piles of stuff connected with beautiful memories. They feel a great love for the people they invite into their homes and to be part of their family life. In this area, they prefer to have emotional safety and security rather than excitement and surprises.

Creativity and Leisure

Gemini likes doing things together with someone. They are neither very inventive nor very independent when it comes to doing things by themselves. They are in dire need of inspiration from interacting with others. They want to discover the unknown in known company. Their creativity is connected to having fun and experiencing beauty, joy, and harmony. They can easily become a bit codependent on their partners in creation.

When Geminis are in discord, they fight intensely against everything they experience as unjust, patronizing, controlling, or destructive. They can even become violently against violence. This sign always strives for equality and equanimity in all aspects of their relationships. They enjoy playing with others immensely and are experts in the noble art of flirtation and seduction. One of their hobbies stems from their chameleon nature—that is to become what someone wants them to be. They can become what is in your dreams…or if you want them to…your nightmare. Their task is to avoid being caught up in one aspect of their nature and to see that they are *one* chameleon, even if they change colors all the time.

Geminis are, in many ways, simple creatures who do not crave too much depth or serious emotion. They thrive within simplicity and can find the superficial enjoyable. As a group, Geminis are the zodiacal experts on understanding the social game. Where others get caught in the play, Geminis are freed by it. The rules that go along with social conduct and relationships give them the guidelines they need to be free to play. They can show more of their true self when they are given the rules and limits of the social game. Without those frameworks, Geminis become unsure about how to conduct themselves in social situations. When they do not know whom they are allowed to be and what they are expected to feel, they become insecure.

For the most part, Geminis are polite, well-behaved, and precocious as children, possessing a vocabulary far beyond their years. But be aware: being a grown-up is also characterized by a special way of using words and gestures. Gemini learns the game easily and enjoys playing but can have difficulties understanding what being a grown-up means emotionally and practically. Grown-ups may easily believe that the Gemini child understands more than they actually do, and so expect more from the child than the child has the maturity to handle.

If you are the parent of a Gemini, it is important to see the differences between mental and emotional maturity. There is often a deep split in the Gemini's inner world between their understanding/mentality and their experience/emotions. Using play and their free time to find a balance between the mental and the emotional is beneficial and important. They need space to develop their emotions and feelings, as well as their ability to think and speak. This is maybe the main motivation behind the creative play of Gemini: to find and create the perfect point of balance between thoughts and emotions. For this sign, creativity and play are as serious as life can get, and finding this balance is necessary if a grown-up Twin is to ever be satisfied with life. In fact, this balance is the foundation that Gemini needs to find if they ever want to grow up at all. If they have to carry out mental work, like being around the written or spoken word, they need to use their spare time to take care of their emotional needs and longings. Even if they should happen to be a single mother with three children, they need to use and develop their minds and ability to think like a grown-up in what spare time they have. As always, they enjoy the game the most when they can keep their balance and avoid crashing into their surroundings.

Health, Order, and the Necessary

Being caught up in daily chores can be challenging for this sign. Geminis can feel anxiety at the thought of going through the motions for the rest of their life. Having order and taking care of all their necessities can feel both terribly constraining and like an impossible task for these fun-loving butterflies. Keeping track of all the small details can seem like just too much for a human being. On the other hand, they can have strong and intense feelings about how things should be done, and the pressure of all that having to be done by a certain time is crushing. Some Geminis just close their eyes and overlook what must be done. They prefer roaming in the inner realms of their emotional fantasies over being present in the outer world. Others seem obsessed with getting everything done and are doing chores and tasks without end. They do not know when to stop or how to take a break and thus end up burning themselves out.

A Gemini's ability to function in their daily life and work is a perfect mirror of how well organized they are in their emotional realm. If a Gemini wants to clean up their act, the way to proceed is always to begin with cleaning up their emotional life and any feelings that are stuck and rotting in their inner landscape. Clean up the inner garbage, and the outer garbage will miraculously disappear. Geminis need to accept themselves in an emotionally healthy way. Fulfilling the dreams of others never fulfills their own. They have to take responsibility for their own emotional satisfaction! They need to examine their fear of being bad or guilty and start taking responsibility for their true feelings and inclinations. Most of them feel guilty when they disappoint others, so they often disappoint themselves to avoid disappointing anyone else. No one has ever become happy or fulfilled through that kind of behavior. Geminis need to accept that they are fallible humans and respect their own true feelings and needs. Gemini has a remarkable capacity to see the underlying emotional reasons for the behavior and shortcomings of others. They have this radar that senses the emotional states and challenges of others which gives them a great capacity for understanding and helping other people with their problems and challenges. This understanding makes them very good at cooperating with and leading others. For Geminis, the greatest challenge seems to be cooperating with and leading themselves—giving themselves the same understanding and leniency that they give to others. The challenge for this sign isn't to see or verbalize the diagnosis, but to see, accept, and make the needed adjustments to address the deeper reason for the problem.

Health for a Gemini is directly connected to their emotional state and is especially influenced by suppressed and repressed feelings. As a Gemini, one of the best things you can do for your health if it's a problem, is to acknowledge your true emotions. If you have severe health issues, psychological treatment will often be the approach you need to follow to restore your own health. The road to fixing physical problems for this sign goes through neither doing nor thinking, but through feeling and getting in contact with the true emotions and love in their hearts. As mentioned, they are often invaluable helpers for others and even enjoy digging deep to find the answers hidden behind the outer facades. This curiosity and eagerness often make Geminis go into jobs like journalism and research of various kinds. But they need to remember that they can't fix themselves! They are wolves when it comes to facing the outer and inner fears of others, but mice when it comes time to face their own fears. There is a simple rule they can follow if they want to have good health and enjoy the bits and pieces of their lives. They have a tendency to try to be the one that others want them to be, but the rule Geminis really need to follow is to do what they love and to be whom they love themselves for being.

One-on-One Relationships

Gemini is in search of lively, opinionated, and visionary relationships. They want others to give them answers and to have clear opinions and viewpoints. This stems from the fact that most Geminis have a large collection of questions. For the most part, they are optimistic, naive, and a bit gullible. They have this belief that everybody really wants the best for everybody else. This is their reason for seeing the best in others—at least before they get to know the other person too well. It is difficult for Geminis to understand that others can be negative and even mean without proper reason. They love to meet new people, especially people with a lot of thoughts, ideas, and opinions. They enjoy being with others who are engaging and interesting. Mostly, they enjoy listening as much as talking, especially if the people they are having a conversation with talk about interesting experiences in an entertaining way. The sharing of stories is often more important than the emotional content that is behind the sharing.

Geminis love a good story and find it far better to have an entertaining tale than to stick to the truth. What is truth, anyway, if not just a viewpoint? Other people are like fairy tales for a Gemini, and as we all know, fairy tales do not need to be true or written according to the rules of logic. In some ways, intimacy with unknown people is easier for a Geminis than intimacy with those they know well. In a meeting with the unknown, there are no layers of old misunderstandings or irritations that can come between them and the other person to create distance. Taken from another point of view, they feel safest with a certain *lack* of intimacy. They are easily overwhelmed and upset if another person wants to share deep feelings with them all the time. In a sense, they feel closest to those who accept that they live in their own distant world of ideas and dreams.

On the other hand, having an intimate two-way discussion and connection is not reserved for a Gemini's intimate partners. They can easily feel just as close to a newcomer as to someone they have known since childhood. True intimacy for Gemini is to openly show the other person their boredom and dullness. Sometimes, this makes close relationships very complicated. Lasting intimacy with the same partner, day in and day out, easily leads Gemini into boredom and dullness. An ideal partner for a really good relationship with a Gemini seems to be a person who constantly expands and opens new horizons on their own. Stability makes a Gemini long for change, while eternal change feels like stability. They need a partner that explores the world by themselves and then shares their new discoveries. Another possibility is a partner who becomes the ever-unchanging foundation that gives Gemini the security and stability that makes it possible for them to be ever-changing and unstable. In that case, the frame they build together with their partner is the base that keeps these partners together. It is neither individual that is seen as the most valuable, but what the two of them create together.

Gemini does not thrive with jealousy and suspicion. For the most part, they can grant great freedom to their partner—and need to get the same trust and loyalty in return. If there is a lack of trust, they feel strangled and imprisoned, like a butterfly that does not have room for spreading its wings. To a Gemini, a partner is—more than anything else—someone with whom they can experience and share the adventure of life; a traveling companion with whom they can dream and discuss everything and explore new horizons in the outer and inner worlds.

Beneath the Surface—Sex and Taboos

In this area, Gemini can be strict and dominating. Intimacy and deep emotion are not only to be taken very seriously but are a dangerous area where Geminis feel vulnerable and are highly self-conscious. As mentioned, they might be easily bored in relationships, but feel very offended if their partner does something that shows a lack of respect for them. Being emotionally dependent on anybody is quite scary and overwhelming for a Gemini. They need clear rules for conduct and very strict morals in this area. The rules have to be very distinct and unwavering: it is in no way okay to have sex or make serious financial transactions without your partner's knowledge and acceptance. Gemini needs to be able to have complete trust in their partner as far as the big topics are concerned, partly because the smaller lies are abundant and even a part of the joyful game. They can accept when you come home six hours later than agreed upon, but not that you have used half an hour of that time to have a sordid little affair. Of course, unless you have an agreement about small, dirty affairs not being dirty at all, but just a spicy part of the adventure of life.

Geminis, who are quick and in a hurry in so many areas of life, often have a sexual stamina and staying power that is surprising. When they have self-confidence, they enjoy building excitement step-by-step. The other option is to suffer from great performance anxiety and stay away from the whole business of sex. Surprisingly, they feel a great responsibility and take great care if they have access to others' money and resources. That is, they take great care as long as they feel somewhat free to do as they like. If things do become nothing but pure pressure and compulsion, they may just give hell and let it all slide without any control or restraint. Generally, this sign is one thing or another: either extremely reliable and sensible or not reliable or sensible at all. They have a remarkable loyalty to those people they have taken into the depth of their hearts. They will stick with their friends and loved ones in any kind of crisis or trouble…but be aware: when everything is like sunshine, they may run away with the first and best flower that they find. They will never forget you if you have been really close to them and their friendships last forever, even if their relationships may end. Often, this sign feels embarrassed when others see that they are a bit prudish, conservative, and moralistic. They want to be seen as free and unrestrained birds. They often hide their inner structure, organization, and discipline from the public. They might react strongly to anyone that tries to organize and discipline them because they have repressed their own inner seriousness and rigidity. One of the reasons that many Geminis avoid responsibility and shun authorities is that if they themselves ever get responsibility or become authorities, they take it extremely seriously.

As a Gemini, you need to know that if you take up a responsibility, you must be willing to carry that responsibility for a long time. You need to choose what responsibilities and authority you want to have instead of being led into the snare by others. It is funny that this sign has great problems with others who think they know everything because Geminis always think that they have the best understanding themselves. One way for a Gemini to break their inner taboos is to be goal-oriented, ambitious, and willing to be an authority figure. As a Gemini, you really need to take yourself and your own goals, ambitions, and needs very seriously. If you ever want to be taken seriously by the world, you must show them that you take yourself seriously by demanding that they do the same.

Education, Adventure, and Life Philosophy

Geminis love to learn and be in the process of becoming something. The future is often more promising than the moment. As soon they have finished one education, they would like another. They enjoy being on the road toward something new and exciting—having arrived is not as attractive. If you remove the dream of a brighter future from a Gemini, you likely remove the meaning of life at the same time. They are curious beings who want to learn everything. They often know at least a little about everything and prefer to expand their knowledge and horizons in breadth rather than depth. Most Geminis are open-minded and free of prejudices. On the other hand, they can be quite intolerant of those who have prejudices.

They love traveling, preferably to far away and exotic places, the stranger the better. They can adapt to all kinds of environments and feel that they learn about life, human behavior, and the meaning of existence every time they connect with something new and unknown. Their prime reason for traveling is human connection. Geminis are not especially interested in buildings or nature but crave human communication—although there exists a variation of this sign that is more interested in art and the symbolic interpretation of life than the real thing. These Geminis seem to be on a quest for something that was lost in the past and might be found somewhere in the future. Somehow, they feel that the future is created through the rediscovery of the past. They prefer education that opens new horizons and involves working in groups. They also like doing things that are off the beaten path and a bit special, while at the same time, financial safety is important. They like to be a bit rebellious—within safe and secure limits. Their rebellion is more about wanting evolution than about searching for revolution. In some ways, they are sensible idealists who want to improve what already exists. Strangely enough, Geminis can easily seem rigid when talking with them about topics like religion, justice, and morality. Mostly, they are emotionally attached to their own view, which is, of course, the right one in their eyes.

As a Gemini, you need to know that you get the most from your open-mindedness when you do not demand that others are as tolerant as you are. Let them have their strange, dogmatic beliefs if it suits them. You need to be just as flexible when it comes to the big lines and life philosophies as you are with the smaller things in life. It is good that you follow your own ideals and your own road, but look out for becoming a weird loon. To realize your visions, you need to walk the thin line that is both flexible and solid. If you become too adjusted, you lose your own way—and the power in all the possibilities. If you become rigid and opinionated, you miss all the opportunities life offers. To make things work, you need to find the balance between your loftiest ideals and the necessity of adapting to the possibilities of the moment. Your greatest adventures and growth come when you manage to be a practical idealist and a theoretical rationalist.

Goals, Profession, and Career

Geminis thrive in professions where dreaming is part of the working process. They need to be connected with something creative that stimulates their mind, intuition, and fantasy. Their inner world must be given space to unfold in the outer. Most Geminis are very good at seeing one thing from many angles, and they easily get bored if they are forced to stick to one perspective or do the same thing over and over again. They can be excellent leaders, especially in environments that have something in common with ant hives. Their nervous systems can handle high speeds and lots of input without becoming too stressed or losing control. In fact, they need this high-speed stimulation to avoid feeling out of control and becoming stressed and frustrated. They really hate work that demands responsibility and seriousness without giving them freedom and ample opportunities for experimentation. If that kind of work is the only option, they prefer mechanical manual labor. Then, at least, the mind is free to roam the higher dimensions of dreams and fantasy. Many Geminis prefer to spend a great amount of time in their inner world regardless of what is going on in the outer. This is because the outer world of time and space has so many limitations and is predestined to be duller than the limitless scenery of the imagination. It is the world of possibility and inspiration that gives Geminis that elated feeling of soaring free and weightless.

Often, this sign holds a multitude of different jobs during their life. In some ways, they seem to be collecting information and experience from the diversity of life. Every time they jump over the fence—because the grass really does seem greener on the other side—they continue building on what they bring from their old field of experience. This sign has a special ability to create connections that are invisible to others. They can create disruptions where there was blind unity and agreement—at the same time, they are experts at building bridges where most of us just see divisions and differences. Geminis know how to work by themselves but enjoy working in the company of others so much more. They like being in an ever-changing community where there is always somebody to fill in for a missing part. In life, they want the music they play to be open to improvisation. Going onstage and playing the same piece over and over again is very dull and boring for them. They enjoy discovering and exploring new sides of themselves and others. They want their professional life to develop from the inside out and are really uncomfortable when somebody presses them into following rigid schematics, schedules, and structures.

As a Gemini, you like to begin by taking a look at where you want to go, and then try to find the people you want to go there with. When your goal is set and your company is ready to go… *woosh*…you like to move at the speed of lightning. It is easy for others to think that this speed is either dangerous or so fast that it is a miracle. The miracle is all the work that the Gemini has done in their mind and on the inner level before firing up the engine. The path seems easy to walk, but that stems from the fact that they have traveled it so many times in their mind that they have taken every possibility into consideration before it can appear. One of the beautiful results of a Gemini reaching their highest velocity is how completely natural it becomes for them to create and be part of a team based on respect for the contributions and the needs of everyone who participates.

Friends, Future, and Ideals

Geminis enjoy a strange diversity of friends. Everybody is welcome, but not too many of the same type. They respect people with visions, ideals, and personal viewpoints. They admire people who are pioneers at the forefront of something and possess the courage and ability to walk their own ways and fight for their beliefs. Geminis thrive in groups and can make everyone believe that they are their special friend, but the ones who really have a deep, personal connection with them know the difference. They will only show their unpleasant and unlikeable traits to close friends. Geminis are proficient at making others see their own talents and unique abilities. They make others feel special and chosen. If a Gemini wants to get into contact with somebody, they will just walk up and tell that person about their curiosity and interest. They enjoy when other people have clear and strong opinions; people who are elusive and evasive in thoughts and words make them insecure.

Personal freedom is a must for this sign. They are searching for a society where every individual has the ability to reveal their uniqueness. Freedom is highly valued, but at the same time, they want rules that make it possible for everybody to have that right. They do not like exploitation and are advocates for equal rights for everybody, no matter how looked down upon. Geminis easily stumble in their own principles since their ideals of freedom often seem to conflict with the idea that no one has the right to do something unpleasant or unwanted to anyone else.

One of Gemini's biggest reasons for having friends is to have someone to share the fun with. They enjoy talking about possibilities but enjoy exploring those ideas in the real world even more. The fact that something is happening is often more important than what is happening. This sign can talk with the same people for a tremendously long time, as long as the topic changes. They are also able to do the same thing over a long period of time, as long as the people they do it with are constantly changing. What makes them bored is doing the same thing with the same people. That is part of the duality of this sign. One half of them needs stability so the other half can be in constant flux. Some Geminis change organizations like others change underwear. They simply love to be involved in new projects together with new people—on the road to new territories. They are known to leave behind a lot of unfinished business that others have to finish and fix…or reap the benefits of. Often, they plant the seed but do not have time or patience to wait until the flower of their effort blooms. There was something new and exciting around the corner and they just *had* to take a peek at it.

As a Gemini, you are well suited to opening windows into new opportunities and spreading enthusiasm, joy, and ideas. You need to follow your dreams and visions if you plan to avoid being numbed by boredom and to live a satisfying life. The truth is that your best friends are always the ones you are doing something interesting with at this moment. You are not very clingy or sentimental if former friends move away to other stomping grounds. Often, your friends are more attached to you than you are to them. As a Gemini, it is of prime importance for your well-being that you throw yourself heedlessly into the future. It is never enough to just talk and dream and discuss. You have to participate in the battle of life, and the prize you want to fight for is the future you see in your inner vision. You have the right and the need to create the reality you dream about creating…and since it always involves other people, you have to learn how to create it together with the rest of us.

Seeking and the Spiritual

Geminis would like to have concrete evidence for the existence of the spiritual world. At the outset, Geminis are open to all possibilities, but they have a hard time believing in anything without solid evidence. Most Geminis are skeptical of dogmatic and established truths, but those who do believe tend to be fanatical. The duality in Gemini shows itself as a syndrome where either everything can be seen as false or true…or there is just *one* truth and everything else is false. Many Geminis are rather contrarian. If somebody says that spirituality is pure love, Gemini protests, and claims that it also must be consciousness…or something else. Geminis have a lot of questions but trouble finding answers, especially the eternal ones. The pity of having just one viewpoint is that you miss the fun of having all the others. To avoid this pain, Geminis easily choose to hold all viewpoints at the same time—or else cling stubbornly to one to avoid the possibilities of the others. In fact, there is only one thing that can make the spiritual realm a reality for this sign, and that is to have a spiritual experience in person. Everything is made of dreams, thoughts, and visions until it is experienced as absolute reality. In this area, Geminis do not believe. Either they know that spirituality is real through their own practical and physical experience, or they don't. When they know it is real, it is not a way to escape, but because spirituality is the truth that is everywhere. Their mind knows that they can argue for any viewpoint they want. Their mind knows that truth is always relative and depends on how you look at "reality." Since their minds can turn everything around, no debate or logic can convince them about spiritual matters.

Spirituality is something much deeper than thoughts and the mind for them. As mentioned, the only thing that can sway them to take the true road of spirituality is experiencing it as an irrevocable fact of existence. When they are moving through the spiritual world, they need to move slowly with great care and thoroughness. As they acquire a deep sense of spirituality, it becomes rooted in the depth of their being and can never, ever be removed. This sign can't lose faith, because they are unable to produce it from the beginning, but it is when they embrace spirituality that physical life gets real and gives them meaning. Their play becomes something more than a game and gains deeper significance!

At the outset, Gemini is a master of the rules of the game, but they do not really understand why the game is played. Since the game has no purpose, they do not take it seriously, and neither do they really care too much about winning or losing. Whatever happens is all right—as long as they have some fun and enjoy the game. With spiritual realization, the physical world of form and space gains a totally new and significant dimension. The reality that was a kind of physical abstraction and game of minds suddenly becomes filled with deep significance and meaning. Then the contrary nature of Gemini rears its head again. As other signs use spirituality as a reason to escape from reality and move into the world of dreams and feelings, Geminis experience spirituality as a vehicle that takes them from the inner realms of fiction and thoughts and brings them into the world of real life. For this sign, the world is the one force behind all that is...made manifest...and if it isn't so, there is no one force behind all that is. Such is the sound of spirituality neatly packed by the clever mind of the Gemini, a master of logic until the end.

Cancer

June 21st—July 22nd

Element: Water
Quality: Cardinal
Ruling Planet: Moon

How to Present Yourself

Cancers enjoy being seen as sensitive and emotional creatures. At the same time, they want others to know how well-protected and invulnerable they are. This can be somewhat confusing for the rest of the creatures of the zodiac. As a matter of fact, Cancers often present their vulnerability in one moment and deny it in the next. They can be the softest of all creatures when they open themselves up, and the hardest and most untouchable when they shut down. As they train and develop their ability to live in the rough world of humans, they learn to find more balance. An important step for them is keeping the door open and accepting their vulnerability without feeling mortally wounded each time they are hurt. Then they can stop to be either bone-hard or defenseless softies. They need to be seen as caring and nurturing and show much of their ability to love by caring and helping meet the needs of others.

One great problem with Cancers is that they sometimes do not know how to take care of themselves at the same time as they care for others. They can ruthlessly and violently misuse themselves in the process of nurturing others. This sign needs to learn—as early in life as possible—that you can never give something you do not have. If somebody is in need of economic assistance, you need to have the financial resources to be able to help them. Likewise, if somebody needs to be loved, you have to have enough love for yourself that you can share without it getting depleted. If they need your time, you have to have enough time for yourself. If they need food, you have to have enough food for yourself. Cancers want you to take their emotions very seriously. They can have a great sense of humor, but do not make fun of their feelings. They accept that others can be more fun and interesting than they are, but if you do not pay attention and are unaware of their feelings, they will leave your company in the blink of an eye. When they are hurt, they might suffer in total silence and show their feelings through absolute withdrawal, or they can take the opposite path and cry long, hard, and publicly, dramatizing their feelings. In rage and fury, they prefer to act out on behalf of others. All Cancers need to show and receive acknowledgment of their feelings. This sign cannot feel completely safe and relaxed around you unless they have shown you their total range of feelings and know that you can handle them and won't desert them when they need you most.

Cancers have a rich inner life as well as a powerful imagination and a lot of fantasies that they want to share with the world. Their relationship with the world might confuse more mentally driven beins, since it is always changing as their stream of emotions moves. As suddenly as a silent stream can change to a thundering waterfall as you paddle down a river, their emotions can suddenly shift from inner silence and calm to rage. In one moment, they can be outgoing and audacious, while in the next they are shy and insecure. Their behavior is totally dependent on the changes that take place in their inner emotional climate. When their mood is good, they feel like they can handle everything with calm and ease. When something has spoiled their day, they feel like everything is ruined and life will never be filled with love and joy again.

As a Cancer, you have a great need to share your feelings with the world. You need to allow yourself to love and show when you need to be loved. You need to give from your heart to others, because the more you give, the more the stream of love flows and the more you have to give. Remember, you are not here to get as much as you give or learn how to share things equally. You are here to learn how to love, and as you see, love becomes who you are. As you nurture your own heart and love yourself unconditionally, you become more and more happy and loving. Remember that you have to be the person that you love first. That is the starting point of the great experience that life as a human being can be for someone born in the sign of Cancer.

How to Get the Best from Your Talents and Resources

Cancer is their own most important asset. The key in all matters is their engagement and willingness to get involved. A Cancer doing things without being emotionally or otherwise engaged will not move very fast or get anywhere. The primal force of motivation for a Cancer is feelings. To get going, they need some kind of passion and an inner desire to manifest something and move into reality.

On the other hand, when Cancer puts both their heart and their will into something, the resulting force is great, and the possibility of moving mountains is absolutely present. Cancers are creative and see a lot of possibilities. They have a rich inner world that fertilizes their thoughts and feelings. Cancers have a great talent for moving something out of their inner world and into a beautiful expression in the outer. This can take the form of art and creativity, but their flow of emotions can just as easily find other riverbeds, too. They can have a great interest in nurturing and taking care of others, or they can become excellent cooks, gardeners, or social workers. The deep need to give from the heart makes everything connected with giving and making others grow a stimulating area for a Cancer.

If you were in doubt...they really do care. A Cancer that does not find an avenue for giving might be bottled up and end up like yesterday's stale milk. Then, they can become self-righteous, pompous, bitter, and offended. They need to learn to handle rejection and to give because they want to give, not just to be applauded. In some ways, all Cancers have the abundance and love to give more than they get! Their greatest need is to find a person worthy of being given something from the storehouse of the Cancer's abundance. They might find a lot of satisfaction in sharing with animals and plants, but most Cancers need to share their love with humans.

The most important resource of a developed Cancer is indisputably the ability to love. Love is a resource they have, not a commodity they can sell or make deals with. In fact, as soon as love has become a trading commodity, it has ceased to exist for the Cancer. A mature Cancer loves because of what is in their own heart, not because the receiver deserves to be loved. They have the rare ability to show unconditional love, something that makes them well-equipped for taking care of their fellow human beings. Cancers know that care and compassion have different faces, and most of them learn to be both professional and personal at the same time, as they know the proper difference. Some Cancers have to learn the difference between giving because they have love in their heart and loving because they have a personal and individual interest in doing so. As they really understand the difference between personal and individual involvement and just loving because there is a flow, they learn to give without being drained. It is like a river in their heart...and they learn the difference between just going with the flow and using the river as a way to go wherever they want with their little boat of individuality.

Communication and Immediate Surroundings

Can Cancers love to talk about other people and analyze the motivations behind their movements. In fact, they like to work through everything that has happened in the outer world in their mind. They can talk for a very long time about small details and occurrences and love finding new ways of looking at life. They love to be around people who know how to use words and enjoy using their minds—but those words have to be something more than empty theories and hot air. The words have to be connected to the real world. In some ways, Cancer has direct inner access to the great mysteries of the heart and eternity, but those mysteries are not something to just go ahead and talk about, nor something that can easily be put into words.

Cancer loves organizing their day and surroundings and strives for perfection in the small things. They are delighted by everything that helps them gain more order and clarity in life, especially if those things are elegant and technical as well as useful. They like to talk about what can be made into reality and are known to get caught up in details and pedantry in their daily life. Half of them have a tendency to be overly structured, while the other half seems to be fighting against the chaos that dominates their lives. Most Cancers just love to make plans. They create structures and organize the future into small boxes so they can know how things were, are, and will be. They love security in the small matters of life. They like predictability and do not enjoy surprises that disturb their plans. They like to live in safe and predictable neighborhoods. They like to have things that are known and recognizable in their immediate environment. They easily become insecure and a bit lost if there are too many new impressions. They prefer to be around close friends and known people, rather than meeting a lot of "noisy, strange," and unknown people.

Cancer often uses language very precisely, where every word has a special meaning and is used in very specific ways. Words are not general containers but specific labels. Cancer is often careful with what they say to others. Almost without exception, they are polite and well-behaved with proper and decent language. They do not like foul words or sloppy and careless language. Often, they go to great amounts of trouble to avoid hurting others with their words; they try to be nice, precise, and truthful. Often, they prefer to talk about things that seem neutral, like the weather. They try to give words to their true feelings while, at the same time, they try to see the positive and loving side of everything without condemning or judging—a feat that is not always easy to accomplish. At times, they stumble around and create a lot of messes as they try to avoid the pain and hurt that so often accompany words and real life. An undeveloped Cancer may start a sentence with "Don't take it personally"—and then follow up with a list of personal, judgmental, and hurtful descriptions. When Cancers are mad or embittered, they can hurt their fellow human beings with uncannily precise, cold, determined, and dry use of words. It is important for Cancers to know that they need to use language to express their true and deep inner feelings and thoughts. Language is not doing the best job for them when used as a knife—to cut things apart and see how they work separated from the whole. For Cancers, language is best seen as a bridge that can be used to fill the gap between your own heart and understanding and those of your fellow human beings. cers love to talk about other people and analyze the motivations behind their movements. In fact, they like to work through everything that has happened in the outer world in their mind. They can talk for a very long time about small details and occurrences and love finding new ways of looking at life. They love to be around people who know how to use words and enjoy using their minds—but those words have to be something more than empty theories and hot air. The words have to be connected to the real world. In some ways, Cancer has direct inner access to the great mysteries of the heart and eternity, but those mysteries are not something to just go ahead and talk about, nor something that can easily be put into words.

Cancer loves organizing their day and surroundings and strives for perfection in the small things. They are delighted by everything that helps them gain more order and clarity in life, especially if those things are elegant and technical as well as useful. They like to talk about what can be made into reality and are known to get caught up in details and pedantry in their daily life. Half of them have a tendency to be overly structured, while the other half seems to be fighting against the chaos that dominates their lives. Most Cancers just love to make plans. They create structures and organize the future into small boxes so they can know how things were, are, and will be. They love security in the small matters of life. They like predictability and do not enjoy surprises that disturb their plans. They like to live in safe and predictable neighborhoods. They like to have things that are known and recognizable in their immediate environment. They easily become insecure and a bit lost if there are too many new impressions. They prefer to be around close friends and known people, rather than meeting a lot of "noisy, strange," and unknown people.

Cancer often uses language very precisely, where every word has a special meaning and is used in very specific ways. Words are not general containers but specific labels. Cancer is often careful with what they say to others. Almost without exception, they are polite and well-behaved with proper and decent language. They do not like foul words or sloppy and careless language. Often, they go to great amounts of trouble to avoid hurting others with their words; they try to be nice, precise, and truthful. Often, they prefer to talk about things that seem neutral, like the weather. They try to give words to their true feelings while, at the same time, they try to see the positive and loving side of everything without condemning or judging—a feat that is not always easy to accomplish. At times, they stumble around and create a lot of messes as they try to avoid the pain and hurt that so often accompany words and real life. An undeveloped Cancer may start a sentence with "Don't take it personally"—and then follow up with a list of personal, judgmental, and hurtful descriptions. When Cancers are mad or embittered, they can hurt their fellow human beings with uncannily precise, cold, determined, and dry use of words. It is important for Cancers to know that they need to use language to express their true and deep inner feelings and thoughts. Language is not doing the best job for them when used as a knife—to cut things apart and see how they work separated from the whole. For Cancers, language is best seen as a bridge that can be used to fill the gap between your own heart and understanding and those of your fellow human beings.

Home and Family

Children are not the priority for a Cancer—their partner is. Children are an extension of family, while the parents are the trunk that the branches of children stem from. A grown Cancer without a partner can easily feel lost and all alone in the world. For many years, the family they were born into was sufficient, and they have difficulty letting go of the parent/child connection. At some point, most of them do feel the pull and longing to create their own family so strongly that they manage to leave the known and find their own, new home sweet home. But again…a partner is not just a partner…a partner is what you need to create a family. So, asking a Cancer about what is most important—their children or their partner—is like asking a scientist what came first, the chicken or the egg.

For Cancers, a partner is part of their foundation for wholeness. This deep and symbiotic connection to a partner tells us that it is more emotionally demanding for a Cancer to leave their partner than it is for any other sign in the zodiac. As far as homes go, they can just as easily live in small, cramped caves as in big, fancy castles. The most important factor for them isn't the architectural design, but the person or people they live with. In many ways, Cancer is adaptable and able to put their partner's needs before their own, but there has to be some balance in the relationship. There must be equality and mutual respect. At the same time, the home of a Cancer is their castle, however small and humble. Choices about decoration and style are very important for this sign. They need space to reveal their sense of aesthetics and beauty within the four walls of their home, but they don't just want to have it their own way. They want their partners or families to participate so they can make the home a blend of the needs and preferences of all who live there. They want others to have their desires as well…in a way that makes them feel good about having their own. It is an interesting experience to participate in this "who wants what" game for non-Cancerians.

Justice at home is important for them. In fact, there are few things that make Cancer angrier and more disappointed than injustice among loved ones. They want their home to be a place for peace and togetherness…and you had better behave according to their standards for peace, or else! Cancer feels terribly bothered and harassed if their home is a place where conflicts and quarrels are daily occurrences. Their home is supposed to be a p(a)lace of peace, harmony, beauty, and comfort. In their book, it should be the place where family members can withdraw and regain balance, harmony, and inner peace after having traveled the tumultuous waters of the outer world. If Cancer is really out of balance, their home stops being the safe haven it is meant to be and instead becomes a battleground where they fight with others about who is supposed to do what and how the daily chores ought to be distributed justly. Having agreements with their partner about who has responsibility for what in the family is essential for inner peace. Cancers need a partner who understands their special needs and sensitivity and who can treat the other members of the household like children and parents: with the proper delicacy and sensitivity. A Cancer wants home to be a place for soft voices and beautiful sounds.

As a Cancer, you have to become very aware of the fact that you need to create and live in places that are peaceful and harmonious. To make this possible, you must give others the same leeway and space as you yourself demand. If you are able to find this balance, you will have a great ability to build relationships that will become the fertile ground for an abundance of joy, love, harmony, and beauty.

Creativity and Leisure

Cancers enjoy doing thrilling and slightly dangerous things in their free time. In daily life, they prefer safety and often seem like the most caring and nicest people you would ever bump into...but when the shades of night reach their inner landscape and they want to give free rein to their shadows, the black leather might come on and their inner demons might walk out with a big grin on their faces. This does not imply that they are the zodiacal version of Jekyll and Hyde, but rather that they need to have a space where their inner shadows can express and fulfill themselves. It is like they have a wild wolf inside, and every now and then, they must throw away their sheepish uniform and bare their fangs. It is important for them to have a security valve where they can release the steam and forcefulness that their everyday persona does not embrace. They need space and the ability to explore their own depths and the feelings within that they mostly are too kind, well-behaved, and reliable to acknowledge and connect with.

If Cancers are completely maladjusted, they are probably possessed by this shadow and make it their job to show their seedier side to the world. Then, their hobby will be to show unexpected kindness and care. Cancers love to have secrets. They enjoy shady, erotic dates with a lot of steam and deep passion. They like to feel the throbbing dark undertones of passion and everything that stems from deep and strong sexuality. They thrive in the animalistic intensity of feelings. For a Cancer to deny this deep inner longing and connection with the nonverbal, powerful, and physical aspect of love is like being a shark that has to swim like a goldfish in a small, round bowl. Cancers need to allow themselves to challenge destiny every now and then. If not, they become so "nice" that they can hardly stand their own boring company.

In some ways, the spare time in the day is the most important time of day for the Cancer. This is when they are free to do what *they* want to do. This sign has an affinity for consuming and passionate hobbies: they do not do anything half-heartedly. Enjoying life and freedom is a question of all or nothing. In a sense, their relationship with their own childish longings is similar to their relationship to their children. Either they give it 110 percent or they are taking the day off. This sign plays with at least the same intensity as they handle the serious stuff, and Cancer is just as loyal to their spare time activities as to their children. They seldom let go easily and stay with a project until it is finished...and the children until they are very much grown-up. In many cases, it is difficult to separate the personality of this sign from their hobbies. If they are a stamp collector, that is what they are known as: "my neighbor the stamp collector."

But alas...when it is over, it is over. If Cancer walks away from a hobby or a person they have befriended, it is a final goodbye. Finished is finished and that is that. Cancer does not play the game of two steps forward and one step back—and that also goes for love, war, and spare time. Empty phrases like "let's take a break and wait and see how it goes" are absolutely wasted on this kind of astrological creature. They are not like a switch with a dimmer. The switch in their heart has just two positions: on and off. They can be friendly and go along with others in a very docile and nonprovocative way so long as their inner switch and passion are in the *on* position, but the moment they turn that switch *off*, you get an idea of their true strength and passion. Once that switch is flipped, they are about as docile as a bear with cubs.

As a Cancer, you need to be aware of how important it is to show your true interests and inner feelings to others. You must let others know and taste your real power and true passion. Then they will know better than to block your path just for fun and will also give you more respect and not take you for granted. Even better, you will be allowed to follow your own passions and be true to your own heart without having to be sneaky or fight for it. In some ways, it is as simple as showing the world your true love and being true to your own heart and deepest passions.

Health, Order, and the Necessary

"No danger, everything will be okay," Cancer says as they fall into an exploding volcano. This sign really does look at the bright side of life with respect to health, future possibilities, and how each day is going to be. They prefer optimism and positivity to reality any day of the week. They enjoy bringing their light to others and sharing their brightness and optimism with the rest of the pack and have an uncanny ability to find meaning and joy in the smallest of occurrences. Cancer might be the astrological sign that most easily finds joy in the small gifts of daily life. In many ways, they take the moment as it is and have this great ability to make the most of it.

Cancers need to find and have meaning in their everyday lives. They like having chores and doing things that feel meaningful—as long as it is filled with meaning, no task is too small or too large. It is amazingly nice how easily they can find something that gives life significance. A smile can be enough, or just making another person happy. It can be a small miracle to see something beautiful like a sunbeam that shines through a tree or to think a new thought or even to just drink a glass of water. On a good day, it seems like life is there just to show Cancer that life has meaning. The challenge comes with the dark tide that washes away that good meaning and makes it feel like there is no meaning at all, neither now nor in the future. As long as Cancers are occupied, the dark tide seems to keep away from the shores of their consciousness. It is when their busy lives stop and the void of idleness seeps in that they have to face the darkness of futility. This makes it easy to understand why Cancers prefer to do things all the time and seldom stop to face the silence and inner emptiness that might live in their hearts. Most of them are incessantly occupied and even enjoy doing things that others dread. They have a tendency to wake up in the morning filled with enthusiasm for the coming day and go to bed at night tired and satisfied with having accomplished so much. It is not the humdrum of everyday living that is the big challenge for this sign. The true challenge comes when the safety of familiar visions and meaning dissolves, and all the things that have filled their life with meaning and enthusiasm seem to disappear. The ugly grin in front of them is the claw of desperation found in the black hole they fell into. As long as they have a bright light to follow, not even sickness or physical difficulties create real trouble for them.

The key to enjoying daily life for a Cancer is to hold the lantern of hope high and steady and use it to shine into the darkness of their deepest fears and loneliness. In truth, they can make a twist on the old saying about hope and life, and their version would go like this: "As long as there is hope, there is life."

As a Cancer, you have the possibility and ability to find much of your purpose in sharing optimism and joy with others. You are good at helping others see possibilities and find their visions for the future. It is important for you to know that you do not always have the answers and yet still hold on to the courage to tell others your true thoughts. One of your gifts is that you quite often have the ability to see what constitutes the right next action for others, but be aware of your need for humility in this area. You do not know anything about what challenges and big choices others have to face. You are not able to tell them how to handle their crises, nor how they ought to handle their lives, you just have a knack for guiding their next step. When you want to help someone find their way through life, you see the challenge straight ahead (for yourself and others), and can be a great help in determining when to take the next step and where to put one's foot. Remember that you do not know where others are headed because the road is created as they walk, and that is also true for your own life, dear Cancer.

One-on-One Relationships

Close relationships and romantic love are serious matters for Cancer. They want partners they can trust and that are reliable no matter what storm is coming. They look for quality and durability in others. They are known to flirt and play with people they do not trust because of their magnetism for danger and sensuality, but if a relationship is going to develop over time, it needs to be solid and feel like it could last forever. Cancers do not waste their romantic love on just anybody. They want stability, maturity, and a willingness to take responsibility for partners as well as close friends.

Cancers are brimming with emotions and swim in internal oceans of sensations and dreams. Like the rest of us, they seek others in the hope of becoming fulfilled and gaining inner wholeness. It is easy to understand that they are attracted to people with clear structure and limits. They need somebody who can create a structure that helps them organize the content of their inner emotional oceans. It is common for them to be attracted to people who are older and more established than they are. Cancers are looking for somebody who can provide both emotional and financial security. If a Cancer is going to get seriously involved with someone, one of the decisive factors is the question of trust. In their soul and gut, they know that if they don't trust the other person, the relationship is doomed from the beginning. Their heart demands loyalty, stability, and staying power from a lasting partner. Cancer isn't easily seduced by glamour, dreams, or flattery; they far prefer quality, reality, and reliability. Being able to trust the word of their partner and close friends is a must for them. The same goes for fulfilling promises and taking responsibility for themselves—and others when necessary.

Cancers are often attracted to strong partners who have their own careers and are self-reliant. They a have a tendency to go for people with standing, authority, and success in the worldly domain. It is easier to seduce a Cancer by showing real quality and strength of character than with romantic chit-chat and flattery. They want somebody they can get support from; someone they know won't run away when the going gets tough. They know that a love that has the strength to endure the test of time is a love that takes time to create and bring forth.

As mentioned, this sign thrives with partners that are self-reliant. This stems from two different causes. The first is that Cancer easily makes their partner addicted to all their care and nurturing. When their partner is addicted, a Cancer might get into trouble because they do not know how to set limits and say no to their loved one. The other reason is that Cancer, besides their great need for emotional security, also craves independence and a life where they can be separate and autonomous. With a partner that is dependent on the Cancer, a relationship can easily become unhealthy and codependent. In that case, it becomes a relationship based on mutual addiction with the need to control one another and a lack of freedom. For a Cancer, that is very close to hell, while a relationship based on mutual respect and love is close to heaven.

As a Cancer, you need to be very aware of the importance of not needing your partner to take care of you. It is just as important to limit how helpful and caring you are toward them. Treat your partner as a grown-up that must take responsibility for their own tasks and challenges. Do not treat your partner like a child, thereby creating a spoiled brat. This balance is not necessarily found by seeking equality and justice around who does the work, earns the money, or carries the burdens; balance is found by giving each other support, trust, and great leeway to give what they have to give. Most important of all is trust—trust that their partner gives out of love and only what they have to give. Fairness in a relationship with a Cancer thrives best in accordance with the basic idea around human rights promoted by many socialists and popularized by Karl Marx: that each shall give in accordance with their ability and receive in accordance with their needs.

Beneath the Surface—Sex and Taboos

The sexuality of this sign is a multifaceted story. Cancers can be quite kinky and experimental, or they can be very traditional, with clear-cut ideas about what is morally acceptable and what isn't. In fact, with this sign, you do not know what you will get until you have taken a peek behind the curtain.

Cancers do not want to be seen as different, even when they feel a bit odd and hide behind a veil of normality. Only people who are closest to a Cancer are allowed to see their "strangeness." They are capable of having weird fantasies, ideas, and opinions, but their main path to intimacy is always through a sense of closeness, belonging, and emotional trust. It is when they really feel safe and secure that they can start to display their real, strange uniqueness and eccentricities, showing you that they do not really need you. When they have you close enough, they can begin to behave in distant and impersonal ways. As strange as it may seem to the rest of us, real intimacy for a Cancer is feeling fully at liberty to be uncaring, independent, distant, and totally free. The more room you give a Cancer for being unpredictable and crazy, the more easily they can be intimate with you. When a Cancer really knows in their heart that they love you and know that you can handle their weirdness and accept that they can be totally distant and impersonal, then they can finally relax and feel safe. Intimacy, for them, is not this cozy closeness and compassion that they can share with everybody. No, it is the trust they bestow upon you as they share their strange secrets, fixations, fetishes, and fears. They enjoy playing games where they behave strangely and detached in intimate situations… and this, they can only do with people they are intimate enough with. Cancers who are in long-term relationships that do not have room for their fantasies and special needs will often be attracted to the idea of situations where they can live out their taboos for a night or even just a few hours. They often dream about being intimate with more than one person at a time. They do not necessarily need to realize these dreams, but they need to have them without morally condemning themselves. Often, just having that exciting fantasy is enough. At the same time, most Cancers enjoy experimenting with the erotic side of life. It is not unheard of for them to use different gear and fetishes to get the experience they seek.

The most important thing with sexuality for Cancers—besides sexuality as a means to create new humans and as a sign of eternal love—is the energetic state that is available. The energy rush that gives this great sense of freedom is the secret for why they love sex so much. Personal intimacy is more a means than the goal of sexuality for this sign. This might be difficult to understand since Cancers are so occupied with emotions, intimacy, and the personal in most areas of life. Some Cancers are very creative and innovative in this area, while others separate the experiences of love and sex…and stick with one of them…or neither, in the worst-case scenario.

As a Cancer, you will benefit from becoming very aware of the fact that you do need freedom in this area as well as space and the ability to explore and get to know your sexuality. You will benefit from a partner who gives space to your originality and you need a partner that is willing to explore and move along nontraditional paths in these matters.

But first of all, you must acknowledge, embrace, and accept that which is uniquely you. Only then, when you have fully accepted and befriended your own sexuality will you be able to experience the blessings of sharing your deepest being without feeling caught and inhibited in any way.

Education, Adventure, and Life Philosophy

In this area, Cancers know how to go with the flow. Most of the time, they act on the best of any possibility, and very often they end up in positions with responsibility and authority. This stems from the simple fact that they have an uncanny tendency to take initiative and show responsibility. Their education and choice of direction in life may seem like coincidences, but as time goes on, it becomes clear that this is not the case. Cancers have a quality that is called intuition and are prone to follow its guidance. Going with the flow can seem like a lack of direction and initiative. However, in reality, it comes from the inner ability to sense where life wants to guide them and to do things that, to them, seem so obvious. In some sense of the word, they are pragmatic and do not waste too much time fighting their fate. When they do fight their fate, they use a lot of energy to fight small things and resist small challenges. Almost without exception, they go along with the big challenges and directions in their lives. They seem to accept the frames and larger structures around their lives easily, but their willingness to accept the smaller details within those limits… that's another story.

Many of these creatures have a vague dream and inner longing for something they really want to do. Finding words for this dream is difficult, especially in their younger years. A Cancer does not really know what that dream is or where they want to go, so they go with the flow, as mentioned. As their lives expand and they grow in stature, their dreams start to become more tangible and real. They begin to know their inner longing from a deeper place and start to see the patterns they are woven from. They begin to perceive how every step they have taken and every decision they have made has led them to the exact point where they are in the moment. Some Cancers try to deny their intuition. They do not go with the flow but either try to desperately hold on to the expectations of others or just as desperately avoid fulfilling them, even if those expectations are incredibly similar to their own longings. If they are caught in this situation, they start to feel that life has no real meaning or value, and in a way, it's true: life has little significance for a Cancer that does not follow their longings, love, and intuition. If those misguided Cancers wake up, they will suddenly realize that everything that has happened and every wrong step they have taken has led them to exactly where they are, which is the place they need to be to reach their destination and true goal. So, everything is just as it is supposed to be anyway.

It is almost unnecessary to say that a Cancer will thrive the most when they choose their beliefs and their education with the heart, not the mind. They need to learn to understand justice and find the laws of their heart. They grow by opening their heart and sharing what flows from within their heart with others. The most significant area of education for Cancers is to understand how the inner life of emotions and love is reflected in the outer world. The formal education they might have has no real significance or importance. To understand how all life is interconnected and how love works as the basic drive to create life and a meaningful life is the alpha and omega for the Cancer. By learning from that school and the teachers that come from and speak to the depths of their hearts, Cancers learn to understand the significance and deeper purpose of themselves, society, and the world they are part of.

Goals, Profession, and Career

This sign enjoys creating their own unique profession. They are attracted to being a pioneer and doing things their own way. They feel comfortable with a profession that has plenty of strain and challenges. It is good for them to feel that they have to find, use, and hone their will to fulfill their function. In some ways, they are warriors that enjoy fighting for the cause of somebody else. If they fight for their own interests, they become too vulnerable and sensitive for the tough profession of fighting. They easily feel guilty and grow afraid of not being kind and good enough. They need somebody else to fight for, or at least some injustice to fight against. They thrive when serving as an advocate for the downtrodden and oppressed. They are also very well suited to being champions for causes that are based on every person's right to freedom and to have love, care, and respect in their lives. In fact, what Cancer wants most is peace, but they are here to learn to fight for the right to peace. A Cancer that isn't willing to fight for their goals in life, or that doesn't have any visions, will easily be overwhelmed by a state of passivity that makes them more and more lazy. In the end, they become unable to handle any kind of conflict or unexpected challenge. Cancer is so vulnerable, sensitive, and filled with good intentions that they really need to grind themselves into something more powerful by clashing with materials that are harder and more ruthless than they are. If they try to avoid this process and upcoming conflicts by retreating inside their personal bulletproof shell, they risk being caught inside that protection, seemingly unable to ever break free and get out into the real world again.

As a Cancer, you need to remember that the world really can benefit from your full presence. There is always something or somebody out there that is worth fighting for.

As you might understand, the soft and good-willed Cancer has an uncanny ability to get involved in great conflicts and power struggles in their work. Sometimes this stems from hiding their head in the sand and avoiding the conflicts for so long that things escalate like a volcanic eruption and drive them out of their hiding. For this sign, addressing professional conflicts as early as possible is highly recommended. The best way to go is to face challenges before they grow into something big and hairy that evokes fear in the soft heart of this astrological creature. Cancer needs to take a clear stand and fight for what they have chosen. They benefit greatly from summoning up their guts and straightening their spine so that they have the courage to state their true opinion. If Cancers get involved with people that are greedy for power and have a bag full of dirty tricks, they experience this, because they need that sort of challenge to get into contact with their own repressed need to fight for what is noble and just.

If you want to become the knight on the white horse, you have to meet the dark shadow and the trolls that are into abuse, power games, and scaring the shit out of their opponents. If Cancers really want to fight for love, goodness, and tenderness, they must dare to throw themselves into the unknown and uncharted territories of life and human behavior. In fact, any Cancer has the possibility of living a charmed life filled with opportunities and expansion into new areas. The only real obstacle that exists is the Cancer's tendency to cling to the known, which feels like safety. In the professional arena, Cancer will benefit from throwing themselves into the unknown one time too many rather than one time too few.

Friends, Future, and Ideals

Usually, Cancer is quite nostalgic and has more dreams based on their past than dreams of what is yet to come. In some ways, they do not want to create something really new, but rather to recreate the old in an even better way than before. The result can easily be that they become stuck in the past and repeat the same things with the same friends over and over again. That can be nice, at least for a while, but there will be a moment when it has just become an old habit repeating itself. Be aware: when the feeling of an empty void starts to fill the interior of Cancer, it spreads fast and grows like a dark, brooding thunderstorm.

As a Cancer, you can learn a lot by recognizing the early stages of boredom and quickly moving into action. There is a limit to how long you can be patiently satisfied with standing by and standing still. You have to move ahead in the end, even if it means that your distance from the past that you want to live in forever will grow. This sign does not want to cut their ties to the past and happily looks forward to a future not much different from the now—especially if the now feels good. But the future always comes, even if it is unexpected and highly surprising for this sign. For many Cancers, circumstances must grow really unpleasant and negative just to make them move on with their lives. As a mule, they overlook the carrot and start to move only when the whip begins to hurt. This sign will benefit from understanding that it is sensible to move toward an unknown future since life always has the possibility of becoming even better and greater than it already is. Once more: it is not recommended to postpone moving ahead until you have to unwillingly tear yourself away from the remnants of a life that was once, in the distant past, nice and pleasant.

Cancers often dream about a future that is even safer and more filled with comfort, pleasure, and money than what they have in the moment. They are on the search for a life that is filled with creative possibilities and space, and free of pain. They are also fortunate enough to be one of the signs with the greatest ability to enjoy the good life. They often make friends for life and are good-natured creatures who enjoy sharing their good fortune with friends. They are social and find great pleasure in good food and sensual stimulation and luxury. They simply love taking it easy and just doing nothing for hours. Some of them harbor dreams about a future that is more artistic and creative than the one they inhabit at the moment, but they are not prone to building castles in the air. They want tangible dreams about the future that seems possible and reasonably sensible at the moment of dreaming. Cancers find it too painful to have ideas that they know are just lofty dreams. If their dreams are too unrealistic and/or unreasonable, they have to fool themselves into believing that their dreams can become reality if they want to keep those dreams.

As a Cancer, you need to be aware of the danger of aiming too low. If you do, you will just crawl around with your eyes glued to your existing reality and never lift your mind toward the yet-unrealized possibilities that hold so many opportunities. You need to acknowledge your own ambitions and be willing to work long and hard to make them into reality. The truth is that Cancer can't really get the safety and security they want by clinging to the safety and security of the now. It is only when they dare to venture into the unknown and move into the uncharted terrain of the future that they start to understand what it really means to feel safe in the now. Then they are safe, not because they know what will happen, but because they have lost their fear of the unknown future.

Seeking and the Spiritual

In some sense, Cancers do not need to seek. They feel in their heart what their life is about and what is of importance. They are spiritual by nature because they have this inner experience of love as the basic force of all life. Of course, this is an insight they can suppress, deny, and bury in the unconscious—but the truth flows in their heart even if they do not acknowledge the existence of any spirituality at all. Their search is for words, thoughts, ideas, and experiences that can help them understand the truth that is already embedded in their soul and heart. This inner voice, which does not seek out the Source but comes from the Source, often makes Cancer choose one of two opposing paths.

The first path means that they become totally uninterested in anything spiritual. They may have kept some remains of it from childhood, but they do not waste time or thoughts on that kind of stuff. They prefer to focus on what gives meaning, pleasure, and joy in this earthly life. They easily become so engulfed by family, personal love, drama, and strong emotions that they have neither the time nor the need to throw themselves into a spiritual quest.

The other choice is to fervently seek out spiritual answers—or maybe just to find the significant questions. In some ways, they already have the answers, so the harder task for them is finding and giving voice to the right questions. What is it that decides whether they take the worldly or the spiritual path? One factor that forces them to seek the true essence of things is when life becomes so intricate, difficult, and painful that they simply have to look for solutions somewhere other than the worldly domains. Most Cancers pray to a higher force in difficult times. When everything eases up and life is simple, however, they often say thank you to Spirit for keeping them company and put a lid on their spiritual quest—at least until life again becomes so difficult that they have to search for the old faith that is stored somewhere deep down in their chest of treasures.

The other factor that leads Cancer to the true spiritual road is the voice of their deep longing. If they open to their inner world of deep longing for unity and belonging, they take step after step on the road that leads to unity with that which is behind all. In both cases, they understand that other individuals and earthly pleasures do not possess the ability to satisfy their deepest longing for unity and love. They also see that they can't satisfy the spiritual need that others have for love and unity, regardless of how much they are willing to give and sacrifice. Often, it is like they suddenly one day wake up and think…"It was nice eating these crumbs, and there are a lot of them, and they taste really nice, but why not go straight to the main meal?" One of the greatest joys and pleasures for a Cancer is to open their heart to the never-ending love meal that is always served by the spiritual force that has created and is the universe. But be aware, the road to this fully served dinner is not to be found through the heart alone. To reach the depth of acknowledgment, experience, and alertness that is necessary to satisfy their longings, Cancers also need to use their mind and understand the game that is going on, which by the way, is called "life."

As a Cancer, you have to use your head, be clear in your thoughts, and ask the right questions. You have free access to the understanding that is embedded in your heart, but you still have to learn how to handle it and what to do with it. It is divine logic and consciousness that are the keys to the inner chamber of your heart. The treasure is there, and you know it, but you need the key of wisdom to access the endless flow of abundance that stems from this inner Source. "Seek and you will find" is an old saying. "Listen to the answer, and you will understand the questions" might be a more appropriate saying for those born in the sign of Cancer.

Leo

July 23rd—August 22nd

Element: Fire
Quality: Fixed
Ruling Planet: Sun

How to Present Yourself

Leo needs to be seen and noticed, however, as a Leo, the most important thing for you is not being seen by others, but having respect for yourself so *you* can enjoy what you see in the mirror. If you try to win the respect and appreciation of others by being the hero that they want you to be, you will be stuck as a character you do not want to be. It is like a lion trying to be the king of hyenas—not a suitable task. As a Leo, you have a lot of warm enthusiasm and joy that you radiate and share with others. If you are addicted to them liking and approving your actions, you will be trapped like a lion in a small cage. Everybody that has visited the zoo and seen frustrated lions pacing back and forth knows that this is not a good solution. As children, Leos often feel that they take up too much space and dominate others with their energy. Making a futile attempt at being invisible and unrecognizable does not work, but neither does taking up all the space or craving all of the attention all of the time. Being the one and only can be very lonely and demand a price that is too high, even for a Leo. What a Leo needs is to give hope, inspiration, and optimism to others. They need to open up with greatness and abundance.

Scarcity, smallness, and stinginess fit them very badly. It is important for them to be larger than life, not just to give nice gifts and play the game of greatness. They have to trust their own exuberance or else they start to feel like sheep in wolves' clothing—or if they play too much for the gallery, like lions in rabbit suits. Lions are born with the true understanding that there is just one thing that can be the center of the life of any individual being, and that is that individual. It is important for all Leos to see and acknowledge this. They need to feel comfortable with being self-centered, which is something completely different from being egotistical. When the sign of Leo really acts out of the fire of their own inner center, they can give all their gifts to others freely. Coming from this place, Leos can give compassion and love, togetherness and unity. However, if they try to make the other person the main focus of their life, they lose themselves and do not really have much to give. The same goes for trying to make themselves the center of other people's lives.

It is important for Leos to know that others have just as much right to be seen and take up space as they do. In some sense, Leo needs to begin by developing the necessary amount of self-respect, after which they can give and have the same respect for the individual miracle that is every other person. They need to see that the feelings, thoughts, and experiences of any other being are just as important to that being as the Leo's feelings, thoughts, and experiences are to them. When Leo has understood and incorporated a basic respect for others and is true to their own integrity in daily life, they can choose to open up their life freely. They can let the true richness of their warmth, energy, and abundance flow unhampered into the world. They can give freely and the rest of us can enjoy the warmth from their fire and their genuine joy in giving. But Leo: be aware! The moment you want to get back as much as you give out, you stop the flow, and what was a rich ore of inner gold becomes a self-absorbed trickle of old coins. In the worst-case scenarios, the glorious Leo is changed to a whimpering, dissatisfied, and self-obsessed child.

As a Leo, you should strive to be giving, warm, and radiant, and know that you are an individual that has great respect both for yourself and for others. Be the person you really would respect others for being, and respect others for being the person they would like you to be. As you hone yourself into a person you really can respect, you can freely show your true face to others. I can guarantee you that they will respect you.

How to Get the Best from Your Talents and Resources

Leo is the harshest critic of their own accomplishments and creations. They want everything they do to be perfect. Even if they always show off like they are the best, they have an insecure inner critic that always whispers in their ear that they could have done better. They also have clear ideas about right and wrong and can easily become quite judgmental and moralistic. In some ways, Leos are so critical of their own accomplishments that they just can't take another critical voice. In general, they want to hear only praise and good words from others, since they manage to take care of the other side of the coin themselves.

Some Lions get numbed and pacified by sheer performance anxiety and do not dare to use their creativity for something that involves a risk of negative feedback. Others just think they are rhinos and push away any kind of criticism or opposition like blind bulldozers. The only voice they listen to is their own inner one that tells them how magnificent they are...a conviction that, in reality, stems from the fear of not being enough.

To get the best from their many talents and gifts, Leos would do well to open themselves up to advice and suggestions about how things could be better and more efficient. It is good for them to strive for the very best and give themselves a lot of credit for really trying, even if the result, every now and then, is far from perfect. They grow by analyzing their own accomplishments to see what worked and what could be done better next time. They grow and make gains by constantly searching for ways to develop and better themselves and their creations. This process might begin with a willingness to admit their shortcomings, but it continues with a willingness to do the work of correcting their flaws, even if it is very painful and humbling to admit that work is needed. To get the best from their mighty and grand personalities, they have to embrace humbleness and a willingness to work with the flaws that come from an abundance of small details. It is their energy, enthusiasm, and personal engagement that gives Leo individuals such charisma and power. When they want to create something worthwhile in the world, they must be sensible, practical, and realistic.

A Leo needs to have a clear concept of their inner and outer ethical standards. They need to see that the same rules apply to them and others. An immature Leo thinks that they can allow themselves to do things that others should not, since they are so special. When they are a bit more advanced, they keep their own path very clean and tidy but allow others to make more missteps and do not demand that they have the same standards of ethics that the Leo lives by. It is of great importance for Leos to master the noble art of forgiveness. They need to forgive others and themselves for their fallibility and shortcomings. It is nice to try to embody the greatest and noblest ideals and standards, but it is also impossible to meet those standards every minute of every day. At the same time as they strive for the great and glorious ideal, they need to see that part of human greatness comes from rising above their fallibility and lowest desires, not from being free of them.

A true hero is not one without weakness, but rather one who admits their weakness but is not conquered by it. Greatness is not to be flawless, but to be great in spite of your flaws and fears. As a Lion, you are very well equipped to see the great and promising potential and possibilities in others and in yourself. You get the most from this quality when you don't judge yourself or others but are willing to keep moving forward on the yellow brick road with many precise and tiny steps.

Communication and Immediate Surroundings

Leos are masters of encouragement and friendliness—when they want to be. A Leo in balance and in good spirits is very forthcoming and friendly to anyone they are in contact with. This is the sunny side of their communication and, as with all areas of their sunny side, is very bright and shining. They have this knack for making their words sound and seem personal, whether they talk to you alone or if you are part of a crowd with hundreds of listeners. This stems from the simple fact they themselves are personal and speak directly from their heart and soul. They talk to individuals, and the individual that is listening happens to be you. It can be flattering and great for the ego to feel this personal interest and contact oozing from a Leo, even though it actually just comes from the way these creatures are.

When Leo loses inner balance and control, the picture is radically changed. A Leo that has left courtesy and a smiling face behind will stretch your ideas about what rude, hurtful, and bothersome comments are made of. They do not seem to have heard about the golden in-between. Leos seem to be either friendly, forthcoming, and sophisticated, or unpleasant and unpredictable—and guess whether they know how to use flattery to get their way. Seen from the opposite side, Leos are the most naive and easiest beings to fool with flattery and by sucking up to their egos. To get them to do what you want, just tell them how fantastic, great, and amazing they are.

Most Leos are like big, purring cats that enjoy company and love to talk with other people about nice and uplifting things. They also love to make plans and exchange ideas and visions. You can only begin to imagine how much this big, sensual, and cozy being enjoys surroundings that are luxurious, stylish, and exquisite. They feel so much better in an elegant restaurant than in a dumpy one. Since their egos seem to be reflected in their surroundings, it is quite obvious that they like their surroundings to be expensive and beautiful. They especially need to be surrounded by visually pleasing things and sights. They are really bothered by ugly noises and voices that quarrel—unless they are the ones doing the quarreling.

One thing Leo disapproves of is talking about difficulties and problems, especially their own. They like to talk about what is good and shining in their life and just bypass the unpleasant and inconvenient. They can live by the motto "out of sight, out of mind." This makes it difficult to talk your way through the real, deep problems with Leos. This sign prefers to cling to their nice and cozy illusions about reality for as long as possible. They are true masters of avoiding thoughts about anything it bothers them to think about. They even can forget that a problem exists, like the true masters of denial they really can become.

As a Leo, it is smart to remember that the visual impression a person sends you isn't necessarily congruent with their inner nature. You also must remember that sweet and pretty words of praise and beauty can just as easily be calculated or unconscious lies as the truth. You have a strange tendency to trust the untrustworthy and distrust those who are trustworthy. You need to learn how to address the unpleasant and hurtful stuff without losing control and ending up like a wobbly, spinning top. To find the quality, harmony, and joy that you seek in all your relationships, you need to avoid being caught in the web of flawlessness, facade, and superficiality.

Home and Family

Leos are very deep and tightly knit in their relationships with their family and have ties that stretch for eternity below the surface. They often feel that there are a lot of secrets and "dark" things that need to be hidden from the public regarding both their childhood home and the one they establish as adults. What happens inside the walls of their home stays inside those walls. They feel a great need to control their home situation and can easily create situations that give birth to power struggles and strong emotional conflicts of interest with their closest family. Most Leos will create and/or encounter situations where they have to fight a very deep and fundamental fight around who has the power at home. Who dictates what is to be done, and when? If their home is their kingdom, there are bound to be fights with those who do not want to be the subjects of a king with absolute power.

Letting go of their ties to their childhood home, and especially to their mom, is difficult for all Leos. These emotional ties are so strong that they will never melt away completely, but when this sign has left the heaven (or hell) of childhood, there are no return tickets available. However, it is a great challenge and undertaking for a Leo to learn emotional sovereignty. They are in dire need of someone with whom they can share their inner secrets and emotions. Their home is, almost without exception, the one place where they can display the weaknesses, shadows, and fears that they hide from the rest of the pack. The "work" of the family is to see this and to learn to love the Leo individual as they really are, without all the splendor and regalia. When they do, Leos become the most purring, lovable, and affectionate beings you can imagine. They then offer their sexuality as a gift to their partner instead of using it to conquer and reign. Sexuality, for this sign, is very connected to wishing to create a family. For an immature Leo, sexual power means that you are the strongest specimen, and the best others can find for building their own self-esteem. In the mature Leo, sexuality is a sign of strength, togetherness, and unselfish love. The mature Lion is very loyal and needs to receive the same loyalty and faithfulness from their family. They demand and give 100 percent—no more, no less.

Leos do enjoy homes that are great and impressive (like a castle), but inside the home, there also has to be some kind of den that they can withdraw to and block access to for everyone else. There, they can think and relax in the absolute knowledge that no one will ever arrive unexpectedly. This is their secret place, where all thoughts are allowed to be thought, all words are allowed to be said, and no taboos exist. As mentioned, they become very strongly attached to a place: a house and the belongings in their home. Anything that is connected with a memory or a good emotional experience—and feels like part of who they are—is very hard to let go of. If they do let go, it is final. If you ever disappoint a Leo who has held you dear so deeply that they let you go, you will know what I mean—bygones will be bygones. The immature ones will hate you forever; the more mature ones are just indifferent. Leos do not appreciate changes in their home environment. They like for everything and everybody to be in the proper, designated place. They like home to be a place where everything is safe, and nothing has to be rearranged or dealt with before things are okay. They want home to be the safe haven that they can use as a base for going out into the world, where they are occupied with spreading and sharing their warmth and shining light.

Creativity and Leisure

Leos love to play. They want to have fun and are physically brave and expansive. They love to do new things and experience unexpected opportunities and adventures. They love to be on the go and traveling is really quite excellent for them. The only real trouble with having fun and traveling is that they do not always know where the limits are. So, every now and then, they learn about those limits in unpleasant ways. They have a tendency to move beyond their capability and believe that they can handle challenges that are far above their capacity. Seen from another angle though, it is often this very enthusiasm, lack of restraint, and ability to see their own limits that gives Leo the opportunity to grow beyond their former limits and thus develop more greatness and face more challenges. As grown-ups, they are good at giving their children freedom and inspiration. They thrive around people who are independent, courageous, and self-reliant. They might even have problems understanding people who are not this way. They do not really know how to handle people who are filled with anxiety, resistance, and other traumas. The exception is, of course, when the Leo themself has gone through those things and thereby knows the nature of the problem from the inside.

Generally speaking, a Leo handles prosperity and success far better than adversity and failure, both personally and professionally. They are good winners and sore losers. Some of them grow egos that are terribly inflated if they have too much success, but even those people don't go too hard when it comes to being condescending and arrogant toward others. Adversity, on the other hand, is something they have a problem processing. Losing is so painful that it often just catapults them out into deep darkness. Most Leos experience losing as a rejection from life, and if there is one thing they really can't handle, it is rejection. They take rejection very personally, which comes from the simple fact that everything *is* personal for a Lion. They easily feel like others are thwarting them. Leos can get so occupied with a problem that their eyes are glued to the hindrance and never slide in the direction of the solution. What really helps them through adversity is holding their hopes and glories high. A mature Leo will give others hope, faith, and light in the coldest and darkest of circumstances. An immature Leo wants to stand in the spotlight of others' admiration and be carried by their hope, beliefs, and enthusiasm.

Leos love surprises and thrive when flirting and playing games. They are masters of showing you that they like you and enjoy your company and what they would like to do with you if you would like them to. But they also know that a flirt is a flirt and do not necessarily have any need to move from flirtation into reality. Knowing that they are attractive and sought after is often enough. They enjoy the dance, but all their hidden moves and flirting have nothing to do with reality and eternal promises. Leos like to have ambitions, even in their spare time and childlike games. They get deep satisfaction from reaching and fulfilling these goals. So, for them, playing is never just playing, just as the serious is never only serious. As mentioned, Leos are benevolent, tolerant, and giving… at least when their inner Sun is up and shining. What they dislike the most is stinginess, both in themselves and others. As a Leo, the best thing you can do with your leisure time and creativity is to fill it with something funny, entertaining, and instructive that promises to make the world a better place to roam for yourself and others.

Health, Order, and the Necessary

Leos are mostly disciplined and often enjoy training to keep their bodies fit. They prefer things that are solid and structured and stay where they are supposed to stay, and that goes for bodies as well as workplaces. A Leo needs and enjoys order, routine, and systems to hold the pieces of their life together. Leos might be spokespersons for democracy, but not the kind of democracy where everybody is supposed to do everything and have the right to the same influence as everybody else. It is important for them to know who the captain is...and who is supposed to fulfill the orders given by the captain. They like a hierarchic structure where responsibilities and functions are clearly divided and given.

Leos are often very good at building organizations and structures. In that respect, they are practical, result-oriented, and want to utilize the time and abilities of themselves and others as effectively and productively as possible. They want results from their undertakings and have little interest in endless meetings and idle talk about mere ideas. To others, they may seem inflexible—and in truth, they can be, but most of the time they are effective, even if they have a tendency to get hung up on certain ways of doing things and get a bit too stiff and self-conscious. Every now and then, Leos need to raise their eyes from whatever they are doing to see that the old ways don't work anymore.

I can assure any Leo reading this that you will never be out of work. There will always be something somewhere that should be fixed or organized in an even better way. In some sense, you strive to finish your work off, but fortunately for you, there is always more coming in. This stems from the fact that the work of life does not have an end, but also from the fact that Leos are very responsible and often do the jobs of others in addition to their own. Leos are easily annoyed and irritated by those who seem careless and irresponsible. They can have difficulties when they must cooperate with people whose work methods include inspiration or delaying things until the last minute. To them, this is not serious and too lackadaisical. It is important for this sign to learn the difference between laziness and lack of effort versus the more chaotic and inspired ways of doing things that are abundant in the work ethics of many creative people.

Leos need to cultivate a serious relationship with their own physical body and health. Sometimes they can become so serious about health and body issues that their greatest health issue becomes their own stiffness and fear of losing control. Softness and flexibility in their bodies is something to strive for. Leos are known to laugh loudly and often, but they really hate to be the laughingstock of others. They are very prone to an overdose of self-importance. Developing self-deprecating humor is one of the best medicines for a Leo. This medicine might have a bitter taste in the beginning, but self-deprecating humor tastes better and better as you become used to it. In more practical terms, Leos benefit from healthy food, stable eating habits, and a regular diurnal rhythm. When Leos become fat, it stems from an inflated ego or laziness and a strong craving for the sweet stuff. Most Leos have a great resistance to illness and bad health as long as they have emotional and practical stability, a required minimum of self-deprecation, and the necessary daily dosage of order and structure in their lives.

One-on-One Relationships

In close relationships, Leos go for passion, but they are also on a quest to find true friendship. They have huge ideals about relationships and are attracted to people who have the same theories and longings in relationships. They see their own worth reflected in their partners; consequently, they are looking for someone who is attractive and makes them proud. They want their close ones to be extraordinary and unique and are seldom attracted to mediocrity or anything seen as common. Quite often, Leos end up with problems in their relationships, since reality has trouble meeting the quality and standards of their idealistic expectations. To many partners, it might be a challenge that Leos want absolute freedom, absolute passion, and total tolerance...all at the same time. If they find a person who is able to meet their very high standards and ideals, Leos themselves have a hard time meeting their own ideals. Maybe the hardest challenge for a Leo is the time when they are dependent on their partner or while their partner can manage without their company. In their ideal world, jealousy is beneath them but in reality, it is a very common emotion for Leos to experience. They have great difficulties with allowing their partners the same freedom and space that they demand for themselves. Their big and passionate hearts make them burn with great force when love hits them, but as we know, fire needs oxygen in order to burn. If a Leo does not get some distance between themselves and their loved ones, both the Leo and their chosen one start to feel suffocated. If it becomes too exhausting to draw the breath of life, then passion dies. Leo needs distance and space to keep the hot flame of intimacy and passion alive. At the same time, they may deny themselves that space, since they want to always be close to their loved ones.

Leos are always looking for an equal partner. In job situations they like hierarchy, but at home, there has to be equanimity. This feeling of equal worth is a necessity if they want to maintain both self-respect and respect for their partner. In some sense, they need someone whom they can try to dominate all the time but who has the same strength and inner power as the Leo. Every Leo will strive to be the boss and number one in their relationships, but at the same time, the only people they can have a really good relationship with are those who don't allow them to get their own way. This does not come from egotism or something shady, the need to be number one is just in their nature. It is the immature Leo that finds and sticks to a partner who is weak, compliant, and easily manipulated. The mature Leo finds romantic partners and close friends who have strength and power equal to their own. Of course, these relationships are much more fun to be in, since it is much nicer to play with someone who is a match for you. No lasting satisfaction is born from the fact that you are stronger than a weakling. All Leos can learn and grow a lot through their partners. They need these intimate relationships if they are ever going to understand the deeper levels of self-worth. In fact, a Leo's closest relationship is their main resource for understanding the nature and true worth of all human relationships. There, they are introduced to the noble art of respecting and helping others, while at the same time keeping their dignity. Throughout this process, they learn to grant other people the same rights that they demand for themselves.

Choosing a life partner might easily be the most important choice a Leo ever makes. As a Leo, you have a tendency to become stuck in your first choice, unless they—for some strange and unfathomable reason—leave you. It is important for you to go for someone who is just as strong, or maybe even stronger than you are. You must remember that your partner should not only have the same ability as you in handling the world, they also need the inner power to handle the challenge that is you. As a Leo, you have the potential to become a great, adorable, and fantastic partner, but to achieve your potential, you must be very willing to learn what you need on the road and have humility enough to admit that the master teacher is your partner.

Beneath the Surface—Sex and Taboos

In the world of fantasy, there are no taboos or impossibilities for this creature. Questions about morals and ethics in the real world, though, are another story. Leos do not generally lack ethics in their behavior, even if their inner world is a non-moralistic and uninhibited place. However, some of them react with violence against their own inner frivolity and lack of ethos, becoming totally clogged up with morality and fanatical standards. In that case, they suffer from severe cases of guilt just for thinking or dreaming about something that their moralistic mind finds improper and unfitting. If so, they feel disgraced and belittled by having the slightest want or need that isn't in total harmony with their ideals.

As in all other things, nothing is impossible when a Leo has chosen to cross their Rubicon. As Caesar said: "The die is cast (*Alea iacta est*)." In the outer world, Leos might often stand out as proper, well-behaved, and exemplary. What they do in private is not the business of anyone besides themselves and any other people they're doing things with. Having a perfect facade with dark things hidden beneath the surface is not an uncommon occurrence for these animals.

Integrating their inner visions and dreams with the real life of the world is of prime importance to Leos. If they do not acknowledge their inner world, they will end up being possessed by their unfulfilled wishes. High on the list of things that most Leos hide from the world are their vulnerability and weaknesses. In fact, they are very empathetic and compassionate and cry over the slightest of things. They work hard to hide this sentiment and lack of toughness, but as the Leo heart expands and swells in tears or in love, they have to give in and stop trying to keep both feet solidly planted on the ground. They have to surrender and just allow themself to drift away on the pink clouds of unquenchable feelings.

As far as sexuality goes, Leos can play the game in two different ways. The first is to have sex with everything that moves and is attractive, and then, of course, the whole thing becomes a bit superficial and impersonal. If this is the case, they do not really see the other person, since they are having sex with their own fantasy rather than the actual person they're with. The other possibility is that they focus all their sexual energy on their chosen one. In that case, that person becomes the center of their universe and all their attention. If you are their chosen one, they will worship the ground on which you walk. Leo truly knows the art of loving absolutely and with no restraints. What you both need to know is that it takes a lot of work to keep love alive through the humdrum of real life, and this is the real secret of a Leo with a successful sexual life: they have learned to keep their dreams alive, how those dreams can be nurtured and grow even greater by the meeting with reality. It is an ongoing dance of passion and tenderness. In their heart, this Leo knows that the other person, whom they love so dearly, is the playing ground where reality and dreams can meet and mingle.

Education, Adventure, and Life Philosophy

In one sense, the life of a Leo is always a journey that has just begun. The possibilities and educational capacities of life are never-ending. This eagerness and longing to get going keep this sign young and alive. Leos are sensible when it comes to manifesting their projects in the real world, but enthusiasm, passion, and impulsivity are what keep them going. If they become too realistic and stop seizing risky opportunities, life will become a dull project for them. If there is something that makes life unlivable for this sign, it is boredom and dullness. As a Leo, you can just as well admit to yourself that you need excitement, pressure, adventure, and challenges to have a life worth living.

Starting new projects is always fun. Leos often unexpectedly expand beyond their known horizons, and age is no hindrance. In some ways, Leos remain eternal children. They never stop loving, exploring the unknown, going to new places, or venturing to see what is yet unseen. At the same time, they want to have a stable foundation where nothing changes and that they always know they can return to. In their travels, Leos do not care so much about luxury and comfort. They appreciate those qualities, as always, but that's not what they are after. They are in the market for experiences and new impressions. They want these impressions to be connected with physicality and action: they enjoy some hardship and external obstacles that have to be conquered. You know they just adore being victorious, and to become a victor, you have to go through some kind of challenge. Leos are in the market for challenges that force them to use their full will and determination to get to wherever they are headed. They do not necessarily need mountains to climb—just to act like they are climbing one. The worst thing you can do with a Leo is put them in a place where nothing happens, and everything is totally relaxed. It takes about half a second before they become bored and restless. A true vacation for a Leo is not filled with peace and quiet, but with active recreation.

Leos enjoy learning about the newest of the new and staying at the forefront of development. They are often self-made innovators and love to see the unfamiliar and rare when they travel. This king of the jungle abhors standing in lines and being just one among the common masses. Lions have a tendency to become reckless and careless in their play. They might be too strong and hurt the people around them without meaning to, but when the damage is done, they just shrug and say something like, "If you want to play the game, you have to take the pain." One piece of advice for Leos is to take a look at your age, general health, and physical state before you throw yourself into challenges like snow racing in the Himalayas or walking among the crocodiles in the Amazon. But whatever your age, you need to have the taste of adventure on your tongue every now and then. Without these kicks, you doze off and feel more dead than alive. Another good piece of advice: don't put more at stake than you can handle losing.

Goals, Profession, and Career

Leos are productive and have great staying power when moving in their chosen direction in life. They do not see the point of trying to become or do something that just isn't within reach. Consequently, they are both realistic and determined. Leos need to be part of the results they create. Most of them are creators of their own opportunities and want to be unique and personally invaluable, not just a piece in the puzzle.

They are investing in their own value and building their own image. The most important product sold by a Leo is not their vision nor the idea, but themselves and their ability to meet your expectations.

As a Leo, you thrive in a profession that is economically secure and satisfying. You need to create some predictability and stability in your career since you enjoy working within the frameworks of long-term projects and strategies. When you are inspired and on the go, you gladly use an enormous amount of effort and time to develop and carry out your projects and interests. But without a stable foundation and security, you may risk all your work being wasted. Since you like to work with big dreams and long-term possibilities, there may be a long distance between the starting point and the payoff.

The professional Leo is quite different from their personal self. The personal Leo is playful and values experience more than results. The professional is sensible, and serious, and wants to touch the concrete manifestations of their effort. As a Leo, you have great determination and staying power. Your professional self moves like a big truck: it takes time to get up to a high speed, and it will take considerable time to stop if you try to hit the brakes. At times, you might be a little too practical and sensible regarding your own career. It is not unknown for Leos to become too comfortable in a job they should have left because it has become routine and insufficiently stimulating. You thrive in professions where something new is developed, be it thoughts, processes, or products. You enjoy having a job where you can influence the value system of the larger society. You are at your best when you create something you deem beautiful and long-lasting. You are good at falling into line when you have clarity around your tasks and responsibilities, but you still must be able to work at your own speed and in your own manner. You have your own ways of doing things and your own way of implementing your ideas. If somebody tries to push you or make you do things you do not want to do, you become an immovable rock. No one can coerce you to do something you do not want to do. Sometimes you can choose your whole career out of pure stubbornness, something that isn't a very good idea.

You need to dedicate your life to doing something you find valuable. You are the tool, and the goal is to make something worthwhile out of your life. Your nature is to always seek opportunities that increase your value and the value of the work you are doing. At your best, you are extremely giving and sharing. To reach this potential, you must become secure about your own value and your ability to create something significant and worth sharing with the world. When you are in that position, you are the very best at inspiring others and letting them know how magnificent and fabulous they are. Your own greatest reward for an excellent piece of work is not the admiration and applause of others (although you enjoy that too), but to see that what you have done works and really makes the world thrive and makes it a better and more beautiful place than it was before.

Friends, Future, and Ideals

"The more the merrier" is how you feel about friends. They do not need to be close, but they do need to be fun to play with. Leos enjoy being a part of a group and thrive the most when they are the center of an event. Friends and acquaintances are often where Leos go when they are hunting for new ideas and inspirations. Leos like to be around young people and often have friends that have been on Earth for less time than they have. They can feel bored if their social life becomes too repetitive, old-fashioned, or accountable. They like to feel young and up-to-date. Leos do not seek friends for emotional intimacy or depth, but to create an arena where they can discuss opinions, ideas, and possibilities. They enjoy having opinions and discussing them with others—some will call them a bit opinionated.

Leos are filled with ideas about how things are going to turn out. These ideas are more like speculations than visions. There are some possibilities they want to avoid and others they want to experience, but for the most part, they are open and curious. They believe in human potential and cultural development. Most of them are optimistic about the future and believe that humanity is growing in knowledge, wisdom, and the ability to get things right. In an underdeveloped country, most Leos would be more interested in developing the schools rather than farming. They believe in the power of knowledge and the mind. They know that understanding and conscious awareness give people the opportunity to create a better future. Most Leos are knowledgeable and great hunters for information. They want to know everything about the latest discoveries, both in their specific profession and about the general state of development on the planet. They walk with their professional feet on the ground, while at the same time, their visionary heads soar into the unknown future. They look for opportunities to take the best of the now into the best of the future. More often than not, they have a lot of words and ideas that they want to spread to the general public. Leos do not really care if the ideas they spread are original or taken from others. The only thing that matters to them is that they get credit for being the ones to share the information. If they get the acknowledgment for being the messenger, others can get the credit for being the creator in this respect.

Leo has two major categories of friends. The first category consists of the friends they have for life and feel are their equals. These friends are quite few, and Leo feels a great sense of loyalty and admiration for them. The other sort is made up of acquaintances with just a little hint of friendship. Their relationship to these friends is superficial, and they can easily be exchanged with new ones. As a Leo, you need to know the difference between those who are just passing by the window of friendship and those whom you want to give your unwavering loyalty to and have a deep friendship with. Another important thing to remember is that you do not create the future by yourself! That means that you have to learn how to co-create with others that can share inspiration, ideas, and true friendship with you.

Seeking and the Spiritual

Spirituality is, like all other things, a very personal matter for the Leo. Either they have a relationship to spirit and the divine power that is behind all that is intimate, personal, and emotional…or they couldn't care less. Leo is not interested in lukewarm relationships without passion. What decides the quality of their relationship to the divine isn't sensibility, reason, or logic, but pure emotion. The high road to spirituality for this sign is the inner world and the experience of energy and emotional unity. It is very simple: the less a Leo feels unity and love as the main force in the world, the less of a connection they have to spirituality. The more Leo experiences a deep sense of belonging and unity with the universe, the more spiritual they become.

This predator must follow their intuition and feel the truth that comes through their inner acknowledgment if they are ever to catch the spiritual prey in the jungle of physicality. They have two gears; either they deny the existence of spirituality, or they hunt for it with all their senses at full alert. The key to their spiritual experience and understanding is never found in the mind, but always in the heart. The name of this key is love. This love is not something distant, but more like a mother that nurtures life and all beings with power and beauty. It goes far beyond what we see as personal love and lust and is more like perceiving the world as one big family. In some ways, Leo as a sign is very connected to the individual and personal identity. This spiritual experience is the opposite and can be called the *feminine* way to spirituality, which involves surrendering and having an experience of unity and compassion for all that is. They have to find the Goddess that does not demand or challenge but instead receives and loves without conditions.

As the circle ends, this also becomes the highest expression of an individual born in the sign of Leo: loving without condition and nurturing without craving any form of compensation. The spiritual, mature Leo feels oneness with everyone and does not create divisions where some are on the inside and redeemed, while others on the outside are condemned. This Leo has understood that "love thy neighbor as thyself" isn't meant to be symbolic, but to be taken literally. Leo has understood that on a deep level of existence, you *are* your neighbor. Thus, the only way to really get the self-love that Leo wants so much is to truly love thy neighbor. For the spiritual Leo, this isn't some sort of magical abracadabra, but just the true reality of life. Since everything is personal, so is the divine. It isn't megalomania when the spiritual Leo says the words "I am God." The truth is that since everything that exists is God, the Leo must also be God. This animal does need to connect with a very individual and personal aspect of God. They need a God whose love is truly unlimited and whose love does not just exist on an abstract or theoretical, spiritual level. They need a God whose love includes this world, and the ramification of that is that the spiritual Leo truly feels love for everything and everyone. True spirituality for this sign is quite simply to be a vessel for unselfish love…no more, no less.

Virgo

August 23rd—September 22nd

Element: Earth
Quality: Mutable
Ruling Planet: Mercury

How to Present Yourself

Virgos often want to be seen as innocent, trustworthy, and reliable. They more often than not wear a mask of politeness, essential goodness, and benevolence toward all. This outer display of harmless benevolence is worn partly because it has some truth and partly because it hides their true thoughts—and even more importantly, their true feelings. As a Virgo, you need to check that your appearance is in harmony with your inner world and experience of life. You thrive when you are clean, pure, and well-dressed. You are also known for taking your time to find a suitable outfit that doesn't provoke attention or single you out in any way. You want to get things right but can easily get them wrong if you do not take your time to think through a situation and what kind of signals you want to send before you get dressed.

One thing you need to learn is that lies do not suit you. In all situations, you are better off with honesty than even the whitest of lies. Okay, you do not want to hurt anybody, but be aware: it is more hurtful to be lied to than to be told the unpleasant truth in a clear and compassionate manner. Give others the same respect that you want them to give you—and that includes believing that they are capable of handling your truth. As a Virgo, you can be quiet, modest, careful, and shy. You need to be aware of the game you play—if you are not, you will hide your qualities in fear of having people trample your heart. Show others how much you appreciate compliments and praise. You are one of the star signs that does not need to worry about feeling grandiose or becoming too self-important. Your trap is more like becoming too much of a critical judge. The rare occasions in which you do seem arrogant stem from the insecurity and fear hidden behind your "I know better than you" facade. Be honest and show others that you are interested. Do not live in the shadow of your fear of rejection. You can be an excellent adviser but be careful not to lose yourself in the constant needs of everybody around you. You must learn to cut the crap instead of being too polite to interrupt—or to just walk away when necessary.

As mentioned, you can be very critical and sharp-tongued. Let others see this side of you early in the game. Then, they won't be so surprised when your sharp tongue overrides your shyness. Be aware of the danger of making your well-groomed appearance into a shield that you hide behind. Make it instead a tool that lets you express and share the contents of both your clever mind and your sensitive heart. Others might not easily see through your carefully arranged defenses, but you often use your sharp, critical brain to hide your tender heart. The truth is that you are a rare mix of trust and skepticism, cunning and naivety. Let others know that these two sides coexist within you and that they even have a very good and cooperative relationship. When you remove your mask and truly show the world both your cunning and your naivety, your relationships with the world and all other humans will be greatly enriched. No longer do you need to hide your true self, although every now and then you need to protect yourself by knowing how to withdraw from unpleasant and unwanted situations and circumstances. In this manner, you will find your way into the pleasures and possibilities of this world much more quickly and joyfully.

How to Get the Best from Your Talents and Resources

Virgos often have a multitude of talents. Their problem seems to be figuring out what to choose since they often want to do everything at once. Virgos love beauty but do not want to be seen as extravagant or vain. Every now and then, a Virgo forgets to listen to their real longings and is preoccupied with what they think they are supposed to want. This stems from the fact that ideas are often more attractive in theory than in practice. Virgos can be so polite, nice, and idealistic that they get stuck on a track that they do not really want to be on. This is one of the reasons why a Virgo tries to keep all options available. But then, fortunately, life has this strange tendency to make reality out of the choices you are avoiding. However, sometimes a Virgo may not see the writing on the wall, and they let the last train leave the station while they ponder where they really want to travel with their life.

As a Virgo, you are not very good at doing things by yourself and need other people to help you see your talents and find the direction you want to take with them. You need others that support, push, encourage, or need you to get going. Without other people to give your actions significance, you easily become passive and unable to get things done. You have a tendency to become economically dependent on others, but you need to remember that they, more often than not, are just as in need of your support as you are of theirs. Every now and then, others do not discover your value and talents until you disappear. It is good for both you—and everyone else—to make others aware of how much you are really sharing and sacrificing for them. Give them at least the possibility of appreciating you before it is too late. It is no victory for either of you if they miss you when you are gone.

Independence is a bit difficult for this sign since Virgos need reciprocity and sociability in their working situation. As a Virgo, you might work long and hard, but if you do not look out the window, you might find that others have harvested the fruits of your labor while you were busy. This happens because you are very good at supporting and helping others, while it is not as natural for you to support and help yourself. You do not want to stick out or give anybody the impression that you believe that you are better than them. You want to be seen as humble and modest, even if you secretly know that you are more logical and doing a better job than many other people. It is important that you give yourself the respect and acknowledgment that you want to get from others. You need to accept that even if you and other people are equals, you can give yourself credit for having done an excellent piece of work that is better than average.

One of Virgo's greatest talents is utilizing their own skills and resources at the same time as helping others develop and get the most from theirs. When they really get going, Virgos cooperate with people in a way that is based on reciprocal support and trust while each individual is still independent and free to do things their own way. Virgos utilize their talents most efficiently and satisfactorily when they can give inspiration and support to others and be part of a team while still being free to follow their own directions and explore all their talents. As they learn to receive support and inspiration in the same natural way that they give it, the Virgo can start to reap the great benefits of true cooperation.

Communication and Immediate Surroundings

Virgos need a lot of communication and a feeling of closeness with the people they see on a daily basis. Generally, they feel out of place in large groups where nobody knows each other and far prefer small, intimate settings with people they already know. They form strong bonds with family and close friends. Even if they often walk lightly on the surface of conversations, their feelings run deep. They are searching for people whom they can explore these depths with by sharing ideas and having conversations. Strangely enough, it can be uncomfortable for them to talk superficially with people they do not know because they feel like they are hiding their true feelings behind meaningless words. On the other hand, they love to talk lightly with good friends. Virgos feel that once their emotions are known, they are self-evident and do not need to be shown or talked about. Often, the emotional undercurrent is what's most important, so the words do not seem to matter that much. Virgos always catch the underlying sensations and emotions within the people they talk to, even if they are often completely unaware of this process or how it works. They prefer to describe it as good intuition and an ability to use their brains to reach the right conclusions. Most Virgos immediately know whether they like or dislike a person they meet, and that impression seldom changes with time. So, very often, Virgo catches more of the undercurrent of the emotions, motivations, and desires of the person that they are talking to than the true content of that person's words. This gives Virgos a problem. They try to be rational and logical, but their inner radar catches the irrational and illogical signals that the mind sends unconsciously.

Virgos only trust people they know are worthy of being trusted with their secrets, and this trust implies that its recipients understand what words and opinions were meant for their ears only and what they are free to spread to others. As long as a Virgo does not trust your ability to be discreet, they will not tell you their real thoughts or feelings. If you are not worthy of this trust, they will keep talking to you, just not about any areas where they feel insecure, weak, or vulnerable. For them, it is a huge step and takes a lot of confidence to share their innermost thoughts and feelings.

Virgos seldom state a strong opinion unless they mean it 100 percent, but they do have a tendency to think and talk in black and white. They seem to have very strong sympathy or resistance to things and often think in terms of right or wrong without seeing all of the many shades of gray. They easily become very occupied with and feel intensely about the topic that is discussed in the moment, even if they aren't that interested half an hour later. This is thanks to the fact that they have only two gears when talking to others: either they are not interested and not very engaged, or they are going in at full intensity. It might be surprising for others when a Virgo talks about something as if it is life or death in one moment, and then in the next breath, they switch to something new and seem to have forgotten all about the first topic.

Virgos are very strongly connected to some people, while most other people are kind of floating by them in a fog of impersonality. The more polite a Virgo behaves, the less you as an individual mean to them. If they do behave rudely in front of you, you are either a very close friend or an archenemy. Rudeness means that they are showing you a bit more of who they really are and what they really feel. You are either counted as a worthless piece of shit who does not deserve any better or as a good friend who is worthy of seeing their true inner darkness. If you pass that test, then you are evaluated and found worthy of being their real friend, since you can handle their sharp minds and tongues without stomping on their sensitive hearts.

Home and Family

Virgos like a big family that gives them a sense of security and permanence. They feel like part of a secret clan and are very giving and compassionate toward their near and dear. They can take a lot of shit from family that would have left them running and screaming if it came from anybody else. As for homes, Virgos thrive in large houses with a lot of open space. They are known for their cleanliness, but many of them are quite chaotic and too occupied with matters more important than housekeeping. For them, home is a place to dream, learn, and read. Often, the house is filled with books, brochures, and things they need for whatever strange project they are interested in at the moment. They enjoy being at home where they can think and talk about what they are going to do and all the possibilities there are. They need to have a feeling of space around the house. If they do not have a garden, they at least need to have a porch or a collection of Japanese bonsais in the living room.

It is important for them that their close ones are healthy, happy, and cheerful. It bothers them greatly when someone in their family is sick or feeling down. They sorely want to help and make everything fine again. Of course, when everything is fine, they are free to tell bitter truths and spread scary ideas and information. They need a home where discussions and sharing opinions are accepted and wanted. Virgos, who in so many areas of life are good organizers and know where their limits ought to be, can easily become limitless and out of order in their own homes. They seem to be either focused perfectionists who are endlessly working to make their home brighter, better, and even more beautiful and perfect, or they go the opposite direction and let everything slide into chaos. Then, home becomes the only place where they can be totally relaxed and allow their inner tornadoes to run free.

The Virgo likes to improve everything they are in contact with, and this goes for everything inside the home—including the people. Be prepared for a constant flow of renovations, innovations, and new stuff if you live with a Virgo. They love everything that is new and free of all the bacteria and other stuff that comes from having a long past. They love the shiny possibility that rests in things unused. At the same time, they can be very sentimental and connected to old and, especially, beautiful things. However, a thing that is too torn up by time often loses its value for a Virgo. The fantastical possibilities that stem from something unused and absolutely untainted by the passage of time and space can give them an almost orgasmic feeling. Often old things, which fill many other people with a sense of security and comfort derived from their age and wear, fill Virgo with a creepy feeling and quite a bit of sadness. They feel this sadness because thinking about the past and all that has gone by and will never come back is a reminder of tremendous loss for them. They like the new coming in but hate to see things that they love and hold near and dear disappear into the jaws of time.

For Virgos, the most important factor in a home is whether it is their safe point of return, where they can be themselves and find their inner strength. If so, then they will use it as a base for their next scary and daring campaign to conquer the world, making it a better, safer, and more beautiful place.

Creativity and Leisure

How to use their time is a very important and serious question for Virgo. They do not like to waste their time with frivolities or nonsense, but rather want the playground of time to be filled with real and quality stuff. They approach their hobbies like their life depends on it. They want to be better and preferably true masters of everything they do and touch. If you ask them to relax and not to be so serious, they probably will send you a strange and surprised look before they go on with whatever task they are trying to master. Relaxing might be a bit difficult when your relationship to what you do for fun is at least as serious as your attitude toward work. Virgos are tremendously critical of their own performance and can often block themselves completely because they have standards that are impossible to meet. Play is bloody serious for most of these creatures. They do most things in the opposite manner of the rest of us. They start with the hardest and toughest, and as they feel more secure, they might be able to relax and play a little.

As children, Virgos are serious beings who take a lot of responsibility, and they often do not know how to simply be the carefree and happy-go-lucky children they are supposed to be. Virgos take their childish world just as seriously as adults take their adult world. As parents, they take responsibility and feel the burden of parenthood very strongly—sometimes much too strongly. They easily become so responsible and controlling that the way children naturally open up becomes a bit stunted. As parents, Virgos need to give the correct boundaries for the age and stage of development their children are at, and then leave them to work out the details. They must let their children explore and experience the toughness of the world by themselves, even though they will inevitably get hurt and bruised in body and soul.

Virgos are not in favor of unexpected or spontaneous changes of plans. They want to know what they are going to do and when so they can be prepared and ready for the task of having fun. This preparation gives them the good feeling of being in control, and then they can relax with the knowledge that everything will work out fine and just as planned. Taking a Virgo on vacation is most likely to succeed if the quality of food and accommodations are high. Virgos do not go on holiday to relax. They want to use that time for something useful, like seeing art, learning a language, or just exploring as much as possible of their surroundings and opportunities. They tally up what they have done in numbers, and the higher the numbers, the greater the success of the journey.

Every now and then, Virgos become frustrated because they have to choose a limited number of all possibilities and opportunities presented to them. Often, it takes some trying before they learn that they get more satisfaction by doing a few things properly than by trying to do everything at once. They can be difficult for others to understand. Sometimes, their keen, even obsessive interest in something disappears the moment they become masters and have learned all the tricks. For Virgos, this is natural. The challenge and fun of the game was to master something and learn how it is done. Once they know the game and do not have much left to learn, the fun is gone. There is a thin line Virgos need to tread to really enjoy life and have fun. If a challenge is too great, they feel useless and get depressed about their own faults and the things they lack. If the game gets too easy, they are bored and feel like it is a waste of time to play since they do not learn anything new. The perfect place to be for them is somewhere they can enjoy learning something new while already knowing enough to feel safe and enjoy it. When they have all that, they can develop a tremendous ability to enjoy themselves, while at the same time, their play is useful and leads to the creation of beautiful future opportunities.

Health, Order, and the Necessary

Virgos want to finish what needs to be done before they start in on the fun stuff. The only problem with this strategy is that they never finish everything that needs to be done. More often than not, they seem to be engulfed in an endless row of necessities that all have to be dealt with before they have time to begin their real life.

As far as health and order go, Virgos are incorrigible perfectionists on behalf of themselves and the rest of humanity. They hunt for systems that work better and more efficiently. They want all the little wheels to be oiled so the big machine runs silently and flawlessly. One of the problems is that humans are part of this clockwork: to make things work effectively, not only the Virgos but also all the other participants have to be perfectly adjusted and coordinated. Virgos have the highest of ideals and often make it their task to align the real world with those ideals. Well, this sign must learn the hard way that their longing for perfection is far from shared by all of humanity. Some people even prefer to enjoy life and have fun when it is unhealthy and unwise. At times, the Virgo needs to improve everything, and everybody is experienced as unwanted critique and a nuisance by the rest of the zodiac. It is good for Virgos to learn to leave others alone about their shortcomings and inadequacies.

This sign does not like hierarchical structures or the fact that others are allowed to make the wrong decisions just because they have a higher rank. Incompetent leaders are a nightmare for them, and it is guaranteed that they will give advice and try to educate any such boss about the right way to do things. When this isn't possible, the Virgo turns to deep bitterness and dissatisfaction. If that happens, they should go looking for a new job instead of destroying their life by working at a place they hate. Virgos can find it hard to be the boss themselves, as they easily become so considerate and afraid of making bad decisions or misusing their power that they end up seeming—or being—weak and easily manipulated. They have good qualities for getting people to work well together but have difficulties with making unpopular decisions.

Health is of prime importance to all Virgos. Illness is seen as scary and very unpleasant. The reason that many people with this sign are found in the caring and helping professions is that they want to fight disease and suffering by all possible means. They want everything to be healthy and well organized so that everyone can be healthy and in good working order. Some of them swing far to the opposite side and will not touch any sick people or have anything to do with illness, bacteria, or pain. They just can't stand the strain of being confronted with inner or outer infections or a lack of cleanliness.

Virgos need to find their own method of handling the stress and demands of everyday life. One of the basic pieces of the method they choose, though, should be letting go of feeling responsible for everyone else. Virgos also need to find the diet and way of life that best suits them and give others the freedom to do the same. They even have to understand that things that are right and healthy for them might be bad for others...and vice versa. They will benefit from developing a high level of tolerance and understanding of the fact that we find meaning in life—and stay healthy and effective—in different ways. Understanding this is, in fact, a prerequisite for realizing the Virgo dream of effectiveness and the maximum utilization of their talents and resources.

One-on-One Relationships

Virgos often believe that others have caring and loving intentions behind their actions. This is why they sometimes overlook the red alert that pops up on the screen of the unconscious, and it's why they can often find it so hard to understand what makes others tick. Since they seldom lie to hide their dirty tricks or to get a personal advantage, they end up just as surprised each time someone else speaks with a forked tongue.

In their partner, Virgos seek out a dream and try to weave reality from fantasy. Emotions are important and their vision of the eternal and immortal love is significant. They want a partner who is sensitive, artistic, and compassionate. They are known to fall head over heels for poets, mystics, and other dreamers that do not have their feet planted on the ground. Virgos often find someone who is elusive and hard to get ahold of. Their inner eye sees that person's undeveloped potential, which the Virgo can then grow and develop. A Virgo intends to recreate their loved one as the partner of their dreams—a project that always works out to be an unending and impossible task and the partner often just slides away. In the worst-case scenario, they end up in a relationship where both sides use their lives and abilities to save and change the other person instead of taking responsibility for their own needs and development.

Virgos are also known to become the victims of unreliable beings who just take advantage of their good intentions. This sign sees the world with a clear and precise eye but seems to be blind as a bat when it comes to their loved ones. It is as if the longings of a Virgo's heart make their sight like looking through water, where everything is a bit hazy, blurred, and difficult to measure in size and distance. What this sign needs is a partner who is reliable, open, and tolerant and who can accept and love them just as they are. They do not need another critic (they already have enough self-doubt), partly because this partner can teach the Virgo to be less judgmental and reserved, and partly because Virgo just needs a partner with a large and spacious heart. A problem for Virgo is that this big heart often has space for others, too.

In many cases, it still works out quite well, since most Virgos are more insecure than jealous. If they know that their partner cares for them, they can accept that their partner also cares for others. Virgos can be quite naive about their partners, but they have the memory of an elephant. If you make unforgivable mistakes, like hurting them badly or betraying their trust, those mistakes will never be forgiven or forgotten. Virgos are shy and do not easily show their sincere, tender feelings, but at heart, they are true romantics and love getting presents and hearing loving words. They love every small token of affection and every time they are that they are truly appreciated—and by the way, they want their partner to be neat, well groomed, and aromatic. If Virgos are given the necessary amount of attention and love, they can be very tolerant and accept even the biggest flaws. If they feel a lack of attention, they can become harsh critics and extremely nitpicky.

Love is overwhelmingly the most important factor in a Virgo's choice of partner, and Virgos are very reliable and faithful. It is very important for them to choose the right person from the start since it is so hard for them to let go. Once they have begun to love, they go on loving and do it without reservation. All that is good and well, but they will benefit from working on not becoming too dependent—or even codependent. Addiction is never a good choice for Virgos, even if the addiction is love for a person. Virgos often try to become one with their partner and need to understand that it is space and separation that allows the love between two individuals to reach its maximum potential.

Beneath the Surface—Sex and Taboos

In this area, Virgos might have a surprise or two in store. Their public and personal images are cerebral, prudent, and well-mannered. They avoid behavior that is provocative or shocking. But what might happen after the curtain drops? That is another story. In very private and intimate settings, Virgos can be quite vulgar, direct, and even overwhelming. Their front pages are squeaky clean and shining while their shadow self is a bit ruthless and crude.

Virgos may harbor secret dreams about driving big, heavy machinery off into the night to just fuck with whatever catches their eye. The same goes for those who on the outside seem to be more careful and cerebral. They drive the car, and in bed, they enjoy being the rider. Well past the initial stage of shyness, they want to be in control and are excited by being direct and even pushy. At the same time, they want style and tenderness. They like to be seduced, but once the temperature reaches a certain degree, they want to be the seducer. Virgos do not break taboos just to shock people or do something "bad." Their main motive is that they want to go beyond their own limitations and explore unknown territory. They want to do this exploration alone as an artistic search or with someone whom they trust 100 percent. Some Virgos might do things that make them feel dirty and disgusting, but this always comes from some form of self-contempt or a deep inner sense of being soiled.

Virgos must learn to handle their own intensity and power instead of getting scared by it. They will benefit from accepting the force of the torrent that every now and then goes through them, then learning to handle that power. Often, Virgos are polite just to hide how ruthless they can be if you look far enough beneath the surface. A Virgo who has shown you their raw and unrefined shadow is either your eternal enemy or someone who trusts you with their life. Virgos want to be kind and fear being bad and malevolent. They need to have this sacred space behind closed doors where they can explore the parts of their personality that they won't allow themselves to access in the outer world. A positive side of this ruthlessness, however, is the power Virgos feel when they fight for their beliefs. They can avoid unpleasantries for a long time, but if something is unjust enough, they attack the problem like a reborn Joan of Arc. Beware when you meet them: behind their potentially bland and dull facade, there is a warrior lurking. They often act like the most dangerous kind of dog: they do not bark before they bite.

Most Virgos have to be pushed to their limits before they bring up the things that are normally hidden deep down in their inner well. This is why they often end up in extreme and demanding situations: they need these challenges to really get going and reach the potential that all their power and inner talents have bestowed upon them. It is a delight for this sign when they can let go of all the consideration and care and just go full speed. As mentioned, be careful that you do not buy into the passive personality that the Virgo maintains. If you do, you will be totally unprepared for what plays out when a Virgo's will of iron takes command, and the shy and reserved facade falls to reveal the face of the true warrior that lives within their shell of politeness.

Education, Adventure, and Life Philosophy

Education is a very serious matter for Virgos, and they are occupied with learning things that can be useful in the future. They love to learn new things, but traveling to unknown areas is a different, riskier adventure. Mostly, they prefer to travel to places that are known, safe, and civilized. They can be skeptical of things they have never seen or experienced and like to feel safe even in unknown territory. They prefer traveling to learn, eat something delicious, or just enjoy life. They do not feel that they have to travel to find hardship and challenges, which in their opinion, are already bountifully present in daily life.

Virgos prefer traveling first class and find no reason to deny themselves luxury or comfort. Beauty is very important for Virgos exploring the wider world. They want to see the sights of pretty people, buildings, and nature, and they happily avoid ugly people, dull buildings, and polluted areas. They enjoy smelling, sensing, and observing, and do not necessarily have to be involved in any activity.

As far as life philosophy goes, Virgos believe in what is practical and workable—while at the same time, they desperately long for miracles. They do not understand why they would travel just for the sake of traveling: they want to have destinations and plans for their travels. The more they know about the good restaurants and where to go to get exactly what they want, the more they enjoy the trip. They often miss out on many opportunities since they have a tendency to reject things that are new and unfamiliar. On the other hand, if they have caught the scent of something they find exciting and instructive, they are insatiable hounds sniffing for every opportunity. They can be collectors in the sense that when they have an interest, they collect all available material around this chosen subject. In this manner, Virgos often prefer to bring the world into their home instead of leaving home to see the greater world outside. In some ways, it seems easier to relax and really enjoy the exotic stuff when they are in safe and known surroundings. Strange isn't very exciting for a Virgo, but as soon as they start to understand the inner workings of something, they always want to know more. Their longing for information and knowledge is often what raises them from the couch and makes them take some steps into the unknown, especially if the knowledge they are pursuing is something they think will become useful in the future.

Virgos want to get paid for the time and effort invested in traveling, studying, or thinking long and hard on any topic. Again, they are this strange combination of extravagance and stinginess. They can work very hard for a few scraps of knowledge, and in the next moment let go of everything they have studied over a long time. Since Virgos want to work with something that opens up new possibilities and opportunities for the world, they need an education that takes care of their longing for something practical as well as beautiful. Most of all, they are indulgent and want pleasure from their travels and studies. In fact, they easily become eternal students, since they often find more enjoyment in learning something useful than in actually using their knowledge to do something useful.

Goals, Profession, and Career

This sign needs a job that offers a variety of activities and sources of stimulation. Virgos seldom stay in one workplace for life and often change jobs the way others change outfits. Virgos want to use their brain at work and needs to work with people with whom they can exchange thoughts, ideas, and opinions. They do not like completely sedentary work, but neither do they enjoy work that is physically demanding. Their voice and ability to communicate will more often than not be two of their main professional tools. This sign is also known to have multiple jobs and career paths that they pursue at the same time. This tendency fits well with their insatiable thirst for information and ever-better qualifications.

Everything connected to communication and knowledge is an interesting potential profession. Virgos do not necessarily have grand ambitions or feel the need to reach a high position, they just want to do something that satisfies them and keeps them interested. It is not a good idea for Virgos to allow themselves to be promoted into a position that gives them too much responsibility or takes away regular contact with their coworkers. Virgos are usually excellent communicators and are able to explain almost anything to anybody. In the working world, they seem to effortlessly create a feeling of cooperation and togetherness. They know how to dress for a multitude of different roles and how to have equal relationships with people of both higher and lower ranks. The respect they have for others is never based on position, but always on the qualities of a specific individual.

In many ways, this sign is an excellent tactician and diplomat in the work sphere. Virgos automatically hold their personal emotions and reactions at bay and react to any needs and situations that arise with clear professionalism. Every now and then, they become mired in inconsequential details and their efficiency disappears, but when Virgo keeps a clear goal in mind, they are able to juggle a lot of tasks and get things done at an impressive speed. They work best when they are a tiny bit stressed and have to juggle just one ball too many. No matter the situation, they know how to be personal without becoming private. Virgos are not always very good at seeing and grasping new possibilities. They are better at seeing what needs to be corrected or changed than what is beyond the horizon. At work, they make better team travelers than solo pioneers. They need to get inspiration and enthusiasm from others. They enjoy being part of a group where everyone does their allotted share and the whole becomes something far greater than the sum of its parts. Virgos like to work in a tight-knit environment and prefer getting so close to their coworkers that they know all the nuances of each other's thoughts and feelings. Appreciation and silent acknowledgment from these close connections mean a lot more to them than effusive praise from some unknown admirer.

Virgos have high standards for themselves and want to do everything better than their best. They are incurable perfectionists who sometimes end up numbing themselves and feeling inadequate. They have to learn to give themselves praise for all the things that they can do and have done well, instead of only ever looking at the things they find unsatisfactory. At their worst, Virgo clogs things up with unnecessary details, endless useless discussions, and a lack of ability to make clear decisions. At their best, they are inspiring, creative, inventive, humorous, and admirably effective.

Friends, Future, and Ideals

Virgo likes to be part of a world and society where everybody is like a big family. In that world, everybody is fulfilled, safe, caring, and cared for. The prerequisite for a successful party is that there is plenty of food for everybody—Virgo's fear is that guests will end up leaving hungry. When Virgos want to change the world and build a better society, they start at home. How can people learn to be caring and responsible for the world at large if they do not practice caring and responsible actions with those they are around in their daily lives? Virgos feel pretentious and false if they do not exemplify the ideals they try to convey to others. As far as friends go, they are quite sentimental and care very much for the people they hold in their hearts. Virgos wants to meet their own ideals and find it difficult to ask other people to do something that they wouldn't or couldn't do themselves.

When Virgos have a close connection to a group, something that easily happens in a work situation, they have a hard time cutting those ties and moving on to another place/group. In the worst-case scenario, they stay in places and with friends that they outgrew decades ago. Virgo does not strive to mean something to the masses. They want to have significance to the people they hold close and feel a personal connection to. They are very loyal and feel much responsibility for their social families. Sometimes, Virgos can get a bit worn out because they take too much responsibility for people who want to take risks by themselves. Virgo's favorite hobby is being cozy and with close friends. They would like to make the whole world into a cozy club where everybody is fulfilled, loving, and respectful of each other's feelings.

Virgos are very aware of the emotional state of their friends and will go to amazing lengths to avoid hurting them—but friendship based only on old memories or similar interests mean nothing to this sign. They crave emotional connections; the experience of love and inner belonging is by far the most important factor in their friendships. They need to have friends that they can talk to about the endless stream of topics that pop into their minds, but feeling good, emotionally safe, and appreciated is even more essential. It is among true friends that Virgo can show their tenderness, vulnerability, and true kindness. When they trust you, they can show you their true, soft, and eternally giving self without the risk of being used or abused. It is so good for them to let go of their skeptical defense system and relax, trusting that they will be loved, cared for, and seen just for being themselves.

If you are a Virgo, you need to remember that every now and then, you must withdraw and take care of yourself. This is not a sign of losing interest in your friends, but of needing to recharge your batteries every now and then. Since both your heart and your head are so actively engaged when you are social, you need some peace and quiet to just sit, contemplate, and get in contact with your own center. As a Virgo, you need to always remember how your big heart functions. Friends aren't just friends—they are family. In some ways, Virgos are perfect for living in communes and being part of an extended family, both on a practical level and as part of their visions for a future and an Earth where all of us love each other and love being with each other. Their hopes and dreams for the future are nothing more or less than a paradise of love.

Seeking and the Spiritual

As far as spiritual reality goes, Virgos are often curiously divided. A Virgo believes and does not believe at the same time. As far as Virgo is concerned, they are critical and logical and do not accept anything that is not understood by their rational mind. Virgos are doubters and skeptics who want everything to be explained and proven beyond a reasonable doubt. They want to do research and tests so they can mentally understand God and eternal endlessness. When this sign is totally dominated by the brain, they will deny any kind of reality that can't be measured, weighed, and explained.

At heart, though, Virgos are true mystics. They have this natural inner understanding of the nature of love and compassion and long to embody this state of loving purity. In their poetic hearts, life seems like an endless and magical quest they would love to see open like a rose—with endless beauty. Virgos often begin their journeys as innocents. Then, as the world passes them by and hurts them with its cruel ways, they become doubting, logical, and skeptical. Their innocence is lost, and their eyes shine with skepticism, criticism, and scrutiny. As they go through the work of processing all the information out there and satisfying their needs for logic and criticism, they slowly begin to revert to their original state of innocence, this time with an awareness of having chosen innocence and naivety. This vacillation between the mundane skeptic and the spiritual simpleton is often as confusing for the Virgo as it is for the rest of us. They seem to be changing the angle of their view of reality from one moment to the next.

In fact, Virgos often find it terribly difficult to decide what they really think and believe. They can end up in a place where they never fully give themselves to anything. They can become a doubting believer or a believing doubter, but if they finally have made a decision, that decision suggests total devotion. They can't make such a decision without facing the full consequences of their chosen truth. Because of this totality, they often hold the great questions of life at a certain distance, while at the same time, they are very busy examining what they steadily hold at bay. A Virgo who converts to Catholicism will feel a great need to go into a monastery to really take in the full consequences of their beliefs. One of the big tasks this sign faces is the challenge to unify the mundane and the spiritual in life: to be fully present in a "small" way—where they must face and take care of thousands upon thousands of trivial things and tasks—and at the same time devote themselves to the mystic, unnamable, and sublime. In more prosaic terms, the heart and head must walk hand in hand. To a Virgo, true love is visible in your actions, and true spirituality is shown in how you live your Earthly life. When Virgos have accepted the full consequences of spiritual reality and surrendered themselves to a higher power and the intentions of their souls, they will become messengers and vessels that show the true essence and existence of the spiritual through their words and their deeds.

Libra

September 23rd—October 22nd

Element: Air
Quality: Cardinal
Ruling Planet: Venus

How to Present Yourself

To be a Libra is to be in pursuit of harmony and balance. This can occur in many different ways. One well-known method is to bring opposites together and try to unify them. In real life, Libra often ends up feeling like they are stranded in the middle of things, trying to hold loose ends together. They have a special propensity for sliding into this position, even if they themselves say that others have placed them between the two warring parties. Desperately, they raise the white flag and try to get everyone's attention while the bullets zoom by. Of course, this situation often has the effect where the Libra themselves becomes like a warrior.

As a Libra, if given the choice, you would pick the peaceful solution—but life has taught you that if a sword is drawn, you better be ruthless. Justice is very important to this sign, and you will be especially warrior-like and ruthless when you see or hear of grave injustice toward others. You might be docile as long as it is you who is treated unjustly, but when you fight on behalf of others, your opponents should take great care. It might be difficult for others to know your true heart since you always try to be friendly, even toward those you don't like. In fact, you are often especially friendly toward those people, since you have to hide that you dislike or even detest them. This often makes it hard for others to know the difference between you being polite and well-behaved and you really enjoying and wanting more of their company.

Libras are advised to be extra careful with white lies. As a Libra, you might be seduced and affected by your own good intentions, lose sight of your true aims, and believe that what others want is what you want! When you know what you want, you wish for the people you like and love to want the same. You want to do these things with them at the same time as you wish for them to want the same things by themselves. In fact, you often try to make others believe that they made the decision to do what you want them to. You do not want to coerce others, but you do want them to do things your way. This game can become quite complicated and confusing for you and those around you. Be aware and avoid using others as an excuse for not finding a path in your own life. What you really want is to do things with equal partners and share with those who want to share and to be shared with. In fact, your desires are quite easy: all you want is togetherness and mutual respect, and so that is what you must show others.

Appearances are important to Libras. Harmony and beauty are highly valued. You might become superficial and caught up in appearances, but there is no reason to hide the fact that you need the world to be beautiful. The more you accept that you want to make the world a more beautiful place and allow yourself to be vain in that way, the better your life will be. However, be aware and see the danger inherent in hiding behind the pleasant and nice. It is important for Libras to promote beauty instead of just trying to avoid the ugly and grim. Real beauty is created from the raw materials of a life well lived. Harmony is created by confronting the challenges of disharmony and discordance. As a Libra, it is important to show the world the depth of your love and joy. At the same time, you must know how to tell unpleasant truths in a relaxed manner. Do not fear the envy of others—you are allowed to enjoy all the praise and acknowledgment you can get. When you find your true inner harmony and balance, you will automatically create more harmony and balance in the world you are dancing with.

How to Get the Best from Your Talents and Resources

If there is one thing Libras are serious about, it is getting to use their talents and abilities. In fact, they might become so serious about it that they never seem to get anything done. As a Libra, your desire to get things right is so strong and deep that you might feel like a fish; always swimming upward, but never breaking the surface. However, when you swim toward the attainment of your goals, you do so like a hungry shark. You give it your all, and you want to dive right into the core of the matter. All superficiality is gone as you search for the inner depths of your soul, which is what you really want to earn a daily living by utilizing.

You need this intensity to give your very best. Many of your hidden talents and resources are brought into the light because of this intensity, and your typical politeness might disappear when real values are at stake. You know that when it comes to utilizing your abilities, it is your will and effort that serve as the deciding factors in how things will end up. You have to be aware of the fact that others feel criticized when you criticize their actions and the results they achieve. You might call your critiques impersonal, but I can guarantee you, they are not! You might stomp your heavy boots right down onto the bare toes of others through what you call "professional honesty."

As a Libra, you need to be 100 percent emotionally engaged in what you do. You need to have a certain amount of passion about something before you can mobilize the necessary amount of energy to get started. If you lose this deep feeling of passion and importance, you can easily end up feeling like what you do is boring and meaningless. At the same time, you have a strong inner drive to succeed. You crave so deeply to be successful at what you do and what you find valuable. For you, failing is barely something you can live with. To you, your birthright as a human seems to be success, therefore being unsuccessful feels like being a failure—not just in what you do, but as a human being. You feel that your basic value as a person is strongly connected to what you do. You can fool others through social games and careful facades, but deep inside, you know that it is your actions that show who you really are and your true value.

Libras might find it hard to let go of any project they are involved with before they feel finished—then they let it go completely. They might surprise both themselves and others with this ability to utterly change directions in a blink of an eye, and they might be just as surprised by how relieved they are to let go of things that were once very near and dear to them. It is like their life has been totally dependent on something external for a long time, and then suddenly, they stopped needing it at all. Libra's intensity gives them the advantage of being able to develop their talents and resources all by themselves. When Libra starts cooperating with someone else in this area, the collaboration has to be deep, serious, and without reservation. In this area, Libras have only two attitudes: on and off. More often than not, Libras are financially independent, even when finances are closely connected with their ability to develop and market their talents in the public space. They really hate being helpless and dependent on someone else in the area of finances. This does not mean that they have problems with tying their resources to others, such as a spouse or an investor. It just means that they want to know that they are able to manage on their own if necessary. Most Libras have a lot of talents, but many of them stay undeveloped. As a Libra, you must accept that using your talents to the fullest is as emotionally challenging as it is rewarding.

Communication and Immediate Surroundings

Libras have a great need to vocalize their ideas and opinions. They think they know the truth, but they want to tell it to you in a nice and positive way. This sign craves meaningful discussions, especially around the big topics of life like faith, the future, politics, and justice. They prefer to keep the conversation philosophical and do not enjoy too much small talk or discussion of personal feelings. As a Libra, your private life is something you can live out and still keep private. Do not step into the minefield of a Libra's inner secrets and feelings—you may spring a trap and become caught in unexpected explosions.

Libras are enthusiasts who always look for new opportunities and possibilities. People may even call them opportunistic, as well as claim that they talk a bit too much. The more engaged a Libra is, the more difficult it becomes for them to stop talking and start listening. Libras instinctively seek out harmony, but they often have a hard time really listening to the deeper meanings communicated by others. Since they believe that they already have the answers, why bother listening carefully to others? They are often thinking about how to reply instead of hearing the ideas of others. You may believe that they agree with you, but it might be true that they are just trying to avoid conflict and visible disagreement.

This sign likes most people and loves having friends—the more the merrier. Every now and then they are known to lose their own identity to a sea of friends and acquaintances. They have to withdraw from time to time to find their own inner core and build new personal strength. They like to have the answers and can have a hard time admitting when they are wrong. The immature Libra has a know-it-all attitude and never concedes that they are wrong—or just don't know. These people want to create harmony, unity, and concordance but end up creating turbulence and controversy.

Remember: words aren't necessarily connected to actions for a Libra. Words come from the realm of ideals and philosophy; actions are based on emotions and reality. All the same, honesty and fairness are of great importance to Libra. Libras seldom lie, even though others are sometimes confused by the fact that their actions aren't always in accordance with their ideals. In fact, Libras are so full of ideals, optimism, and ideas that there is no way they can realize all the possibilities they might want to engage in. At times, it is good to know the difference between what they consider to be your options and opportunities, and what they themselves would have chosen in the same situation. They give you the advice they think is proper for you, even if they would have done the opposite and they are generous with their advice. They really believe in your potential and strive to support you 100 percent—as far as ideological and theoretical support goes. In fact, this ability to see the best in others and to believe in their talents and potential is one of the nicest and loveliest abilities found in almost every Libra. Even if a Libra is disappointed by you every now and then, they go right on believing in your talents and believing that you will eventually make it if you try hard enough. They believe that you can walk on the Moon and love to talk about how great it will be when you finally do.

Home and Family

Home and Family are important cornerstones in the life of a Libra. Libras build much of their self-image around their history and origin. In many ways, their sense of worth and ability to contribute to society is based on their roots and traditions. They need this feeling of weight and belonging that comes from the past since they can so easily lose themselves in how others see them. They need an inner sanctuary where they can rest in tranquility and savor the feeling of being carried by all those who have come before. In their home, they need stability—something tangible that does not change in structure. They are often very proud of their ancestors as well as their home and family. This might be the one instance where Libras are not interested in quick or fancy solutions, but instead, honor proven quality and durability. Libras can be out of balance if they do not have this foundation in working order. Details like unpaid bills or even the fear of not being able to pay bills can be quite traumatic. As Libra builds close ties with people, houses, or things, they have a significant problem with letting go of them. Friends come and go, but the cornerstones stay. In these areas, a Libra might find it difficult to move at all since they so easily become addicted to the known. Their solidarity with and loyalty to their children, parents, and other family members is seemingly endless. In many ways, they feel that it is their responsibility to make everything work within a basic family unit. One result of this fundamental care for those near and dear is that they can take worrying over everything that might go wrong for their loved ones to unknown heights.

For Libras, the Scale Bearers, home is also a workplace. Sometimes they switch and make a home out of their workplace and vice versa. They are very structured and aware of time and know how to run things efficiently when at home. If order is lacking, however, they feel overwhelmed by the thought of all that should be done and the need to start doing it immediately. Libras need this order at home to be able to function properly. In other areas, they are weak to temptation and often just go with the flow. They have an amazing capacity for self-discipline when they are at home by themselves. They are unbelievably efficient when there is nobody there to disturb them: they are like trees with enormous root systems. If somebody does threaten the safety of their home and loved ones, all doubts and difficulties with decision-making disappear as easily as dew under the hot Sun. They protect what is nearest and dearest to them by every possible means necessary. Their sense of responsibility is unlimited in this area.

As far as the interior of their homes, Libras enjoy simplicity and a kind of frugal, classical elegance. They have an ability to make things so simple and at the same time so beautiful that others often admire their taste and ability to get it right. Their secret is having a clear and defined style as well as maintaining a high degree of quality with every single piece. They avoid the flashy and do not feel like opening their homes to all kinds of strange people or things. They like to have defined limits as far as what and whom is allowed to pass over the threshold and into their sacred sanctuary of a home. They create a structure where their chosen few feel safe, looked after, and very comfortable.

Creativity and Leisure

Libra just loves when something unexpected happens during their leisure time. In this area, they are inventive, creative, and lovers of strange hobbies. They enjoy spending their time in the company of others who are hunting for the unexpected and like to be part of groups traveling through unknown territory. They have the ability to melt into the group, but if the group goes in one direction and they want to go in another, this zodiacal creature easily switches to their own path. They look ahead and are seldom victims of sentimentality. If there is a sign that loves flirtation, it is Libra. They just are delighted by the display of sparkling energy and emotion that accompany a daring, flirtatious comment.

Libra has a surprisingly open relationship to sexuality in its many variants and disguises. Most of them are tolerant, and many Libras enjoy experimentation and trying out different possibilities. At times, their sexuality might seem a bit impersonal. They can seem to be in it for the energy rather than the person they are with. This can be confusing and sometimes very hurtful to others. Libras might give their partner an enormous amount of energy and attention in one moment, just to be gone and disinterested in the next. Immature Libras often have a problem maintaining their energy and interest when things become too personal, intimate, or responsible. So, if they seem to flirt with you, don't take it too personally. Flirtation is a game, and if you do not want to play, Libra will just go looking for another playmate.

Libras do not feel that they are unethical or using others. Quite the opposite—they want you to have the very best. However, the rules of the game state that everybody can do what they like, and nobody is allowed to take away that freedom from another person. Presenting demands or rules to a Libra in the early stage of a romance is doomed to end badly. One of the main qualities you must demonstrate on the road to permanent residence in the Libran heart is a willingness to trust them. You also need to show that you feel no need to control or restrict them. This sign knows that carrying control freaks around in their heart will inevitably end up as an intolerable situation for both parties.

Libras are quite good at presenting themselves from their best angle. They know how to use and get the most from their many talents. They have this strange ability to be mesmerized by humans, projects, and ideas, and the moment they are smitten with something, they have passed the point of no return; but when the trance is gone and they have lost interest, it is equally final and absolute. Then they just smile and look around, wondering where the next unexpected adventure is going to pop up.

Health, Order, and the Necessary

Health is something this sign cares about on a day-to-day basis. One day, they might be very structured and have very long-term plans for the future and their general health. The next day, they might be far more occupied with fulfilling whatever desires they have in the moment and having some fun. In a strange way, Libras are equally dependent on chaos and order. It seems like they need some of the flexibility and unpredictability of chaos to create order. Having too strict of a schedule makes them feel bad. They need to have some kind of rule to break in order to stay healthy and satisfied.

You see, Libra's health is closely tied to their emotional state. When tired and sad, they feel a bit sick. If their body insists on staying healthy, they can only manage to develop some of the symptoms of whatever they catch. Put another way, Libras are known to become very ill in almost no time at all, but they are also known for their ability to heal in almost an instant. Illness gives Libras the ability to relax and do nothing—something they otherwise might feel guilty about. Libras have a tendency to go to extremes as far as work ethic and health go. They can be forever indulgent and just want to relax and enjoy things all the time, or they can be workaholics who do not know when and how to stop and take it easy.

Libras often have high ideals when it comes to health, hygiene, and order and find it better to have a clean bill of health—unless they want to get sick for the attention. Often, this is the only way they can really get care and attention from their surroundings. When they feel appreciated, and the dark clouds lift from their burdened souls, they heal quickly and in mysterious ways. This sign isn't very occupied with details; they might seem like they are, but in that case, it is just that the Libran sense of beauty and aesthetics has the upper hand. If it wasn't for this longing for beauty, Libras would let most things slide and only do the minimum of any boring necessities. On another note, Libra is not scared by illness—not their own, nor that of others which is convenient, as they like to be of service to the sick and downtrodden.

It is of great importance that this sign feels like their actions have significance and contribute to the well-being of others. The boredom of day-to-day routines only feels meaningful when it happens in the process of bringing some kind of love, beauty, or harmony to others.

Libras can be very financially astute and tidy as far as the big things are concerned. They are a lot more lackadaisical when it comes to small amounts of money and day-to-day matters. One of Libra's greatest talents is their ability to organize things for others. They can see the big picture and have an amazing overhead view of the situation. They need to live for something bigger and greater than their own ego's satisfaction. They will become careless and lazy if they do not have some kind of vision or love to give them a purpose in life. If they have become ill, they will benefit from getting as much sleep as possible. Another healing factor for Libras is picturing themselves as healthy in the future, as well as being fulfilled by the love of doing something really important and meaningful. In reality, their inner fantasies and images are often more important for their healing process than what actually goes on in the physical world. In turn, this ability to create from their inner vision gives Libras a great ability to manifest their dreams, fantasies, and creativity in the physical world.

One-on-One Relationships

Libra is known to be very impulsive and daring when it comes to love. When the magic arrow of Cupid pierces their heart, they put their brain into sleep mode and follow their passion. Libras throw themselves into the arms of their chosen one, even if said chosen one is very different from them and an unlikely prospect for lasting love. In fact, Libra is attracted to the challenging task of creating harmony and love with someone who is nearly impossible to predict or influence. They value independence in their partners, but nonetheless, they want to tame the wild stallion.

Libras are in search of balance but need to find the other side of their own coin to create the unity they so long for. This is much of the reason that Libras so often end up in difficult and demanding relations. They somehow enjoy the drama of all the time spent trying to get some balance and harmony: it gives the relationship a sense of purpose and growth for them. Besides, being split apart is a prerequisite for coming together again and again and again. Libras like their close relationships to be active and are known to choose people who are so occupied that they seldom have the time or opportunity to meet. In this sense, a

Libra's life can be filled with dramatic departures and sweet reunions. The worst thing to a Libra is a dull life with a dull partner. They can live with a lot of peculiarities, but not with boredom. They like their partners to be direct, simple, and brave. They like to admire their partners for their power, actions, initiative, and courage to fight for what they believe is just and true. At the same time, Libras enjoy feeling a bit more delicate and sensitive than their partner. Since they themselves often have a hard time making decisions, they want a partner who is able to make swift and forceful choices. This works out well as long as the partner can satisfy the inner longings and wishes of the Libra, but if they start to act without regard for the Libra's wishes, the relationship will quickly grow discordant. This creates a lot of potential for daily fights, which can easily become an addiction for the sweet Libra. Peace can exist without conflicts being solved beforehand and growth can happen when a partner challenges the Libra and forces them to face previously unknown facets of their own nature and personality.

The worst possible partner for a Libra is someone that sits around all day and never does anything. They need someone with the energy and will to get going. Libras are more than willing to work and accept sacrifices to make a relationship succeed. In fact, they need to work with the relationship to get it to work! The challenges of a relationship are necessary to keep up the Libra's interest and energy. As mentioned, they fall in love head over heels, but they might as easily lose interest if their partner grows dull or too easily available. Some Libras have a problem with always falling in love with impossible or unattainable prospects. In a sense, Libra does need to have relationships to feel alive and well, but once they are in one, they are monogamous with their partner—although, that monogamy easily translates into a series of monogamous relationships.

Beneath the Surface—Sex and Taboos

Most Libras are quite self-indulgent. They are highly sensual and like a partner with whom they can feel safe and cozy around when it comes to physical pleasures. They enjoy strong partners, even if they themselves prefer to be slim and well-sculpted. Many Libras are the kind of person that really thinks "the more to the merrier" where the body mass of their partners is concerned—at least as long as size does not hinder motion. Their appetite for sensuality and sexuality is strong and long-lasting. They do not need to feel like they have touched their partner's soul in bed but rather are quite satisfied with simply enjoying carnal pleasure in an atmosphere of safety and intimacy.

Libras are known to have great sexual needs and stamina. Many of them feel that their body craves sex in a similar way to how it craves food. Libras also have a great appetite and seldom get tired of eating, even when they have enjoyed the same dish over and over again. At the sexual table, they are both gourmets and gourmands. In some ways, sexuality is connected with a sense of possessiveness for this sign. They conquer and take you into their possession through their sexuality. Understood from this angle, it is easy to see why they do not thrive by having a lot of brief, loose sexual connections. They want to possess and "own" the one they are having sex with and do not like to share their partner.

The differences between a Libra's contradictory needs can be hard to handle. They have this constant tendency to want to satisfy their sensual needs and be swept away in a moment of exhilaration, while on the other hand, they also have a great need to have and live in a stable and secure relationship. If Libras do not find the right balance, this contradiction becomes an eternal struggle where they move back and forth between extremes. This kind of inner phenomenon is the reason why Libras can be extremely jealous if their partner is unfaithful, but will make up excuses if they are the one "lured" into living out their own darker side with someone else. If Libra hasn't found a partner they want to be with in the long term, they like to try out different dishes until they do. However, they easily fall victim to their own game and form strong bonds with the first and best person they have sex with. In fact, sexuality is something that many Libras simply use to ground themselves. It helps them be in their bodies and feel like physical life is real.

A well-balanced Libra will enjoy a well-balanced sex life. The more out of balance they are on the inside, the more unbalanced their sexual life will become. When this sign is unbalanced, they have a great need to do forbidden things and explore the taboos and prohibited zones of life. But deep inside, they are quite uninterested in exploring the taboos just for the sake of it. At heart, they just want to have depth, safety, and security with their sexual partner. This need can be quite strong, and it is funny that Libras might feel ashamed over their inner need for safety and security. They feel safe sharing their intensity and daring nature, but shy about sharing their normality and need to feel safe and sound. They want to possess everything that they adore and find beautiful, and that includes their sexual partner. If Libras have something all to themselves, they can feel safe in the knowledge that no one else can steal it. Libras always have this need to find a true balance between the deep longings of their soul and their need for Earthly safety and wealth. One of the most important elements of finding this balance is finding someone who can provide them with Earthly security and a great sex life at the same time. This is what they always are hunting for, even if they do not like to admit it—to others or themselves.

Education, Adventure, and Life Philosophy

Curiosity and a love of learning new things are important driving forces for this sign. Libras are chasers of gossip and information that can lead to even more information and knowledge. They hate doing the same boring exercise over and over. They want updates and the latest and greatest of any developments on the horizon. At times, they confuse mere words with truth and believe that a big collection of facts amounts to wisdom. They tend to spread themselves thinly, either because they have such diverse interests within their chosen fields, or because they have a hard time concentrating on one thing at a time. They tend to try to learn everything at once. They love to be on the move and explore new environments. Libras are very adaptable and easily make friends with others. Often, they just peek into an area, grab a small taste, and gobble it up while they politely mumble: "That was very nice, but I have to move on to the next experience."

Libras enjoy a good discussion and love to share their thoughts and opinions. Often, the exchange of ideas and thoughts is more valuable to them than finding the right answer. In their own way, they know that a question has many different answers, and they are more interested in collecting a diversity of truths than finding the one and only truth. In fact, Libra has to see a topic from a number of different angles before they can make up their mind about their own opinion and understanding of the truth. They can also understand both sides of an issue—something that makes it more difficult for them to believe they have the actual truth. But be aware, this only goes for the bigger philosophical questions about the meaning of life. In daily matters, they have a tendency to believe that they know more than the rest of the pack. Libra has the idea that there is a single truth out there somewhere, and if they can just get enough information, they will find it. As long as they do not know everything, they are in doubt about everything. Libras, consequently, are open and curious, but quite closed off to those who think they have found the truth. In fact, Libras often doubt that anyone can know the truth or have answers as far as the big questions in life are concerned.

One part of a Libra's journey in life is finding and exploring what is beyond known limits without forming a fixed opinion about it. To people whose convictions come from the deeper layers of the heart, this may seem a bit superficial, as if Libras just lack the soul and guts needed to take a stand. However, as far as Libra is concerned, one major goal of human life is the ongoing journey toward the unknown—not just getting there and possessing all the right answers. The best part of the Libran adventure is the excitement of being on the road and the joy of finding the good and exciting questions. Once they have found all the answers, the fun is over. When they know without a doubt the differences between right and wrong, truth and lies, they also know that it is time to close the case and move on to the next chapter of life.

Goals, Profession, and Career

Libras want to give something worthwhile to the community. They want the work they do to be sustaining and to put their heart into it, whatever it is. Libra is in pain if they have a halfhearted relationship with their vocation. This fact makes them work with great intensity and, at the same time, great vulnerability. Since their projects are their children, they get very sensitive about how their work is perceived by others. This attitude makes them a bit moody if somebody disagrees with their work, tries to ditch it, or simply wants to change parts of it. As long as everybody is nice and supportive, however, they are the most pleased coworkers you can find.

Libras are very social and have a great need for emotional contact and even intimacy with their coworkers, who in many ways are their second family. To function, Libras need to feel safe and wanted in their work; if they do not, they become moody and unstable or start to hide everything behind a thick shell. Emotional balance is alpha and omega for the working Libra. At times, their work is so connected with the longings of their heart that they feel closer to their colleagues than their friends and family. This makes it hard for Libras to change workplaces. They often worry about how their colleagues will manage if they are not there to help. Libras love to feel needed and indispensable. They are also known to miss their former coworkers and feel that they can't go on without them. Even if they left their job because the emotional pressure and load were too heavy, they are going to miss the humans they worked with. Even when they didn't like their coworkers, they will still miss them in a strange way.

It is important for Libras to have a job that has significance, one that the world really needs. They do not enjoy working just to make money or have fun. Libras need to have a job where they feel they give from their heart and contribute to the larger family of people. Often, Libra has great compassion and care for those who do not fare so well in this world of ours. They often love to work with unassuming people and basic projects, so long as their work helps people that are disadvantaged. It is self-evident that Libras do not want to work by themselves. They need to be part of a stimulating and tight milieu. They thrive when doing intense work in small groups—ones where they are already familiar with the emotional needs and reactions of all the participants. Then, they can relax fully and let the best parts of themselves come to the surface. At times, they create emotional conflicts because they know that as long as they fear things and hide themselves, they can't really relax and do their best.

Friends, Future, and Ideals

Libras are known for having big plans for the future. They see themselves in heroic circumstances and may feel that the life of their dreams is more in accordance with their true nature than the life they actually live. You can tease a Libra about things in the here and now but be careful when teasing them about their ideals and vision. They are prone to taking themselves far too seriously in these matters. Another piece of advice is to avoid making fun of their friends. Libras will defend their friends fervently. If you are on the lookout for a friend that always calm, stable, and undramatic, Libra is not a smart choice. They may seem very balanced, but in fact, they often create conflicts just to be able to play the hero and be the protector of their allies. In some areas, Libras seem modest, but when public attention is on them, they just love the limelight and want to make the most of it. Such attention gives them a strong sense of purpose and significance. To be frank, Libras love attention, admiration, and being idolized by their friends. They love to be the spokesperson for a golden world and future, one where everybody has freedom and plenty of riches. This sign is known to be very generous and giving with friends and the larger groups they associate with. But be aware: if someone has dishonored a Libra or their friends, that person may have earned themselves a lasting enemy. Libras do not easily forgive people who treat them or their friends condescendingly or without respect.

The best friends this sign can have are people who share their vision for a beautiful and ecstatic future—or even better, people they might begin to live out this beautiful future with in the present. At times, the Scale Bearers feel like they are crammed between their friends. One of the reasons for this is that they want to be in the middle, and of course, the middle person ends up being cramped every now and then. Sometimes they get twice the attention, and sometimes they are pressed in on both sides. Libras have this peculiarity of becoming jealous if their friends are better friends with somebody else. They give a lot in their friendships and want to be the chosen friend among equals. As far as friendship goes, they have steadfastness, loyalty, and the willingness to be there when you need them.

However, as mentioned, if you have disappointed a Libra in a major way, be aware that they can disappear and allow you to blow wherever the wind takes you without doing anything to reel you back in. If your Libra friend feels insulted and has thrown you into the pits of ignorance and darkness, do not even begin the futile project of trying to fix the problem, whether with excuses or admissions of guilt. Just take the hit and accept that this part of your journey together is over. There is no in-between for Libran friends—either you are in the light and their smile warms you every time you look in their direction, or you are just dust somewhere out in the darkness. That same rule also goes for visions and dreams—either they believe in something and see the very best and brightest in it, or the whole project is thrown away. If you are depicted as the villain, the best you can hope for is that Libra will walk on ahead into a new tomorrow. They have another adventure to play out and another friend that can appreciate their light and heroic willingness to be the best friend ever.

Seeking and the Spiritual

This sign is a rare mix of skepticism and superstition. Yes, they know that anything is possible, but on the other hand, they will discuss, argue, and search for flaws and inconsistencies as soon as anybody comes up with a specific statement about spiritual matters. Libra seems like a camel trying to get itself through the eye of the spiritual needle that is the portal into their true soul and deepest convictions. Outside of this portal, they are open-minded and tolerant, but at the same time distant and skeptical. If a spiritual truth is to be accepted, it first must withstand being dissected by the ruthless scalpel of logic and doubt. Libras have this deep longing to find the truth and essence of spiritual matters, but they are not satisfied with just any vague or cloudy meaning. They want precision and the pure core of essence. They seldom accept anything if they do not really grasp it with both heart and soul. Unfortunately, they are often too occupied with life to have the time needed to carry out this demanding spiritual quest. There is also a bit of fear here—if they really accept this spiritual truth, they might have to let go of all the other opportunities and fun that life has to offer.

Libras are good at advising others, but lousy at trusting in their own judgment and decisions. This is why they so often seem to be absolutely unshakable in their decisions. They try to convince you of their choice, and if that works, they start to believe in the astuteness of it themselves. The road of spirituality is in many ways a road of cleansing and purification for the Libra. They have to let go of many misconceptions and stop judging others and themselves if they want to ever get ahold of the spiritual essence they seek. Their spiritual road is not so much about finding as it is about letting go. They need to return to simplicity and understand that a clean soul needs to live in a clean body, in a psyche that is not saturated with the addictions and fears of the ego. It is important for Libras to see that having a healthy body does not open the door to paradise; the key is inner purity and the willingness to serve what lives in the soul. At the same time, they need to meld the inner and the outer worlds together. Body and soul, fair and foul, hand in hand—that is the magic wand.

That is why Libra will not find the true road by being obsessed with either the spiritual or the physical world. As prosaic as it may seem, this sign will find the promised land by walking the middle path. As they see the spirituality of the physical and the physical pleasure and beauty that flows from the spirit, they grow open to the magic essence of spirit that does not just flow through them but, in truth, *is* them. The road to this place is not found through either openness or skepticism but through cleansing the body and consciousness. As this happens, they gain the ability to be very open and naive at the same time—as they can recognize and see the truth of any falsity. As long as Libra has a hazy and distorted picture of who they really are, they are trapped by the mirror of projections. The same goes for any unrealistic expectations of their own potential and worth. For Libras, true spiritual realization begins when they use their awareness to pierce through the false, projected image they have of themselves and begin to catch sight of their true core and essence. Then, they can begin to receive the freedom and essential joy that is available to those that surrender to the one force that vibrates so strongly through every fiber of their soul. As all false images disappear and only the witness and pure awareness remain, their being becomes nothing but pure love.

Scorpio

October 23rd—November 21st

Element: Water
Quality: Fixed
Ruling Planet: Pluto

How to Present Yourself

Showing your true self is a dubious thing for a Scorpio. It is much better that people find you interesting and wonder about who you are but do not know your secrets and deeper motivations. To let them in on your secrets is to give them power, and why would one want to be vulnerable? Life is much more interesting when it has secrets and depths, ones where others have only a vague idea of the fantastic landscape they can sense beneath the surface. In some ways, Scorpios show their nature by hiding it. What they really say is: "If you want to know who I am, you have to risk coming closer to find out for yourself. I do not guarantee that it will be either nice or pain-free, but I can guarantee that you will discover sides of yourself you didn't know existed." Scorpios often maneuver in the undercurrents: silence from a Scorpio can be far more chilling than a stream of hurtful accusations from others. If you know somebody who can give you the feeling of being in the vicinity of a black hole, there is a great chance that person is a Scorpio. Small gestures, precise words, and emotional radiation are Scorpio's way of showing themselves. They can give you attention or reject you. Scorpios will test you before they show you any secrets. Are you worth the trouble? Can they trust you with their true self and feelings?

This method may seem strange, but it has its logic and is seen as a necessity by many Scorpios. After all, if a Scorpio decides to trust you and show you their true self, expect a full package. Some test you by being secretive, seeing how far you are willing to go to get to know them. Others test you by showing off their worst sides at the very beginning. If you can take that, well, then they can trust you. Scorpios like to have control over the situation and use different tactics to achieve it. They can seem very friendly, sensitive, and harmless, or scary and intimidating. As mentioned, if they decide to show you who they really are, they demand the right to show everything. Be careful what you ask a Scorpio for... you might get it! They will show you their dark sides as well as the light ones. Scorpios have this strange tendency to show their very best only to the people they really trust. They often hide their true sensitivity because they know that the moment you know how sensitive, caring, and loving they are, you have the power to hurt them. If a Scorpio has chosen to trust you and show you their true heart, know that you mean very much to them. They do not treat their feelings or relationships superficially; they have to either keep people at a distance or get very close and intimate. It is important for Scorpios to reveal themselves at the speed that suits them. They will never do something because they should do it or because others want it. They are ready when they are ready! It is important for a Scorpio to really dare to show themselves without reservation when they choose to do so.

That means, dear Scorpio, that you need to show other people your vulnerability and weak sides, and you need to show that you care for others and that you need them to be in your life! As a Scorpio, it is a significant step forward to stop hiding the sides of yourself that you think are demanding or difficult. It is a giant step to show others that you do in fact love yourself and think that you have many wonderful and positive qualities.

How to Get the Best from Your Talents and Resources

Scorpios have many plans and visions. They enjoy having unreachable goals and often have such high ideals about what they should do and how they should be that they are doomed to disappoint themselves. Some people might find Scorpios unethical because they often dig for diamonds in old slag heaps: they have no fear of getting their hands dirty. In fact, Scorpios are very ethical and sometimes moralistic, since they have a great need to justify their actions to themselves. They can be deeply occupied with doing what's right and doing good things, but at the same time, they know that you have to move through the dark and unpleasant to reach the light. Sometimes, they believe that there are different rules for them than for the rest of us, and that can make them quite self-righteous. Scorpios need concrete goals to use their talents to the fullest. They are in dire need of hope and belief, and they need the chance to do something even more valuable than what is happening in the moment. Scorpios that lack goals or a quest can easily end up mucking around in slag heaps, having forgotten that they were searching for diamonds.

As mentioned, they can have strong ethics and values, but can also easily adjust their ethics to fit with their goals and desires. Values and ethics are strongly linked with their visions for the future and where they want to go. They can adjust in the same way you adjust how you play the game if you change from golf to rugby. Scorpios know that many roads will lead to their goals, so their ethics are based more on the goal they see ahead than the circumstances they meet on the road. For Scorpios, finding the right way to use their power requires knowing that the end does not always justify the means. They need to become aware of the fact that the method can in fact destroy the goal. It is like wanting peace and having to learn that violence is not the right way to achieve that, because violence destroys the goal of peace. As a Scorpio, you cannot reach and fulfill a noble goal through cruel and rotten means. One of the reasons is that you yourself will become infected by the rottenness as you move down your path.

The Scorpio sees many possibilities, but it is important for them to save their energy and concentrate on one thing at a time. They can use their talents and resources best when they focus their energy in a clear direction. They also need to use their physical energy and have the physical strength needed to move toward their desired goal. When Scorpio manages to make a firm decision and dedicates themselves to their goal, their ability to get things done effectively and successfully is amazing. When they do not believe in their actions or are without a sense of meaning and love, their progress either becomes very cold and careless, or else just freezes and stops. Scorpios have a fantastic ability to create possibilities out of scraps and pieces—when they feel meaning in doing so and let their talents blossom. They do not set clear limits for the kind of behavior they will accept from themselves. Their limits are not found through emotions or instincts but through the development of a system of values based on their desire to use their talents and resources to create more hope, belief, and meaning in the world. Scorpios find the deeper meaning in life by creating it!

Communication and Immediate Surroundings

Scorpios detest white lies and the people who tell them. If a Scorpio commits this unforgivable deed out of cowardice, they will detest themselves for it. It is important for Scorpios to *not* have the same demands for others as they set for themselves. They are the ones who have this great inner urge for absolute and direct honesty. In fact, the honesty of a Scorpio might be challenging for others, so many Scorpios prefer to remain silent and hold their tongues instead of harassing others with their harsh and direct versions of the truth. Some Scorpios have a twisted form of communication—the idea behind their version is that everybody is lying all the time, therefore you are allowed to say anything to reach your goal. When Scorpios are faking and bluffing, they do so with a thoroughness that makes them very accomplished liars. The lies go deep and are carefully prepared, as is most of what a Scorpio fills their life with.

Scorpios take all their friends and contacts very seriously and feel a great responsibility for the people around them. Having too many acquaintances can be very taxing for Scorpios, especially if they are still fumbling around without a clear-cut understanding of the limits of their responsibilities. Superficial conversation is very tiring for most Scorpios. This comes from the fact that meaningless words and superficial feelings do not exist in their inner world. To them, every exchange of information and feeling is serious. Scorpios can be silent for an extended period, but if something really matters, they can speak with great force and for a long time. However, when the topic involves their own feelings and vulnerabilities, they easily end up helpless and at loss for words. Scorpios want to know where they belong in the grand hierarchy of things. They want to know their role and what the expectations are. They demand respect from their surroundings and are willing to give the same. They know how to fit into a system where the roles and functions are clearly defined and divided. When things are up in the air and power structures are hazy and undefined, they feel insecure and want to create order and clarity out of the messy chaos—and of course, the best solution for them is to become the top dog. The worst thing, to a Scorpio, is a lack of respect. An untimely joke at their expense is very provocative, and they might respond to it in the worst possible manner. Only very good friends are allowed to make fun of Scorpios without serious repercussions. Do not misunderstand: Scorpios do have a great sense of humor, especially at the expense of others, but it can be hard for them to laugh at themselves since the most painful thing they can experience is being a laughingstock.

A Scorpio needs to be able to trust your words and your integrity. They are trustworthy and will do everything possible to fulfill their promises. They want to walk the talk, even if the walking may be very stiff at times and perhaps even lead into a pit of destruction. One very good thing is that if you are found worthy of having a place in the heart of a Scorpio, they will always be there for you when you need it. Better friends for the hard times are difficult to find. They will help you with the practical and even take on the unsatisfying job of telling you the painful truth. Of all the creatures in the zodiac, Scorpio is the one that speaks the truth most directly and from their heart.

Home and Family

Scorpios often go so deep into their feelings that they need to have some distance from others. This distance is not a lack of intimacy but rather another way to show it. For Scorpios, the highest and most difficult form of love to attain is giving others absolute freedom and confidence. To feel really secure, Scorpio needs to experience that same freedom and confidence from the people closest to them.

Many Scorpios choose to keep a certain distance and detachment from the people they are closest with. In a way, their feelings are so strong and intense that it would be too much to go around and live with that level of intensity all the time. The home of the Scorpio is often open to everybody, and they like to drag special and unusual humans back home and into their dwelling. Although they have intense feelings for the places they live, Scorpios generally have little problem with moving. They do not feel that they are tearing up their roots—just replanting them in new soil. Their new home is interesting and exciting, and the possibility of exploring new surroundings makes them feel free.

Sometimes Scorpios become so trapped by family life and the place they live that they feel like they are slowly suffocating, even as they cling to the old with all their might. They can become self-destructive if they do not find a way to get out and use their talents and abilities. If family life is a realm of limitations and regulations, the Scorpio quickly grows unhappy. They need to have room to be strange, different, and even a genius. At its best, the home of a Scorpio is a base from which they can explore the unknown. Scorpio demands great tolerance from others, and it is important that they give others the same freedom that they need to receive. In this arena, Scorpio is more open than many realize. They are more than willing to receive the unknown and unexpected when it's on their own home turf. Strangely enough, the person that a Scorpio is most strongly connected to is also the person they can seem most distracted and distant from. When Scorpios, at last, feel safe, they can relax and allow themselves to be just as strange and distant as they sometimes are. Intimacy is a way to gain security for Scorpios. Once they do feel safe, they continue to feel so even when there is a distance and lack of intimacy. Only Scorpios can really understand that the greatest form of intimacy is to not have to be intimate at all. If this freedom is not experienced, Scorpios feel constantly caught in a web of undercurrents, emotional attachments, and demands. Scorpios enjoy life most when they build togetherness on a foundation of freedom, friendship, and choice. It is all about togetherness that gives each individual greater chances and freedom to explore the world.

Many people start relationships at a distance and move closer as time goes by. Scorpio feels most safe and intimate when what was once an emotionally and sexually loaded relationship moves into a deep friendship and love from the soul. Scorpios often have fixed ideas and somewhat rigid thoughts around family life. They have a tendency to create a vision and inner ideal that is not based on reality. To them, a home should be like this or like that, and their family should be equally specific. When the rift between dream and reality is too obvious, Scorpio often either withdraws or tries to force others to live by their ideals. Scorpios need to remember that ideals are something to strive toward, not something to be grumpy about if they're not met, and part of reaching their ideals means allowing others to strive toward their own ideals and dreams. The mature Scorpio looks at family and home as a breeding ground for all kinds of new and exciting opportunities: not a place for making demands, but a place for finding new solutions.

Creativity and Leisure

Scorpios have big ideas when it comes to creativity and figuring out how to use their time as best as possible so they can enjoy life and have fun. They're joyfully swimming in possibilities, but unfortunately, sometimes the Scorpio just floats around like a cork in the ocean. Far too often, their fantasies and dreams are more alluring than reality. In fact, Scorpios are hopeless romantics (even if they won't tell anybody that). Their passion and fire are awakened by their fantastic dreams and imaginations. Often, the real world is a bit dull and lifeless compared with the inner world of richness and endless sensual love. Scorpios easily fall in love—if they have opened their heart to this ability. If not, they do so once and then feel satisfied—been there, done that. If their inner door of dreams is open, however, they can fall in love with almost anybody, anywhere, at any time—because it is love that they have fallen in love with, not the person. Scorpios are privately very sensitive and emotional, but they can seem ruthless and uncaring to others. After all, when their inner dream has evaporated and disappeared, there is no more need for them to stick around the person who was once a vessel for those fantasies. As long as the outer world is connected to the inner dream, they will be passionate, vulnerable, and sensitive—but as soon as the door to the inner dream closes, the outer dream goes too. At that, Scorpio's former partner goes from someone the Scorpio couldn't live without to just another apple in the barrel.

Scorpios seldom go to the effort of, or have any interest in, rejecting someone. It is just that their attention suddenly turns in another direction. Then, the person who has been getting a lot of energy and attention from the Scorpio suddenly feels like they mean nothing when the passion has gone. The Scorpio is friendly enough and does not easily notice how lost and dejected the person they are neglecting might feel...well, there is an exception. Because of the intensity of a Scorpio, love can be so demanding and strong that it starts to feel like a nightmare to the person receiving all of their dark and desperate passion. It can be like the Scorpio pulls their loved one into their own dark world of dreams, and their loved one can easily feel overwhelmed by the sheer intensity and depth of their passion. Scorpios need to understand that they are searching for an idealized person when they fall in love, and once they have, they need to accept reality—which is neither idealized nor changing to match their dreams.

Scorpios really must learn to forgive themselves and others for not living up to the idealized standards, longings, and dreams they have around love. Scorpios are open to most as far as love goes and are often willing to drift into almost anything...at least once, just to test it out. On the erotic stage, they need to learn the difference between fantasy and possibility and to say *now* when *now* is what they really want. On a deep level, Scorpios are always looking for love and they feel most free and happy when they can surrender to their love and passion. The strange thing about Scorpios is that even though they really can get caught in the realm of flesh and worldly love, it is always the deeper and more refined soul of love that they seek. Scorpio's joy in life really begins to blossom when they find that refined love within themselves and dare to follow their soul's need to express that love to the world.

Health, Order, and the Necessary

Scorpios do not like routine. They get bored easily and need challenges in their daily lives. Scorpio enjoys it like no other sign when daily life is a struggle that constantly demands guts, courage, and initiative. They want to test their strength against the world and other people. They must choose between staring at walls that they're trying to tear down and being in constant motion toward new and unknown horizons. The Scorpio does not particularly want peace in their life, preferring action and tests of will. In work, it is the intensity that counts. They do not work at the same speed for long hours, but rather go all out in spurts of intense energy. They can do an enormous amount of work in a short time—when they have the inspiration and energy. If the inspiration is lacking, however, it takes them an enormous effort to get started at all. Their ability to plan and structure their days is not so great. A lot will happen on impulse or at the moment of inspiration, and there will always have to be room for unexpected and spontaneous actions.

Scorpios enjoy working with others—as long as they can do as they please. Having the freedom to choose their own actions at any given moment is of great importance. If they have chosen to accept order and discipline, they enjoy it. They can be the perfect material for soldiers, but if someone thinks they can force Scorpios to accept orders, they are making a great mistake. The Scorpio will do whatever it takes to resist attempts to force them to do something against their will.

This sign needs a lot of physical activity to stay healthy. The worst thing Scorpios can do for themselves in terms of health is sit there passively without doing anything…but they sometimes need a kick in the ass to get started. Give them a challenge and they thrive; give them boring routines and they get bored. In fact, they are in need of daily doses of excitement. Their work should entail some kind of journey or exploration where they never can be sure of what is around the next corner. That journey can come in regulated forms, like working with extraordinary or sick people, or exploring new and unknown areas of possibility.

Scorpios need to give themselves goals and test themselves against almost impossible odds. If they do not test their dreams against reality, most of their potential will stay unused and dormant. In many ways, Scorpios perform best under strain and pressure. They go deep and bring up their best qualities when it really matters. The old saying, "when the going gets tough, the tough get going" was made by and for Scorpios. A Scorpio who tries to avoid pressure and challenges will either become lethargic or start to pester others with their unused energy. The same goes for illness and health. If Scorpios do not use their physical energy, the excess may be turned inward in a destructive way, turning into illness. Very often, physical activity is the best way for Scorpios to handle emotional problems. After training and working out, insurmountable mountains of emotional problems suddenly become small heaps of manure that are easily cleaned away. They need the physical stamina to live with the intensity and passion they have. Scorpios need to know that they have the energy to meet the challenges of their daily lives. It is when they have this security and trust in themselves that they can delve deeper and solve the greater problems that lie beneath the surface, and it is digging into these greater problems and finding new and powerful solutions and methods that offer a hardworking Scorpio true bliss.

One-on-One Relationships

Lasting relationships and sex are two different things for Scorpios. They can come together, but even if sexuality is deep and intense in the moment for Scorpios, there is also something fleeting and transient about it. Most Scorpios are easily erotically attracted to others, but finding someone they want to live with year after year is something totally different. For Scorpios, an erotic meeting is something of the moment—they can even have deep and intense erotic meetings with people they don't actually like. Being in a relationship is something totally different; that involves safety, stability, and trust, which are so much more challenging than having sex. Scorpios are drawn toward people who can give them a feeling of rock-solid stability and absolute trustworthiness. They are attracted to people who can give them stability and a firm foundation for their lives, and hopefully at the same time join them in the depths of their inner oceans.

Scorpios are attracted to beauty and generosity. Stinginess is not something Scorpios adore in anybody...although they do like to sting themselves with a little swing of their Scorpio tail! When Scorpio has established a lasting relationship, it is solid, and they do not let go of it easily. Since they have invested so much and have been willing to work on it so hard for so long, they want it to last forever. As time passes, a Scorpio may start to feel a kind of ownership over their partner. It is like that person is *their* partner. The same goes for very close friends, and Scorpios can easily grow jealous or disappointed, especially if they feel that someone is doing things behind their back. They are not afraid of sharing but very afraid of losing the person they have given their love to with full intensity and no limitations. If a Scorpio sees you as a threat that wants to snatch away their partner or friend, be prepared, as they will fight to keep that person using all available means. Their chosen friends and loved ones are, in a way, their anchors to the real and physical world. Scorpios are normally generous and trustworthy, but they can be overly protective and quite domineering toward their partners.

Scorpios show their interest through lust and intensity, but their true love is most often shown through the physical realm—gifts. Buying gifts and sharing their material wealth are very often expressions of this love. The manifestation of love in the form of things and physical objects is what makes their lover feel real and touchable to a Scorpio. Scorpios seek out what is lasting in the deep zone of love. They can experience intense lust and erotic sensuality and pleasure without really being occupied by the person those feelings are directed toward, or even experienced with. Love, on the other hand, demands time, persistence, a willingness to be present, and a deep respect for the other person's values and needs. When Scorpio starts to think more about how their practical and physical needs can be organized and met than about the satisfaction of lust and passion, they have a serious outbreak of deep love occurring in their heart. But as a Scorpio, you must be aware that if your partner becomes your safety and security, you can easily start feeling despondent and helpless. Remember that a relationship is not a fight or a conquest, but rather a shared adventure and an experience where both parties need to give generously.

Beneath the Surface—Sex and Taboos

Scorpios enjoy fiddling around in the dark and exploring their wild side. They can be tempted to do so with almost anyone, anywhere. But, even if many will not admit it, they are often more preoccupied with talking about taboos than actually engaging in them. They can spend large amounts of time just thinking about things that people are told not to think about. The best way to manipulate a Scorpio is to tell them that something is prohibited and that they're not allowed to do it. That gives them an almost irresistible urge to taste the forbidden fruit. Scorpios are masters at keeping their own secrets, but not always so good at keeping other people's. In a strange way, they do not necessarily feel closest to the people they have the most intimate experiences with. It is the people that they tell their inner secrets and talk to about their real feelings that they feel most intimately connected to. Notwithstanding the way Scorpio circles around eroticism, words are more intimate for them than actions. So, they are far less fixated on sex than they appear to be. As others try to lighten the atmosphere with small talk, Scorpios might try to lighten the atmosphere with some sex. Scorpios sometimes get great pleasure from saying forbidden words and voicing their erotic experiences during the act—but what is harder to see is how Scorpios can be awfully silent about topics that others are chatting about. The Scorpio easily talks about what they do and want to do, but not so easily about their inner feelings and deeper thoughts.

Scorpios feel safe through physical intimacy, lust, and attraction, but there is often something impersonal about those experiences for Scorpios—the same way talking to the waitress at a restaurant is impersonal for most people. Scorpios feel safe when other people are attracted to them or lust after them. They feel safe when other people want something from them but start to feel more unsafe if the other person comes too close on an inner level. It is unsafe for Scorpios to have feelings that make them grow attached to other people. Letting other people close enough that they can really cause pain is a risky game for Scorpios. Therefore, Scorpios feel unsafe both if you show no interest in them and if you get too intimate and personal. They like to experiment with sexuality and intimacy, but they need to have both a certain distance and a great trust in the other person in order to let go of their iron control and highly developed defense system. This can be a problem in long-term relationships, which Scorpios both greatly long for and greatly fear. This ambivalence comes from the great length it takes to get down to the depths and rock bottom of their feelings, and at the same time, from their fear of being trapped and losing their freedom. However, the only thing that can get them to really let go of their cloak of mystery and secrets is true and lasting love. Only then can they feel completely safe and absolutely free to talk about their innermost dreams and desires. As mentioned, while they can share their dreams in theory, it is not always necessary to do so in the real world. That which cannot be spoken about, on the other hand, will grow and grow and force its way to the surface in the end. If you want a Scorpio to be true and devoted to only you, talk about their freedom to do what they want with others—yes, even give it to them. For Scorpios, there must be a choice. If there is no choice, it will be impossible for them to stay away from the forbidden fruit, but if Scorpios have a choice, they can live in chastity, purity, and unwavering devotion because they are the ones who have chosen to give away their freedom. Since that is the case, they feel like the freest beings on Earth.

Education, Adventure, and Life Philosophy

Scorpios are neither the most adventurous nor the most eager when it comes to spending their lives in school or other lengthy education programs. "Home sweet home" could be their slogan. They enjoy being in familiar surroundings where they have control and know the underlying patterns and rules. They prefer to bring the big world home instead of going out to find it. The exception is when they go out and discover a taboo they can explore. The prohibited, dangerous, and unknown have enough force to draw Scorpio away from the familiar and known areas they prefer to have as their base. But still, they prefer for things to be on their own turf and for games to be played in their home stadium.

That being said, Scorpios seek things they see as useful and need a specific emotional reason to get a longer education or go traveling. They do not do things just for the fun of it. They must have a purpose that is connected to their emotional needs. Their inner world seems very large and even endless, so they have more than enough to do just exploring and experiencing the emotional lives of themselves and others. Scorpios enlarge their horizons through close encounters, something they do not have to travel far to find. They most often choose a profession that connects them to people and their inner emotional lives. It can be in the art, in legal rights, in caring and teaching, or something else, but they need to use their talents to read and explore the inner worlds of other people. When they travel to new places, they try to get inside the culture and understand what drives people from the inside. They feel safe on the inside of things, and it is always a bit scary for them to stand on the outside. They like to have an idea of what goes on in the hearts and guts of other people. The first thing they do in a new place is make interpersonal contact and establish emotional links. When that is done, they can move on to the new landscape with inner confidence.

Traveling for the sake of traveling is a waste of time for Scorpios. They want to see what advantage they can gain from traveling to a new and unknown place. Remember that Scorpios can be players and gamblers, but they only risk their money on things they really want to win. The premium has to be worth the price and the effort. Because of this seriousness, they can have a lot of trouble deciding what kind of education they want or what adventures they want to explore. In one moment, they are very excited about an idea, but in the next, something has happened with their emotions and the same thing suddenly feels wrong or threatening. It is almost never the mind that really makes the decision. In the end, it boils down to feelings, guts, and intuition. One great incitement for Scorpios to go on an adventure and open their inner world to new impulses is the longing to do something for others and to be of help. Scorpios are at their best when they open their hearts to something greater than their own needs, so much adventure and joy comes to Scorpios when they really want to nourish and give to others. The philosophy of love, sharing, and giving serves them best in the long run. Their greatest adventure is taking this road of generosity. In the end, it will lead them to what they so long for—an inner sanctuary where they feel absolute trust, safety, and security. To reach this heaven, Scorpio needs to confront their own insecurity and open their heart to the full power of love, both in the inner and the outer worlds.

Goals, Profession, and Career

Power is of prime importance to a Scorpio. They do not necessarily want to have the power for their own sake; the feeling of powerlessness and helplessness is an abomination for them. Scorpios take their choices, drama, and vision very seriously. They want acknowledgment, respect, and attention. In private, Scorpios like to be a bit secretive and peek out at the world from around a corner, but the professional Scorpio wants badly to stand in the spotlight and be seen. It is important to know that the professional and the private Scorpio can easily be like two different people. The professional personality is direct and expressive, while the private one is restrictive and mostly hidden. Scorpios desperately want to have careers that will give them acknowledgment and notoriety. They want success and can push themselves really hard for a long time to reach what they seek with so much fervor and passion. They are not very fond of having superiors and only accept someone as their superior if that person is very clever and competent. If they do give their loyalty to a leader, it will probably last at least until death. Scorpios want the same absolute loyalty from their coworkers. If you are truly on a professional Scorpio's team, you can count on unbending loyalty and generosity. A Scorpio can be very ruthless against opponents and competitors. There is nothing personal about this willingness to use their power to the fullest, just the knowledge that all of us must take responsibility for ourselves, especially those of us who want to rise up and reach for higher goals. Scorpios do not yield without a fight, and it is important to remember that they respect people far more than systems. Therefore they give you respect not based on your position, but on your personality.

Scorpios have a great need to feel like they are masters of their craft and deserve whatever success they have achieved. Self-esteem in Scorpios is closely connected to their experience of realizing a certain portion of their dreams and visions—or not realizing them, as the case may be. They can excel in many professions if they do what they do with their full heart and power. A Scorpio who isn't devoted to their work is almost without exception unhappy and fighting ugly inner demons. Sometimes Scorpios think too much in black and white. They need to see that their method can destroy their target and that truth has more than one dimension. That will help them coordinate their efforts with others in a more flexible and easy way. People are just people, not either with them or against them. A Scorpio who feels safe, appreciated, and respected is one of the absolute best leaders to exist. In this case, they will have great authority, respect for others, and generosity. They will be an excellent strategist because they understand the underlying power structures and have both the knowledge and willingness to do what is necessary to get things moving in the right direction. The most advanced Scorpios find great joy in using their power with love and cunning. When Scorpio really is true to their inner heart and chosen goals, they achieve the best form of acknowledgment a Scorpio can get—respect and acknowledgment not for what they do and what they have achieved, but for who they are and the way they have done things.

Friends, Future, and Ideals

Scorpios take one step at a time on that yellow brick road into the future. They are realists and do not expect to get a lot for nothing. People born in this sign would rather see how far they can get with whatever means they have than work toward fantasy goals that have nothing to do with present reality. A Scorpio always evaluates possibilities before making a decision. They are always a bit skeptical of things that seem to come too easy and seldom trust what is gained without effort. They have the same skepticism toward overly friendly and enthusiastic friends. At worst, they are masters of skepticism, distrust, and pessimism.

Scorpios are almost always very polite and affable toward acquaintances and friends. They listen to the strange plans of others and nod at the right places without showing their true thoughts or skepticism. But be aware of the fact that you will be keenly tested, weighed, and examined if you are a prospect for future friendship. The same thoroughness goes for dreams and idealistic visions. Scorpios move slowly toward the future. This comes from the fact that the future is often seen as the eye of a needle. You need very good aim, precision, and focus if you are to have any hope of getting through that opening. This view of the future means that some Scorpios choose to live without dreams and visions, while others have ideals that are totally unrealistic without a clue about their lack of realism.

Most Scorpios are good listeners, and they are masters of listening without giving advice. If you really do want to hear their opinion, they will most likely go directly to the heart of the matter and tell you what they think without beating around the bush. Giving you specific advice on what to do and how to live your life is a sign of deep trust and friendship for Scorpios. This comes from the fact that they only want to be on the receiving end of such advice from people they trust without a trace of doubt. Neither do they find any reason to take the effort to give this kind of advice to people they don't care for deeply. In their world, they become vulnerable when they show you that they really care about you. Then you know something about their feelings and what really lies in their heart, and that can be scary for a Scorpio.

The Scorpio doesn't need many friends. They want a handful of friends with qualities they can really respect and appreciate; worthy and trustworthy people whom the Scorpio knows will be there for them when needed. Know that Scorpio will be there for you if you are in need. They want friends who can keep a secret and who know how to hold their tongue. They also want friends who will leave them alone when they need to be left alone. Scorpios like to analyze, discuss, and evaluate everything with good friends. They like to be mentally challenged in nice—and preferably a bit luxurious—surroundings…but not too much small talk, please; they like people to be direct and a bit ruthless. When they really go for their dreams, they do so in the same way each time. First, they analyze and cut things down to the bone, getting to the heart of what the dream is about and how to get it rolling. Next, they get going and take the few, calculated, and effective steps that can make their plans become reality.

Seeking and the Spiritual

The main road to the spiritual for Scorpios goes through humans and the human heart. They need to see the holy and spiritual in the soul of their fellow human beings. It is impossible for them to find what they seek only in their inner world. It is said that the realm of God is within, and that is somewhat true, but the Scorpio must seek and find its reflection in the outer world to truly find the spiritual depths within. Giving selflessly in encounters with others will show them how to trust and surrender— actions that are necessary to go deeper into the spiritual mysteries.

In doing this, Scorpios start to understand the depth and profundity of the spiritual laws and become able to live more and more in accordance with them. "Do unto others as you would have them do unto you" can be a simple slogan for Scorpios walking the spiritual path. It might be hard for them to accept, but these are underlying rules that also must be accepted and followed by the Scorpio clan. They can take a lot of shortcuts and sneak around corners to get what they want in the outer world, but this tactic doesn't work for the spiritual path. Going down the spiritual road, they learn that all they send out will return and that shortcuts only mean postponing the payment until later. No act can take you away from the fact that your feelings and inner state are an exact reflection of your spiritual state.

Finding balance in all things is of prime importance for the spirituality-seeking Scorpio. The same goes for learning to be fair but to hold no grudges and make no judgments toward either themselves or others. The outer and the inner worlds have to be balanced. The spiritual and the mundane, the male and the female, emotions and consciousness, and, last but not least, they have to find the balance between light and darkness. Scorpios have a tendency toward extremes. They want to be pure goodness for a while and then they need to do something filthy just to explore and get that beautiful feeling of being truly alive. They need to explore both heaven and hell before they can find balance. They just have to remember that walking the yellow brick road in the middle is also part of the human experience. If they want to experience the full range of human emotions and possibilities, they must remember that having balance, peace, and inner harmony is part of the package.

Creating beauty and harmony is important for the spiritual Scorpio. Being able to stay pure and balanced when the storm rages is the sign of a spiritually mature Scorpio. Scorpios can be masters of letting themselves become possessed without being possessed by the possession. When they really understand that every being is their sibling and that they really will reap what they sow, lilies start to grow from the earth that they have made so rich with their fertilization. The ability to manifest and live their highest ideals and at the same time have a full heart in meeting with their fellow human beings opens the door to inner bliss for Scorpios. It is not the great, glorious act that opens the door for Scorpios, but the pure and humble ability to love on a daily basis; to love without judging the position or quality of what is loved. To love because all life is valuable and to accept that the needs, dreams, and longings of others are truly as important, just, and right as their own. To love whether the object is a pretty flower or an ugly insect. Valor, consideration for others, and the quest to find beauty in both the small and the great things are what distinguish the spiritual Scorpio.

Sagittarius

November 22nd—December 21st

Element: Fire
Quality: Mutable
Ruling Planet: Jupiter

How to Present Yourself

Sagittarius loves to explore and grow in an enthusiastic and open way. As a Sagittarius, you love being interested in things and find great joy in giving joy to others. One of the best compliments you can get is that you are colorful and exciting. If someone is satisfied with being a bore, that someone is not you! Every now and then you become a bit tired of your own speed and exuberant activity and get a sudden urge for peace and quiet. You are extroverted and open, but sometimes you have a great need to share your serious and introverted side with the world. But alas, this activity is also done with great intensity and focus. If anybody knows how to be introverted in a way that attracts attention, it is you.

As a Sagittarius, you often find the middle road a bit boring. You are unusually happy when you are happy and unusually sad when you are sad. You have a great need for action and the feeling of being alive. You want others to be happy and thrive in your company, something which sometimes makes others feel like you are a bit too much. You want everybody to think well of you and find you benevolent. The things you talk about with others are the things that you yourself are vividly engaged in. You really enjoy the enthusiasm and inner fire that make your heart and mouth sing. You know that faith can move mountains, and you enjoy moving those mountains... at least, as long as faith can do it and it doesn't take too much time or manual labor.

Being a Sagittarius, you want to share what gives you joy with others and get them to see your point and be interested in the same things that you are. It is of vital importance for you to be aware of the signals you receive from others. If you're not, you can believe that you are having a lively and interesting conversation, while the other person feels overwhelmed and overrun by your enthusiasm. As a Sagittarius, one of your greatest assets is your ability to be an open conduit and allow energy and joy to flow through you and out into the world. To avoid becoming too much of an annoyance, you have to give others enough space and room. Other people need to feel like they can choose to sit still if they want. Sometimes they feel overwhelmed by your wave of enthusiasm and feel they are drowning and losing their own footing and ability to choose and to say *no thanks*. You can exhaust yourself in the long run by making so many people addicted to and dependent on your go-ahead spirit and engagement.

Normally, Sagittarians have great hearts. They enjoy loose and wavy clothes and feel constrained and constricted in clothes that are too tight and formal. They can be quite open-mouthed and like to speak from their gut...and they appreciate honesty and directness. To others, it seems like the Sagittarius runs on some strange batteries that do not need to be charged, but they need to remember that this is not the case. Every now and then, they need to fill themselves up.

The right recreation (holiday) is a good way to do this. One of their finest qualities is that they can easily become just as enthusiastic and happy on behalf of others as for themselves. They are generous with themselves, and their laughter comes from the heart. Sagittarians easily say yes—sometimes a bit too easily, because they need to make sure they have enough time to do all the stuff they have said yes to. They enjoy themselves most when they are headed toward an unknown but promising future.

In some ways, the Sagittarians are eternal optimists who always see and believe that things will work out for the best and that they can be even better than they are—but as a Sagittarius, you must remember to take care of yourself. One way to do that is to share your insecurities, soreness, and pain with others. That gives you access to something deeper and even more meaningful. It is important that others understand that you have your own inner depth and challenges—otherwise, they might get the impression that your most important purpose in life is to be a great furnace that can warm their frozen limbs and souls. In truth, this might be one of your greatest gifts to others—as long as you remember to feed your inner self with what fills you with warmth, joy, and enthusiasm.

How to Get the Best from Your Talents and Resources

The distance between an excellent idea or opportunity and the long, arduous process of making that idea into reality is very short for a Sagittarius. They are quick to show their enthusiasm but are also quickly caught up in all the work that needs to be done. They have a tendency to become very responsible and put a lot of pressure on themselves when they start to work. They have such high demands for themselves that they frequently choose to let their dreams just be dreams so they can float around in the fluffy pink world of unrealized possibilities. Since Sagittarians find that only the best is good enough, they have a tendency to feel like they always could have done more or better. They are surprisingly thorough and use a lot of time to get the results that they want. In their world, there is a huge gap between the professional and the amateur. In some ways, the Sagittarius can play around and enjoy being an amateur. As an amateur, they can easily learn how to impress others and use their charm to float along, but at the same time, so many things that they want will never be started—it just takes too much time and effort to follow through.

When a Sagittarian's professional identity enters the race, everything changes. They work tirelessly day and night. They are more concerned with putting in the right effort and getting a result than having a good time doing it. Just remember, Sagittarians suck at being semiprofessional. They can do things just for fun and out of love or they can do them with 100 percent seriousness. In the latter case, they need to be willing to do all the tasks thoroughly with precision and total concentration and effort. It is important that they have room in their lives for both approaches to the world. They really need the freedom to just play and be an amateur in some arenas and to be a serious, hardworking professional in others. The Sagittarius need to work and use their talents on things that catch their enthusiasm and attention in a joyful way. But as a professional, they also need big challenges that make them work really hard and sweat like a pig before fulfilling their lofty visions. They need these efforts and challenges to attain the inner security and feelings of worth that only come from reaching the goals they have worked hard to make into reality. The one force that really makes them a professional and expert is the fact that they do not give up, even if the road is long and demanding. They stick to it until they have learned what it takes to get there, and it is this practical knowledge of how to build what they want in the world from scratch that makes them an expert. Sagittarians have a conservative side that is not always so easy for others to see. They like to do many things the old-fashioned way. They do not believe in shortcuts or that they will get something for nothing. Hard work and even more hard work is the Sagittarian's way to success. They can hold up a lot of ideals like freedom and experimentation, but when it comes down to it, they believe in good old-fashioned qualities like responsibility, honesty, respect, and reliability.

As a Sagittarius, it is very important that you feel a deep respect for both what you are doing and the way you do it. You need to be proud of yourself and your contributions to society. Shortcuts do not feel good to you, even when they work. You want quality and get the greatest pleasure from using your abilities to the fullest in your work. You enjoy taking things step by step and building slowly. You must constantly prove to yourself that you are worthy and that the values you have and the things you strive for are worthy. You will always achieve the best results by having one eye focused on reality and the possibilities of the here and now, and the other eye firmly looking at the future dream that gives you the energy and the enthusiasm to move forward.

Communication and Immediate Surroundings

Sagittarians love talking about ideas and possibilities and they have many unusual and rebellious ideas. They love talking with non-traditionalists and enjoy the company of talkative and different people with a lot of interesting ideas. They can fight to their last breath for their own and others' right to have and use their freedom of thought and speech, but they can also become immensely provoked by people who have different opinions from their own, especially if the Sagittarian regards them as intolerant. In general, they seldom have any tolerance at all toward those whom they deem intolerant. They would like to deny others the right to be judgmental and prejudiced, but that need conflicts with everybody having the right to say and think what they want...

As a Sagittarian, your thoughts are not as flexible and logical as you would like to think that they are, but they are very consistent in their own peculiar way. You do not easily change your opinions, and very seldom do so during a discussion. In fact, you can be quite stubborn and cling strongly to your old opinions and views. This statement can feel quite provocative as you read it since you view yourself as a very open-minded and tolerant person. On the other hand, you do change your point of view when you are given time enough to think about it for yourself in peace and quiet. The strange thing is that you quite often do not actually realize that you have changed your view or opinion. You might believe that you have just made a slight adjustment in your position, while to others, it seems like you have a totally new understanding of the matter.

You like people with strong opinions who present them in a direct and straightforward manner. Sometimes you get into trouble because you disregard your own and others' vulnerability. Your need for direct honesty sometimes seems to give you the right to be rude—and ruthlessly so—in the name of freedom and truth. Pay attention to the fine line between honest truth and a blunt lack of empathy. You should not set yourself up as an advocate for everybody's right to have their own gun while talking to a mother whose child was just killed by an angry man with a gun. Truth is a sharp sword that sometimes needs to be kept in the sheath and your truth is not necessarily the truth of others. You have a tendency to believe that you have unique answers and that others ought to listen to your wisdom. Humility and willingness to listen are very useful skills for you to develop. On the other hand, you enjoy knowing people from different fields and walks of life. As a Sagittarius, you may become enormously attached to your own ideas and what you think is important in the moment. The truth is that you could have been just as intensely engaged by something completely different. Remember that words are just that...only words. In fact, the most important thing for you is the exchange of energy that makes you feel enlivened and loved. You need the sparks, but where they come from is not so important. The more you can handle the flow of enthusiasm and engagement from the other party, the greater the possibility of real friendship and love developing. A daily dose of the lukewarm is one of the worst things you can offer a Sagittarius—a daily dose of conflict and contrast is so much more enjoyable for them than shallow boredom.

Home and Family

These Centaurs have some problems with finding out who they really are and which stable they belong in. Some Sagittarians love indiscriminately, falling for almost anybody they get in touch with, while others keep everybody at a distance. This comes from the fact that intimacy only comes in two categories for Sagittarians: the first version is total devotion, and the second is impersonal treatment and nonattachment. Sometimes, this star sign has a problem with sorting out which is which. Who deserves their unlimited devotion and who is just a passing acquaintance? Sagittarians have a tendency to reach for great feelings and love without limits, even when it is not proper or natural and they sometimes keep their distance when somebody really begins to get close to them.

When Sagittarius is in the throes of passion, they are liable to do almost anything to keep the love from their partner coming. They can be heroic and unselfish if that is the method that works—or the crying, howling victims if that is what is needed to keep their partner's attention. Sagittarians must learn to sort out the important from the random so they can know who and what is important and who and what is not. At the same time, they need to see that giving all their love to one person/object is not enough. They need space to love many, and at the same time get their priorities and the different kinds of love right. Sagittarians have this great capacity for love. They need to be able to let it flow and see what kind of love is strongest and where their true heart and responsibilities lie. Sagittarians love to help the ones they love, and so they must be aware that love does not mean sacrificing oneself. Neither is it a good solution to fall in love with victims just because they are victims. In their eagerness to be helpful, Sagittarians might also create helpless victims by making other people addicted to and dependent on their help. The Home and Family should be places of openness and trust, not places where everybody is somehow seen as a victim that needs to be rescued or helped.

The Sagittarius does not feel at home in surroundings that are too rigid and structured but enjoys having a certain amount of fluid comfort in their home. They want everybody in their home to be friendly and caring. They want a home where they can relax and enjoy life without being criticized. They often need to listen to music, paint, look at an aquarium, or just dream the time away. They can enjoy living in small and cramped apartments but also know how to enjoy huge mansions with lots of space. Everything fits them as far as homes go, as long as it gives them an inner feeling of meaning and love. The truth is that if you're a Sagittarius, your inner dreams are the foundation that you build your life upon. As long as reality is in tune with your dreams, reality can have all kinds of shapes and ways of manifesting. If in reality, however, your home and your family are disconnected from your inner dreams, they will be unsatisfying and feel like a swamp—even if they seem like heaven to outsiders. It is the deep inner dream of love and the willingness to follow that dream that gives Sagittarians the courage to love fully and the foundation to create a true home in their inner and outer worlds.

Creativity and Leisure

Leisure time is not a planned activity for a Sagittarian. It is something that just happens spontaneously and without preparation. They love challenges and the unknown. They love widening their experience by doing something unusual and not really knowing what to expect. Things that bring a feeling of freedom, fun, and spontaneity are very welcome and a great way to charge the Sagittarian's batteries. When a Sagittarian lets go of the reins, the outcome can be unpredictable, and they love to let go of all their inhibitions. Sagittarians can be a bit much for others when they let themselves open up without restraint. Sometimes, they can become quite single-minded and inflexible, as well as a bit primitive. Their creativity is greatest when they walk the untrodden paths of life, and they love to do something different and put their personal imprint on everything they do.

Sagittarians are a master at playing games but can become so absorbed that they forget that something is just a game. In the worst-case scenario, they become so preoccupied with getting ahead that they don't notice the perplexed people they knocked down in their eagerness to reach their goal. There is seldom any bad intention in this—just inattentive inconsideration. They have a great need for the space and freedom to open up and should take precautions that they do so under the right circumstances and with people who can handle their wavelength. As a parent, Sagittarians tend to have the opinion that children need to be given a wide berth and have to learn to handle the cuts and bruises that life will inevitably give them. Sagittarian parents are seldom nitpicky or overly anxious, but they might be a bit too optimistic and push their children into doing things the children are not ready for. Sagittarians like brave, courageous, and successful children, and should be aware that not all children are as unafraid or reckless as they were as kids.

One of the things a Sagittarian must learn if they want to create a life of joy and beauty is to see and respect the fears, phobias, anxiety, and timidity of others. Sagittarians want to play and that is great; they just have to let others go at their own speed and by their own rules. They can feel like others hold them back and constantly suppress them when, in fact, it is the Sagittarian who constantly finds challenges and wants to push other people past their limits and out of their comfort zones. The Sagittarian at their best is courageous, entertaining, and a great inspiration for others. In fact, they can teach the rest of us a lesson or two about the fact that the prime essence and meaning of life is to enjoy it and have fun. They are great company if you want someone to roam around and seek joy together with. They are created for adventure—except for the times they are stuck as completely as petrified wood. Remember, the most important thing for the creative Sagittarian is not where they are headed, but that they are on the way...and enjoying the ride.

Health, Order, and the Necessary

In most Sagittarians, there is a gap between their serious and playful sides. Joy is supposed to be completely joyful and not hampered by sad and serious stuff. On the other hand, the serious stuff is taken very seriously and is pursued with great determination and effort. They can just as easily go to an extreme with efficiency and order as they can with joy and play. If they begin to go down the road of efficiency, order, and earning money, they can do so with great determination and for a long time.

Feeling secure and safe in daily life is important for Sagittarians. They like life to be safe, uncomplicated, and easy five days a week—and then like to have pure adventure for the weekend. They hate it when a lack of order in everyday matters stops possible adventures and great experiences from happening. They can be very sensible, even purely matter-of-fact when it comes to the small things, and they can be stingy with money. They know how to be big spenders when life is about play and joy but are miserly when it comes to the daily necessities. Champagne is there to be wasted, bread to be respected and handled with care. Sagittarians like it simple; they want an emotionally uncomplicated and practical life and want to use up as little time as possible on the boring stuff. So, they have a tendency to do the necessary in sudden bursts of effort. Often, they postpone things until their pile of tasks is so big that it just has to be taken care of, and then they want to get it all done so that they can wait as long as possible until next time. Sagittarians hate all the small, fussy things that have to be done and talked about. If they have planted themselves in a chair in front of the television or at the dinner table, they hate being disturbed. They do not want to move their ass again before they have finished their meal or the television program that they are watching is over. Of course, something unexpected and fun can still happen. Other people can be very astonished by the fact that someone who, at times, seems like they are glued to whatever they are sitting in, can move so quickly and with such joy and enthusiasm.

Sagittarians are thorough and enduring in their work. They prefer doing something over hanging around and just being bored. For the most part, they have naturally good health and a strong constitution. They can handle food and ways of living that would give others health problems. As long as they enjoy life and get some decent nutrition and food every now and then, life seems to be nice to them and they stay surprisingly healthy. For most Sagittarians, it takes a long period of malnutrition and misuse of their bodies before diseases start to get ahold of them. Once they have fallen ill it will take a long time for them to heal and get their system in order again.

Sagittarians are surprisingly good at working in teams and collaborating. In fact, it is easier for them to work in groups and teams than to work on their own. They have problems with pushing themselves to do what's necessary when they are alone. As professionals, they can become very critical of their own abilities and performance and need somebody around to tell them how clever and competent they are. They like to work in comfortable surroundings, and there should be access to food in the vicinity. It can be downright destructive for a Sagittarian's enjoyment of working if there is no access to food in cases of sudden hunger. Sagittarians need to get their food, and when they do, they can go for hours and hours, day after day. As an employer, remember to keep your Sagittarian workers well-fed. If you do, Sagittarians are some of the steadiest and most loyal, trustworthy, and enduring people you can find. The same goes for housework and taking care of what needs to be done. They need to be fed with food, compliments, and other people's satisfaction. One of the greatest pleasures you can give a Sagittarian is to show them your satisfaction with their existence in your life and the work that they do.

One-on-One Relationships

Sagittarians are curious about other people. They want to find out what goes on in their heads and what their beliefs are. They want to know anything about everything new and unknown to them. This can get a bit difficult when they are in relationships with people they know well—because then they already know what you think, mean, and what your beliefs are. So, to entertain them, you have to come up with some new thoughts every day. It can be hard to maintain competition with strangers who are always new and unknown. Sagittarians need to have lasting relationships with people whom they can talk with about literally anything. The same topics over and over again will not hold their interest for very long. They want something fresh and inspiring. In many ways, Sagittarians want to have the perfect buddy as their partner. They want somebody to play, dance, laugh, and have fun with. They want the whole friendship package with a sexual and erotic topping just to make it even better. Needless to say, it can be difficult to live up to these expectations for other mere mortals.

One absolute necessity for Sagittarians in close relationships is the feeling of freedom. If they feel free and are allowed to talk about their dreams, fantasies, and freedoms, they can very well be buttoned up and restrained in the real world. But if they are not allowed to talk about their dreams and live in that inner dream world where everything is possible, they will feel bound and gagged. However nice and comfortable it is in their cage, it is not a staying place for a Sagittarian. A Sagittarian must be able to dream, flirt, and play with possibilities to be happy. Time with their partner is essential for this sign. The Sagittarius does not want to be alone often—on the contrary, they want to share everything with their chosen company. They can have an enormous capacity for social life and endless conversation. If you love a Sagittarian, you need to love spending a *lot* of time with them. They need someone to share their ideas, ideals, and thoughts with…all of them! Sagittarians may seem very independent because they love to throw themselves into the unknown—but if you are with one of them, then you are not falling for that crap anymore. You know how addicted and dependent they can become. In their world, what is the point of having all this energy, joy, and all these ideas if there is no one around to share them with? It is easy to be with Sagittarians as long as you don't mind their intensity and need for conversation with you.

Sagittarians forgive easily and are seldom the jealous type. They are flexible and can be dragged into most of the things that you are interested in, but remember, make sure to avoid boring them with endless repetition of the same things. A Sagittarian will never leave or abandon you because of problems or challenges that you create. It is when you become gray, dull, and boring that they might slip away to something more colorful on the other side of the fence. They need to have a stimulating partner and a lively relationship. They always see their partner in the best possible light and are rather optimistic about the future and its possibilities—as long as they are not bored out of their wits. If you want to be nice to your Sagittarian partner, tell them how inspiring, fun, and great they are to be around. It is like a magic formula: the more often you tell them how great and fantastic they are, the greater and more fantastic they become. If you also take the initiative and invite them to do something new and exciting with you, they will adore you until the end of time—or until they start to get bored again (which for Sagittarians are one and the same…boredom is the end of time.).

Beneath the Surface—Sex and Taboos

In many ways, Sagittarians are the simplest and most naive of the creatures in the zodiac. What makes it a bit more complicated with them is their intensity. They often go into things with such fire and eagerness that it is too much of a good thing. Suddenly, what was really easy to start with becomes very complicated and touchy.

One of the most difficult things for this sign is letting others know how dependent they can become, and showing their vulnerability and sensitivity is a scary project. Behind their free and careless exterior, you will find a cuddly teddy bear that wants to hug you forever. The most intimate thing a Sagittarian can do is let you know that they are dependent upon you and have this deep emotional attachment to you. Sagittarians have approaches to sex that are in their usual fashion. The first approach is sex as a playful meeting—as some sort of communication that does not mean something more than that you enjoy sex together. This approach has no expectations of depth or emotional intimacy. With the second approach, it is completely different. Then, their sexuality is very intimate, with great depths and deep bonds. Their emotions are intense and serious in approach number two. There is no more fooling around or just having fun. At this stage, they are more than ready for eternal love, marriage, and whatever it takes to stay together forevermore. At that point, the brave Sagittarian explorer will show their true feelings, longings, and greatest need: to be received.

Often, there is a great need to be taken care of inside this seemingly independent Fire sign. This yearning for surrender and being totally enveloped by another being is something Sagittarians rarely display. At the superficial stage, a person's feelings and tears make the noble centaur run away. At stage two, the more feelings the better, and sentimentality and tears just make their heart thump harder. A good cry is invigorating and erotically stimulating. The flow of softness and love stimulates the sexual impulses and needs of the Archer—the Sagittarius—to reveal themselves like an eternal spring. Sagittarians know how to make ecstatic love and cry out about their wounds and depth at the same time. They surrender totally and experience how lack and closeness, pain and love merge into a deeper intimacy. When Sagittarians have surrendered to this kind of love, they seldom choose to let go of it. They feel such closeness that separating from them is like severing a person in two. Their chosen one can easily feel a little constricted as the Archer changes from freedom-loving and easygoing to the most loyal, dependent, and sincere of them all. Sagittarians are preoccupied with breaking rules and taboos until they reach this stage of real and deep intimacy. At this stage, they become occupied with having a good time and preserving the situation. Beneath that easygoing, devil-may-care, fair surface, you will find one of the most sensitive, loving, and devoted creatures roaming this Earth. If they have taken you into the core of their heart, you will have a room there as long as they have a spark of life left in them.

Education, Adventure, and Life Philosophy

Sagittarians love great plans and visions. They dream about themselves in new and exciting roles and situations. For this sign, the future is a treasure chest filled with promises and possibilities that are just waiting to be found and conquered. As time goes on, the Archer gains wisdom by learning how to be discerning and thus how to tell which dreams really can be conquered and which ones would just leave them banging their heads against the wall of rock-hard fantasies. This might be the most important method used by Sagittarians in all countries to learn about themselves and their relationships to the world: testing their own visions and abilities, and by facing the actual results of their actions, slowly learning the difference between who they are and the person they dream about being. Archers have a great need to make a big impression on the world. They want to be heroes and accomplish marvelous feats. They want admiration and seldom seek an education that leads to a life in anonymity. They want to rise above the masses, and even as tourists and travelers they want to follow an untrodden path. They want to experience and be somewhere that no one has been before. They want newness and—at the very least—to avoid the boringly normal and dull stuff. They want life to be a journey where they meet other free souls who dare to sail under the flag of discovery and freedom.

More than anything, Sagittarians want to expand their horizons through adventure and grand sunsets. They love beautiful nature, especially the wild and untamed part of it, and have a tendency to feel that the bigger the better and the more the merrier. They want to be the creators of their own adventures and want to play the role of the hero. Sagittarians have a tendency to think that they are always right and that they know better than anyone else. It is easiest for them to talk with people who are less informed and not so occupied with getting the facts exactly right. They enjoy sharing opinions and experiences without having to get into too much analysis or too many petty details. They can go for any education if the heart and the enthusiasm are there. Without inspiration and enthusiasm, there will be no education at all.

Sagittarians can do something for a long time—yes, sometimes even finish it off—but they often suddenly start on a new and more alluring adventure. They have a problem with finding the right balance between steady, hard work and the need for inspiration. As mentioned, they want to be heroes in life and rarely find any pleasure in being anonymous and ordinary. They want to help others, but with some flare and greatness. They need to be seen and get a lot of acknowledgment. They like to give inspiration and get praise. They can have problems with being on the top, both because there is a lot of pressure in being the top dog and because they prefer being on the road to somewhere else. They like to be climbing up the ladder, both in life and in their career, as long as they have a vision. Sagittarians never stop learning new things. For them, life is an education and to learn new stuff is to be alive. The most important meaning of life for these creatures is the freedom to explore, seek, and expand into new horizons.

Goals, Profession, and Career

Sagittarians can be very particular and demand a lot of themselves and others in their chosen profession. This is also much of the reason behind their successes. It is amazing how these creatures that have so much slackness in them can be so particular and exact in the way they accomplish things in their professional lives. They can have difficulties in figuring out their goals and making important choices and decisions because there are so many things that look interesting and promising to them. On the other hand, they want to do something special and unique. In their chosen area, they want things to be perfect. This longing can either make them very thorough and careful—or just make it almost impossible for them to move anywhere at all.

The preferred and most convenient solution for Sagittarians is to eliminate so many possibilities that just one is left standing. After having searched and started things all over the place, they end up left with the one thing that has enough potential and quality to still hold their interest. To others, Sagittarians do not seem to be especially meticulous, but in the end, there are very few things that find their way through the eye of their inner needle. Sagittarians like to have a profession where they can use their brains and their practical abilities. They want to make things better for everybody and create a world that is better and closer to heaven than it was when they first arrived on this planet. They like to go for things that have deep significance and eternal value. In some ways, they prefer to have small measures of quality in their profession than large amounts of meaningless success. They also want to have a job where they can use their deductive powers and wits. They love solving problems and finding paths and solutions where others just see dead ends and misery. They enjoy serving in their own way, where they can do small things with grand gestures. If they have found their place and their line of work, small things can have immense importance and give them great joy and satisfaction. As always, they love being right and knowing the answers. They enjoy a good discussion about problems but also want to be recognized and respected for their ability to solve problems by themselves. If the Sagittarius feel that there is nothing to be done, they become very despondent and negative.

In worst-case scenarios, all their positive inspiration turns to self-destructive negativity and hopelessness blown totally out of proportion. Then, they just feel dark despair and have lost every ability to find hope and solutions. So, if you want to help a Sagittarius find the bright side of life, just remember to give them praise and show your appreciation for all that they are and do. As a Sagittarius, you must remember that the interplay between play and seriousness is also very important in professional life. If you just stay on the serious and responsible side, you soon lose the brightness in your eyes and become graver and feel more inadequate with every breath you take. If you just play and completely forget the serious side of life, you will not get anywhere and begin to experience life as a boring and superficial place to be. Sometimes, Sagittarians just go on to be immature children that never grow up or make a real life for themselves. Sagittarians need to take their work seriously and at the same time have a lot of space and humor around their visions and need for greatness.

At their worst, Sagittarians become condescending and always look down on others, believing that they are better and wiser than everybody else. They have so many words with which to say things that they think are immensely clever and smart, but that everybody else finds tiresome and repetitive. At their best, they are inspiring, enthusiastic, entertaining, and good at solving real problems. In addition to that, they are trustworthy and have a great sense of solidarity and togetherness.

Friends, Future, and Ideals

The primary interests of Sagittarians involve humans and human society and its possibilities. They often have a diversity of dreams and hopes for the future, but all of them involve a society where humans are friendly and loving. Sagittarians know how important it is that humans really care for each other. So, friends are of great importance for Sagittarians, and they can go to all kinds of lengths to help their friends in difficult situations. They want every friendship to be something unique and special. Sagittarians can have a lot of acquaintances and a great circle of people they know, but they pick their true and close friends with great care and consideration. They seldom have more than one or two friends of this kind at a time. One challenge for Sagittarians is that the difference between a life partner and a close friend can be hard to see. If you're their partner, it may seem like the Sagittarius is married just as much to their friends as to you.

When many people come together, Sagittarians like to concentrate on one person at a time. This might seem strange to others. If you are spending time with a Sagittarius, they will try to include others in the conversation and company. On the other hand, if they feel like people around them are in a group, the Sagittarian will concentrate on one of the other people and may even exclude others from the conversation and exchange. For the Archer, the logic is simple enough: everybody shall feel included and be invited to take part in things, but when there is already a whole group doing things, then it is a good idea to withdraw with somebody and just give them that extra attention. Sometimes the Sagittarius chooses friends for superficial reasons, like because they are popular, rich, nice looking, and so on. The fact is that Sagittarius, under their tolerant surface, is attracted to people that are or have done something the Archer can admire and respect. In other words, Sagittarians love to swim in the glory of the status and success of their friends. It is like they can suck up this energy and use it to boost their own feelings of worth and success.

When Sagittarians dream about the future, they always dream about themselves as a hero with a lot of other people around them. One of the worst things a Sagittarian can picture is themselves alone with no close human connections. They need people; to have someone there to do things for, to do things with, and with whom to share the results of what they have done. In other words, they have to live for somebody, live with somebody, and share their lives with somebody. They are trustworthy friends—if you have reached that inner circle of friends who do not just live in their minds but are lodged in their hearts. The only way they are going to let you down is if you give them a serious reason to do so by disappointing them terribly in some way. If you want to get rid of them, it is simple: just stop being friendly, or even better, talk shit about them behind their back. They can't stand false friendships or fake people. They seldom lie, even if it can seem like they do because they are prone to exaggerating and beautifying the truth. That is in a different category than lies…at least if you ask the Sagittarius about it. They need to be on good terms and be friends with the people they work with, and at the least, they have to like their coworkers. Remember that even if Sagittarians themselves are not so interested in being or creating beauty, they have a great admiration for people who takes the time and effort to beautify themselves and the world.

Seeking and the Spiritual

Seeking the meaning of life is very essential for the Sagittarius. What's most important for them is the feeling that they are on the road toward something that has deep significance. They are seekers of wisdom, and a life without the quest for answers is meaningless. They love to be on the road toward something greater and better. They often start by directing all their energy toward exploring the outer world. There is so much there to discover and explore, but every now and then, they hear the strong call of their inner voice—a voice that tells them to take their eyes away from the blazing Sun and look directly into the dark depths of the inner world, because it is in the inner depths that they will find their true spiritual path and meaning. They love the beauty of the rainbow but have to remember that it is rain that creates the display of colors, just as it is tears and real depth of feelings that create a truly colorful person and life. An Archer who hasn't gotten to know their inner darkness and just tries to live in bright light and joy will every now and then be dragged into the black despair of desperation and futility. This inner despair and darkness are the best-hidden secrets of Sagittarians and it is not a secret they like to share. Their gift to others is often their ability to see possibilities and create hope and joy, so they do not easily show or share their desperate, dark fear of a meaningless and wasted life with others.

The real spiritual insight and wisdom for a Sagittarius is found on the other side of the abyss of meaninglessness. When they can see the light even in their darkest hours it becomes a true shining beacon for them, not just a toy to play with. This beacon they found lies in the depths of their inner being, not in the understanding of scriptures and ideas. Sagittarians love to share their wisdom and insight with others. They are generous and want others to see the beauty they have seen. Sometimes this longing to share makes them an annoyance to others, who may experience them as pushy, wanting everybody to see things the way they do. The quality of this sharing is totally dependent on how far the Sagittarius has traveled into their own depths and connected with their own heart. There is often just a tiny hair that separates empty phrases from eternal truths as they flow from the lips of a Sagittarius. Their words can be just a superficial dance of smart thoughts without substance, or their words can be truths that are digested through their own experience, pain, loneliness, and deep feelings. This trait is the reason why lively Sagittarians are so often attracted to the sinister, scary, and dark—like moths toward a candle. They know there is something there, behind all the scary and gooey stuff, that will give their lives real meaning and a deeper joy. Somewhere in that secret place, behind all the unknown and unfathomable, there is a pearl; they just know that to be the truth. As lilies grow from mud and dirt, so too do pearls grow from irritation and disturbance. In this way, Sagittarians find their most precious truths and experience by moving through the deepest and most ruthless segments of their own fears and longings. It is by changing themselves on the deepest levels that they change the universe and find the divine answers that they have always been searching for.

Capricorn

December 22nd—January 19th

Element: Earth
Quality: Cardinal
Ruling Planet: Saturn

How to Present Yourself

Capricorns like to present themselves in a decent and respectable manner. They give weight to form and codes of behavior. Often, they can seem a little stiff and formalistic in the beginning, but as they get to know you and start to feel more secure and comfortable with your presence, they begin to relax. Some Capricorns seem to be flexible and relaxed and begin the conversation with some jokes about themselves, but beware! You can laugh with them when they have invited it, but do not try to make fun of them or make jokes at their expense. If others allow themselves to make fun of Capricorns, they will become deeply wounded and disappointed and next time, they will be received with the formal treatment that icebergs give their visitors.

Capricorns, symbolized by a Goat, want others to see them as reliable and responsible. They do not want to be seen as standing out to begin with. Often, they dress elegantly and with great care, or they try to be as neutral as possible. What a Capricorn wants least of all is to make a scene—unless they have planned and chosen to do just that. As mentioned, many Capricorns develop a sense of self-deprecation and make jokes at their own expense—before anybody else has the chance to. In a strange, Capricornian way, that gives them a sense of control and safety. They need to show the world that they know what they are doing and are in charge of the situation and their life. You will have to be very close to these Goats before they openly share their insecurities, doubts, and lack of control with you. They like to seem invulnerable, and this stems from the simple fact that beneath their hard and tough exterior, they are very soft, tender, and vulnerable animals. They have thick armor because they need it because what is within is so soft. If you ever get on the inside of the shell, you will see how sensitive and soft-hearted they really are. They find it terrible to be so soft and unable to face tasks head-on without fear. They still think with horror about that one event fifteen years ago where they really were caught with their pants around their ankles. It was so terrible that they will never, ever let it happen again.

As a Capricorn, you are a bit reserved and easily create distance between yourself and others. One of your best traits is your ability to be interested in others in an honest and direct way. You do not like small talk or walking around corners. You know how to cut the crap and show yourself to be direct and honest. Never try to pretend or ingratiate yourself: that never has and never will work for you. Honesty suits you best. You are like an old-school businessman: people know what they get because you have told them what it takes to play the game with you or become your friend. The next move is up to them. In fact, you do not need to hide behind a cool mask of arrogance, indifference, and self-reliance. It is much better for you to show others how much you appreciate them without being dependent on them. The rest of us do not need to be told that you can manage on your own. We already see that, but we need to know if you want to play with us...do you? More than any other sign, Capricorns need to understand that the strongest people aren't the ones who act indifferent and untouchable. The truly strong people are the ones with so much inner strength that they have no fear of showing and sharing their feelings and vulnerability. Your life will be richest when you can show both your independence and your vulnerability, and that means that you really show the rest of us that you care for us and loves us.

How to Get the Best from Your Talents and Resources

In some ways, Capricorns are a bit peculiar. They have a tendency to do weird things in a traditional way or traditional things in a weird way. They have their own set of values and want to find the solution in their own way and at their own pace. Capricorns can be fixed in their opinion of how things ought to be done. In fact, they have to do things their own way and while at times they can be quite brilliant, at other times, they can get quite lost and sidetracked. They have this strange combination of traditional and nontraditional ways of doing things that confuses other people and, at times, makes it hard for the rest of us to understand what values and methods the Capricorn follows.

Capricorns want to reveal their talents freely, and at the same time, they need order and procedures. They are occupied with creating the right framework for an activity. When a Capricorn wants to change their life, they try to do so by changing the structure around their life, not the content within it. It can be hard for them to realize that sometimes it is them, their sense of values, and their inner feelings that have to change, not just the structure they wrap their lives in. Most Capricorns have a great sense of power and want to influence the society they are a part of. Sometimes they use the power to maintain what already exists, while at other times, they instigate change and open doors into the future. Sometimes, they think they are moving toward the future but are actually just clinging to a past that has already gone by. What they never do is just float around without taking a stand.

Capricorns need to be involved in how things are driven and structured. They can engage in local matters or the politics of the world. They need to be inside a system that they can influence and eventually change from within. A Capricorn finds it much harder to build a new system and a new structure to replace the old than to just expand the old one into something better. An important thing for Capricorn is that they need to create enough space within the system and structure they are part of so that they can use their talents. They need to work independently with wide frameworks and a great sense of freedom to choose between differing possibilities. At the same time, they also need to regularly check in about their ideas and thoughts with other people and their surroundings. Otherwise, they can discover a bit too late that the project they have worked on is impractical and will go nowhere. Capricorns are excellent as part of a creative team. It gives them room to breathe and enough input to get the necessary creative inspiration. This creature needs clearly defined goals and values; climbing and pushing themselves upward is a natural state for mountain goats. The important thing is to find something worth striving toward. A Capricorn without a vision or goals is like a camel in a desert with no wells.

Capricorns can be extremely resilient and enduring. They are also unyielding if they have already set their path and started to walk down it. They have to try out their ideas so they can learn if said ideas are worthwhile or not going anywhere—only praxis can demonstrate if the theories have value or not. The ability to manifest theory in praxis is one of the greatest assets of Capricorns, and they need to be on that road because if they just repeat the old, they become very stuck and inflexible. For Capricorns, it is of prime importance to have the guts and courage to risk making mistakes and getting things wrong, however painful it might be. It is important for them to give others the same rights and opportunities. The risk of doing something wrong is the single most important force that helps Capricorns use their talents to the fullest, so eventually, they get things right—and even perfect.

Communication and Immediate Surroundings

Capricorns have a unique approach to conversations. Sometimes they can be extremely talkative, but mostly they see it as a waste of energy to use more syllables than necessary. In some ways, this sign does not understand where the limits of others are, so mostly they keep themselves and others on a short leash to be sure that nothing runs wild. But sometimes, they just glide on top of a great feeling and talk without sensing when they have stumbled upon topics that are sensitive to other people. They will hardly admit it, but as far as conversation goes, they really do not know what they are doing or how to do it. They try to construct a conversation as they think it ought to be. They can be extremely clear and precise, but a confused Capricorn is more total and thorough in their confusion than other signs. Strangely enough, they can sometimes be so sensitive and soft that it limits to the supernatural. In general, they like to talk about impersonal and general affairs, but there will always be a personal feeling and intention underneath. They like to seem objective while they are in fact deeply subjective. Without that deep undercurrent of personal concern and importance, conversations become dead to a Capricorn.

Capricorns have a hard time expressing their feelings and perceptions except in practical and concrete ways. It might seem like they talk about these practical matters, but in reality, the conversation is always about feelings and longings and the inner world. Do not expect them to be aware of this themselves, since they do not always know what makes them think and say different things. Many of them feel they can express themselves best to people they have recently met. The reason is that they haven't yet experienced being misunderstood by those particular people. At the other end of the scale, Capricorns talk about their dreams and feelings with people they trust completely and have known for a long time.

Capricorns like to dream about things that haven't yet happened. Often, they talk and think about feelings, tastes, and images. The words are like boxes and constructions wired to hold together the soft and vulnerable stuff inside. So even if the messages they deliver seem to be inside hard packages, they are in reality very soft. Capricorns often have strangely poetic minds and can nurture their inner beings by reading or writing poetry. They need to nurture their consciousness through some kind of art. Unless they drink from this well, their words and thoughts become like a dried-up desert—dull and without variation. In reality, Capricorns listen more to the vibration and timbre of other voices than to the content of people's words. It is good training for Capricorns to be more aware of the words and thoughts that others share, rather than just the underlying feelings. For those listening to a Capricorn, it is good to listen more to their feelings and the timbre of their voice than to the meaning of their words. Most of us need to train and practice to be able to do this, because no one is better at hiding than a Capricorn that does not want to be found. On the other hand, once you have cracked the code, they will appreciate it immensely because you will be one of the few who gets what they are really talking about. You can understand what they really mean and think and feel, which often is something much more and much better than what you can understand by just deciphering the words.

Home and Family

The childhood of a Capricorn has often been one that demanded they stand up and fight for themselves. They had to make decisions and learn to trust themselves at an early age. Independence was important for managing family life in childhood. Many Capricorns experience the world as a fighting arena, where they keep scores and take responsibility for themselves. The alternative seems to be getting run down by the wild hoards that are roaming around.

The family life of a Capricorn never seems to be docile and peaceful. Something is happening all the time, and if nothing happens, the Capricorn will push things into red alert. They can rearrange the furniture, throw a party, move, start a fight, or simply make sure they're so occupied that they never have time to just be at home and relax. Trivial coziness and niceties soon become too dull for the Capricorn. To them, family is a place where each and every member fights for their own identity and right to be a unique individual. It is a place where people learn to stand up and fight for their rights. Family is a smithy where the personality is forged. Home is a place where everybody ought to be able to open themselves up without fear of smashing the beautiful and expensive china. Home is a place to live, express, and be free to be and show who you really are. Aesthetics and beauty are always second to the need for free expression and opportunities to act out your needs, although most Capricorns appreciate both. They want homes that are practical and open to play and untidy expression, while at the same time are a place for beauty and order.

Capricorns have a tendency to use family life as an arena for showing and playing out the more raw, uncivilized, and vulnerable sides that they so often hide from the outer world. In the safety of their home, Capricorns can be stupid, incautious, direct, and rigidly possessed by whatever it is that rises to the surface. On the other hand, Capricorns willingly defend their family and will fight to the death to protect them if necessary. They can be a bit dictatorial on the home front but will defend the honor of their near and dear with absolute loyalty and fearlessness. It is important to them that any appliances and equipment in the home are functional and effective. They have no interest in maintaining things with more effort than is absolutely necessary. Their homes will generally be effective and functional rather than cozy.

This sign likes doing activities with their nearest and dearest. Action makes them tick; too much small talk and idleness makes them restless and jittery. They bond with others by doing things together. It can be watching something, playing a game, going for a walk, or discussing things and arguing over them with intensity. To a Capricorn, relaxing at home does not mean relaxing and doing nothing. It means engaging others in an activity so that no one has a dull moment or the time to get bored. Family isn't something that just falls out of the sky for this star sign. It is something you must work to create. Family is the result of effort, choices, and devotion. Like everything else, it is an outcome created by willingness and effort.

Creativity and Leisure

Spare time is when Capricorns want things to be slow and nice. Family time is not a leisurely activity for them. But when they first go off to be completely by themselves, they can be quite lazy and inflexible. Few people can be so hard to move as a Capricorn who has made the decision to have a day off, and this is either-or. Either they do absolutely nothing—and nothing really does mean nothing—or their so-called relaxation has a schedule that is just as tight as any workday. If a Capricorn is going to use their spare time to be creative, they want to see results. For a Capricorn, creativity without results or a final product is a waste of time and space, and their creativity always focuses on things that are useful in some way.

Another side of this seriousness is that Capricorns often do not really know how to flirt. They are a bit slow to understand what is going on and rarely fall in love at first glance. Love is a work of patience and endurance for Capricorns. They want the durable and lasting stuff, not the glittering, short-lived versions. The method to use if you want to seduce a Capricorn is to give them prolonged stimulation of their physical senses. Pure physical pleasure is the fastest track to their hearts. Good food and sensual stimulation are always appreciated. Capricorns do not really understand the concept of having so much pleasure without repeating it as many times as possible. They like solidity and see relationships and their own creative endeavors in the light of eternity. Of all the star signs, Capricorns have the most difficulty understanding the purpose of superficial, ecstatic, short-lived relationships. For Capricorns, ecstasy is something that is built through time and effort. You climb the ladder of love and pleasure step by step until you reach the top and finally surrender yourself to it—and to surrender oneself is a serious thing for a Capricorn. It is not done lightly because surrendering is forever—at least forever in this lifetime. You do not surrender like this to the first and best possibility that comes down the road. You have to think, feel, test, and hold that love in your hands for a long time before you finally let go of all resistance. Capricorns have to know that they are in both a durable and consistent relationship before they can give in so completely, because once they give in, there is no going back or turning around.

This is also why Capricorns often are so good at what they do. Once a choice is made, there is total dedication to it and acceptance of the chosen path. Capricorns can enjoy themselves alone and often thrive in their own company. To engage deeply with others, they have to believe that it is better than being alone. If the new doesn't seem much better than what already is, why bother changing things? You know what you have. In creativity and romance, most Capricorns are late bloomers, while others find their love and/or their vocation just after childhood and stick to it for the rest of their lives. If Capricorns wait too long before choosing, they may never dare to make the jump and never launch either their love life or their career. However, once Capricorn has found their love and surrendered to their own creativity, it is like an avalanche of power flows through them and they can manage almost anything. They are among the rare beings that can produce quality and do so in the same way again and again and again—and then their life becomes filled with an abundance of quality.

Health, Order, and the Necessary

Capricorns often have many concerns about health issues in old age but do not care in their younger years. If they have been a bit rough with their bodies in their younger years, they will have to pay the price as they grow old. Capricorns must take special care of joints like the knees and wrists. They also can develop problems with their lungs if they have breathed in too many toxic fumes in their youth. It can be a shock for these creatures to discover that their bodies have started to grow old and may start to ache and hurt. At first, they won't believe it and will mostly ignore it, but a Capricorn has to accept that even if they mentally seem to get younger with age, their body follows the normal progression of aging.

Capricorns can handle quite a lot of chaos and untidiness. They have an idea about the necessary order and structure and their capacity to implement this order, but they have no problem with messes in those areas that do not need to be tidy and organized for their lives to function properly. One thing that might create real chaos for Capricorns is if they have too many projects going on at the same time. When they do not get things finished, everything has a tendency to pile up. Then the Capricorn becomes stressed and uncertain , and the more stressed they become, the greater the pile of unfinished business. It is like always beginning a new book before finishing the current one and putting all the half-read books in a great "to-do" pile. Capricorns are easy to distract when they are doing boring and necessary things. This is the reason they need so much structure and discipline. That is the only way they can get the job done without becoming distracted and forgetting the whole thing. They are great at finding excuses to postpone things they do not want to do. They often really attack the big things in life with great spirit and courage, but easily avoid the smaller things and just slide around them. Tomorrow is a new day, so why do this small, insignificant business now when there are so many more important things to take care of?

The big things are easy to decide to do. Something just *is* important. But choosing from among the trivial stuff can be overwhelming and tiresome for any Capricorn. All the small piles of dust can be pushed under the carpet—until they become a large pile that causes a real problem. In that moment, the Capricorn rolls up their sleeves and gets going to fix things. The challenges need to be of a certain magnitude for Capricorn to find them worthy of bothering with. So, they often create great trouble in order to have something worthy of being challenged by. Capricorns are often amiable and friendly in the arena of work. They can be friends with both employers and employees. They are interested in and really enjoy listening to others talk about the work they are doing...well, of course, except for when they are busy expressing their own (and, in their own opinion, genial) thoughts about all kinds of things. When they are at their best, they can cut through all the crap and go directly to the point. That goes for a work situation, a health problem, or an organizational difficulty. At their best, their greatest gift is not the hard work, but their ability to find the exact right piece at just the right moment. Precision, timing, and an instinctive eye for the right details are the mark of an aware, interested, and professional Capricorn.

One-on-One Relationships

Capricorns go for intimacy. They want intense, deep, and lasting relationships. What does not last isn't worth investing in. They can really become mushy and sentimental if they go for it and jump into the soft and compassionate side of the story. At first impression, Capricorns often seem to be reserved, cold, and self-protective. They are always looking for the softness and vulnerability in others that they are so afraid to show that they have themselves. Capricorns often seek out somebody who is even more vulnerable than themselves—or someone who seems completely invulnerable. The result is often the same: they end up pairing up with someone who is hypersensitive, very vulnerable, and often a bit helpless in the world. Capricorns feel safe with a partner that is caring and has a great heart—and a partner they know will never leave them no matter what happens. They really detest being left, deserted, or dumped. It is not just unpleasant and painful; it can be devastating and life-threatening for Capricorns to be deserted by the ones they love. Once they have given their love, they cling to it with all they've got. Another strategy of theirs is to get out in a hurry at the first signs of discord—to be sure they will be the one leaving, not the one left. Their image of coolness becomes a problem when their vulnerability and tenderness become visible, so they cling to projecting all the neediness and softness onto their partner and children, as long as it works. But when the truth rises to the surface, they are the one that is addicted to the other person.

Capricorns often pay the price for a secure relationship by giving up their emotional freedom and centering their whole inner life around their partner and family situation. Their only place of freedom from this becomes their work, and this is one of the reasons why work is so important for Capricorns. It is the only place they can breathe freely without hurting their partner. At their best, Capricorns are really caring and giving toward their partner. At the other end of the spectrum, they do not have a partner, but either a smothering and paternalistic spouse or someone who acts like a child. Capricorns always have to watch out to keep their relationships alive. Food, safety, and boredom can easily replace joy with boring repetition. Over time, Capricorns grow accustomed to their partners and start to relax with them. This can involve not seeing a partner for who they really are any more and taking them for granted, but it can alternately involve opening up to the depth and greatness of the Capricorn's total and unlimited ability to love. When Capricorns have started to love, it will go on for a long time. Their heart is like a really heavy truck: it doesn't accelerate too quickly, but it takes a long time to stop once it gets going. No Capricorn can leave a long-term relationship whistling and careless, even if it was the most wretched and meanest of all relationships ever witnessed on this planet. Letting go of attachments and the deep strings tied to the heart takes time, whatever the reality or circumstances. This is the one basic foundation of all personal relationships the Capricorn builds and participates in. It takes time to create those relationships, and it takes time to let them go. It takes time to love and to find the courage to surrender to it, and it takes time to get over a breakup or a loss—and an even longer time to rebuild the ability to trust and surrender again in the future. As for partners and deep relationships, all Capricorns with half a brain go for quality instead of quantity. If you stand in front of one, love them, and want to have a relationship with them, give them your heart, but do not push them. Give them the time and space they need so they can be free to choose to come to you and free to love you because they want to. This open love is often what captures their heart and makes you irresistible to them.

Beneath the Surface—Sex and Taboos

Sex can be a validation of identity for Capricorns. "I have sex, so I have worth and exist in this world." They prefer to have very deep and intense cravings and love to be longed for with intensity. In practice, this does not necessarily have to be erotic—the deep longing and intensity is the most important thing. In many ways, the most important erotic partner for a Capricorn is themselves! They want to perform well and attain value by being attractive. This does not mean that they are selfish or incompetent lovers, rather the opposite. But what is most important to them is not whom they have sex with, but that they get to express their own sexuality. What binds the Capricorn to a life-long relationship is not sexuality but love, care, and common meals.

Capricorns are immensely proud behind their cool image. They really hate to be the butt of other people's jokes, and the closer you are to their hearts, the more difficulties they will have if you make fun of them. That comes from the simple fact that they have given you opportunities to hurt them more and more deeply than most people. Being sexually dysfunctional is intensely painful for most Capricorns. They can be so numbed by their need to perform that they lose the ability to perform. This angst does not primarily show in the public areas of life, but in private; the deeper the intimacy, the greater the possibility for angst. Capricorns do not want to explore taboos or experiment with all kinds of things. They are primarily after what works and gives them the desired result. They have nothing against tradition or the old and well-used road as long as it works, but if those roads are closed, they can end up experimenting with everything just to find a way that works. They are no adventurer by nature but accept adventure if it is a necessary part of their journey.

The most important and dearest thing a Capricorn can give in an intimate relationship is their own true image of themselves, and Capricorns can and will only do this if they know that you trust and respect them. Showing weakness and lack of self-esteem to others is the most intimate act of a Capricorn. Showing others that you need them and their support is a great show of trust from a Capricorn. If you really want to harass a Capricorn, just make fun of them in a very personal way, tell their secrets to the world, and generally show them a lack of respect.

A Capricorn that is out of balance will either just not show that they care for you, or they will be ruthlessly honest and blunt and say everything directly to you without softening the blow at all. In this way, they can say things to others that they do not want others to say to them. They allow themselves to be completely insensitive to the feelings of others...but will demand that you be completely respectful and sensitive toward their own feelings. In a way, they never go into the taboos...that is *their* taboo. However, they gladly will step into yours, because they do not regard them as taboos, just your quirky ways of being. A Capricorn that is in balance and connected with their own heart will show you respect, love, and closeness by offering these things to you. When we have this advanced version of a Capricorn, they know well to defend themselves, but they are also totally open when it comes to giving. The level of intimacy and love in this case is not dependent upon them but upon your ability to be there in the moment with them. Not all people understand that this way of reciprocal affection, respect, and validation is an expression of deep intimacy and love without limitations. But that is what it is when it comes to the more open-hearted and balanced Capricorns that walk around with the rest of us in the forest of humanity.

Education, Adventure, and Life Philosophy

As mentioned, Capricorns do not really seek adventure just for the sake of having fun and new experiences. They want to have a direction and a deeper purpose for their doings. Why expose themselves to all the trouble, danger, and unknown bacteria if doing so does not have a purpose and something they can gain or learn from? Capricorns can be very picky about what they want to study, where they want to go, and generally everything connected to philosophy, education, religion, and culture.

Capricorns do not jump heedlessly into the first and best theory that is offered. They easily become stuck in the opinions and definitions they have already made. They develop their view of life and the meaning of things in a thorough and methodical way. Thought and concepts are there to be analyzed, tested, and evaluated before either being accepted or thrown out with the rest of the crap. Capricorns can be very quarrelsome and fixated on details when big visions and grand questions in life are debated. The good side of this is that they are some of the best when it comes to finding flaws and holes in the theories and ideas of others. If something is put together in a nonfunctional way, be sure that the Capricorn will notice that it is so.

Mostly, Capricorns find their way through life in one of two ways. First, they may choose the area of life they want to explore and work with at a very early age. In that case, they stick to it, focus on it, and specialize their education to accommodate their chosen direction. They constantly expand their knowledge about their chosen field and become experts in it. The other way to go about life is when they start to sniff around for different opportunities in their youth, they constantly move from one area to the other and collects bit and pieces from every arena they have visited—but they seem to be a bit lost when it comes to seeing how this information could be put together and used. The first Capricorn has a clear direction and knows how to move through life. The ones who have tried to go the other way feel confused and frustrated for a long time since it is always a bit uncomfortable for a Capricorn to not know where they are headed. At a certain point, well into what is called maturity, the pieces start to come together and, in that way, create a completely new and hitherto unexpected and unknown picture. What before seemed to be separate and unrelated information and experiences are suddenly creating connections and granting the Capricorn both deep meaning and direction. When this happens, the bewildered and frustrated Capricorn becomes creative, clear on their priorities, and quite satisfied with life and themselves.

Capricorns almost always move toward the unknown by exploring it piece by piece. They can seem to throw themselves into great mysteries and adventures, but on the inside, they analyze, sorts thing out, and try to get a good overview. As adventurers, they are methodical, prudent, and prefer to think and act clearly and logically in a challenging situation rather than be swayed by their emotions and instincts. The more challenging and demanding the situation is, the less emotional the Capricorn becomes. For Capricorns, giving in to emotions is a luxury that comes after one has gone over the logical and practical side of the matter. But when they can surrender to the future with emotions and love, there will be a freshness and purity there that creates a vivid clarity—a rare and beautiful flower to behold.

Goals, Profession, and Career

It is not always so easy to see, but one of the most important things for Capricorns on the rise is their ability to create connections. They need to have some people to play with and exchange ideas, thoughts, and possibilities with. They can easily be bulwarks of strength, but they also sorely need advisers. A Capricorn who lacks the right people to play with will very soon get stuck and not go anywhere. Capricorns have difficulties with building a career just for the sake of having a career. They need something—or rather, someone—to be the reason for their efforts. In the worst-case scenario, they create success as revenge against all the bloody bastards that didn't believe in them. They can make the effort for their country or create opportunities for others, but the best case is when they make an effort with and for love.

Feeling equality with and respect for their coworkers is of prime importance to a Capricorn. They are dogs for justice and think you will be repaid for effort and results. The person that works, takes responsibility, and is competent shall be duly rewarded. The principle of equality does not mean that all are equal or that everything is equally valuable, but that you will be rewarded equally for the same effort and result.

Often, it seems like Capricorns are only interested in results and reaching their goals, but at the same time, they are very aware that the most important factor in reaching their goals is other people. They have great respect and admiration for humans that can get things done and get results. In the same way, they might easily have contempt for those who are not able to accomplish anything. The American division of humans into winners and losers fits nicely into the philosophy of the not-so-advanced Capricorn. The biggest problems for this star sign are when they themselves have limited or no success and limited talents and opportunities. A task of prime importance for Capricorns is to see their own and others' true inner value, instead of measuring everything against success and results in the outer world. Capricorns need a vision, and they need someone to share that vision with. Without visions, Capricorns easily become creatures of habit and without imagination. They grow skilled at following routines and repeating the same actions over and over. So, they are dependent on their visions to move away from the deadening security of just repeating what they already know how to do.

A dissatisfied Capricorn is a great nuisance to their surroundings, and especially as they grow older, they are better as leaders than as followers. At their best, they are friendly, professional, caring, and excellent team builders: they know how to cooperate. They will be loyal and trustworthy to their coworkers and friends but ruthless against their enemies. Sometimes, others may wonder whether the professional friendliness of a Capricorn goes deeper. Do they show you their weakness and insecurity? If not, see the relationship as purely professional. At the same time, that professional loyalty and love is still a very deep and strong love for the Capricorn.

Friends, Future, and Ideals

If you have friends that are Capricorns, you do not need to have enemies. That does not mean that Capricorns are lousy friends but rest assured that sooner or later, they will step up and accept the great responsibility of telling you the truth about yourself. They think and feel that honesty and the art of speaking from the gut have to be the true foundations of any friendship. The more advanced specimens of this astrological sign understand that this directness goes both ways. The more immature ones crave the right to tell you the direct truth and their honest opinion about everything, but feel they have the right to become bitter and offended when you do the same thing.

Dreams and visions for the future are seldom laid out for public consumption by a Capricorn. Those are a very private matter, and Capricorns enjoy that other people do *not* know where they are really headed. They have a feeling that as long as nobody knows what they really want, nobody can thwart and stop them. Another far more important reason for this secrecy is that if they tell others about their goals and ambitions, and then they fail to reach them, that would be unbearable. Capricorns want to be left alone with their losses and shortcomings. In fact, they are not very keen on sharing the moment of victory with others, either. Some Capricorns hide their ambitions so well and so deeply that they do not know about their ambitions themselves, so these seemingly humble beings can really surprise both themselves and others with the fierce hunger for success and acknowledgment that surges in them when the opportunity arises. In some cases, these Capricorns have hidden their ambitions so deeply that they never arise, and the Capricorns just walk around without any visions or plans for the future. A Capricorn without visions for the future is not a very happy Capricorn, but these ambitions do not need to be personal. They can involve work, a company, the country, creating a better world, or even the national soccer team, but Capricorns do need to have some kind of vision for the future to be remotely happy.

Friendships go very deep for Capricorn. Once they have given their loyalty, they are often willing to give their life if it is really needed. There are things more important than surviving for Capricorns, and two of those things are that they can rely on and trust themselves—and that entails being true to what they find right and righteous to do. Sometimes they can be loyal to the point of absurdity and they can also get into big trouble and end up disappointed because others fail to live up to their standards. Nothing hurts more for a Capricorn than betrayal from a friend. They are known to test people before giving their friendship, just to be sure that they will never be betrayed. In some cases, the testing is so hard and takes so long that the friendship never gets the chance to flower. Their friendship is intense and strong once it is established, though, and there is not much room for superficial conversations or meaningless activities. Deep talks and committed actions are what happen. This is something they have reserved for the real friends they trust with their full heart—with showing themselves as they really are. The biggest trust a Capricorn can give to you is to show their flaws, weaknesses, longings, and vulnerability.

Seeking and the Spiritual

Even if Capricorns like to act skeptical and practical, they are philosophical seekers and mystics on the inside. They are truly, desperately looking for the meaning of life. In many ways, Capricorns are the true believers of the zodiac. They are always trying to find an explanation, searching for the answers, but wherever they go, they seem to end up with the same question: "What do I really believe?" The whole of life and the concept of reality is based on this question for Capricorns. They can believe in Santa Claus, Christ, Darwinism, nihilism, their grandmothers' sayings, or the long-term strategy of their firm. The important thing is that they desperately need something to believe in. If a Capricorn asserts that they believe in nothing, they will assert this belief with intense and fanatical energy.

But Capricorns are not satisfied with just believing. Belief is just a kind of instinct that gives them the motivation to find the meaning of life, the same way hunger gives people the motivation to get food. But Capricorns also want to know. They want to know more than others and prefer to be the ones telling the truth. This need can greatly diminish a Capricorn's ability to be open. In this area, they may be caught in a rigid and hierarchal system. The Capricorn wants to be the teacher and have the rest of us be the students. A more advanced Capricorn has understood that we all in, some sense, are both teachers and students. This Capricorn has left the spiritual hierarchy and moved into the circle of spiritual equanimity. In this circle, meanings and truths are personal and relative. They have understood that there is more than one truth, and so there is not just one truth that has to be found by any means necessary. They have learned respect and tolerance on the spiritual and philosophical level of existence. In a deeper sense, they see that it is not about right or wrong but about being true to the meaning they put into life. At the same time, most Capricorns are aware that they never arrive at the end of the path and are eternally seeking out and occupied by exploring the limits and possibilities of their own consciousness.

Capricorns have to be careful not to become fundamentalists—either the atheistic, materialistic kind or the spiritual kind. Whatever roads they have chosen to walk to spiritual insight and an open heart, the way goes through embracing tolerance and humility. One thing all Capricorns will need to do is see that spiritual truth and essence always follow the melodies of joy and freedom. They will find the deepest and truest spiritual understanding and truth through dancing and playing and realizing that life is a great and miraculous party. It is through seeking their own inner space that Capricorns start to find the freedom and openness that their spiritual quest is about. All the keys to joy and bliss are buried in the depth of the Capricorn's inner heart.

Aquarius

January 20th—February 18th

Element: Air
Quality: Fixed
Ruling Planet: Uranus

How to Present Yourself

Aquarians want others to really see and acknowledge them as the unique and individual beings that they are. Name and number don't do it for Aquarians. They want to be seen as something different and special, not some kind of clone or copy of someone or something else. Every now and then, the result is that they create a performance that is a bit strange and difficult for others to a get handle on. They often try to be very special because they are so very afraid of being boring and uninteresting. As long as Aquarians try to stand out as special and interesting, they actually seem like quite normal nobodies trying too hard to be somebody. It is when they behave in ways that are, to them, perfectly relaxed and normal that their unique and special qualities become visible. Aquarians like to be regarded as unselfish and considerate of others. They can go far out of their way and far from their plans to hide their egoistic motivations. They often label their needs and wishes as "what's best for everyone."

As an Aquarian, it is important that you find the right balance between your own needs and preferences and the needs and rights of others. You really need to acknowledge yourself, and that means both your selfish needs and your longing to do something beautiful and good for others. Your relationship with the greater community is of prime importance, as you easily can feel that you are left out and not wanted. At the same time, it is important for Aquarians to show that they are something special, not just a face in the great crowd of anonymous community participants. In a way, it is like they want to stand with one foot on the inside and the other on the outside. It is quite understandable why their position sometimes becomes a bit stretched and unbalanced—because the different camps where their legs are rooted can be quite a distance apart and they can easily be caught in conflicts between those sides. It might not be visible on the outside , but Aquarians are experts at being divided within themselves.

Most of the time, they do not need help from others when they disagree. Often, they do not feel that they can do exactly what they want to do, and at the same time, they feel that they should have been better molded to fit in. On the other hand, they are very social, enjoy togetherness, and thrive in groups where they feel accepted. Freedom and togetherness are equally necessary for the well-being of an Aquarian. They need to be accepted for their thoughts and ideas. It is important that Aquarians show the rest of us what they like, need, and prefer. As an Aquarian, you really want to be open, tolerant, and unbigoted. You become unhappy if you get caught in the net of your own or others' pettiness and lack of tolerance. You need to spread your wings, but you have to give the same rights and freedom to others. You thrive when you have freedom, opportunities, and a well of ideas. The alpha and omega of a good life for Aquarians is to accept, love, and be curious about the strangeness and diversity of people and the world at large—and to have the same acceptance and love for your own strangeness and unique experience of yourself and your relationships to the rest of us and the universe.

How to Get the Best from Your Talents and Resources

Aquarians are born idealists. They want to do something good for the world and improve conditions for everyone. They are born with visions around their own role and potential in the theater of life. Their values and understanding of how to handle physical reality are rarely completely realistic. They have ideas and feelings about how things ought to be and long for an idealistic and romantic world where that really means something. Sometimes, it is like the limitations and boredom of the physical world are not their concern. They have a hard time accepting the limitations of the world as it is and want to stretch it and mold it into something greater and bigger than what it is in the moment. It can be quite destructive for an Aquarian to be caught in a busy, day-to-day reality where the meaning of life is reduced to trivialities and the maintenance of the status quo. The basic value of being alive disappears when the ability to choose and seek something better seems lost.

However, it is not the outer reality and actual situation that is of the greatest importance. Instead, it is the inner feeling of possibilities. If they have the opportunity to manifest their ideals and longings in some sort of action, they can be alone on the top of the world or inmates in the worst jail on Earth and still experience life as deeply meaningful. They want to create heaven on Earth, and that longing is more important than whether it is practically possible to do so. The dream is what has the greatest value. It is akin to how love has the greatest value regardless of whether it is effective or dependable or in line with common sense. To love is more important than the result of the love. Aquarians have arrived on Earth without a map for the roads they shall walk. They have to draw it themselves, find it, and even create it as they move ahead. The most important thing for an Aquarian is to protect, respect, and keep connected with the naive, creative dreamer that they truly are. I can guarantee that every Aquarian will meet resistance, and at some point, become disappointed and desperate because of the cruelty, hardness, and lack of meaning they find in the world.

If, as an Aquarian, you choose to become bitter and so disappointed that you believe the world has no room for you and your dreams, you will be caught in the shadow of your own values. The right way to go is to try to set an example by living out your true values—even if others don't. The point is not that *others* should live by your standards, but that *you* should live by them. That is the way you can proceed to make the world a better place. Make sure to connect your ideals with humility. Live by your highest ideals but respect others for not living by theirs. Your greatest gift is tolerance against intolerance, friendliness against the unfriendly, and giving freedom to those that bind others! Through giving these gifts, you will be able to change things, which is of prime value to you. You have many great resources, and you will get the best out of them when you stay true to your own dreams, even if others tell you that they are unrealistic and not in line with reality. Just smile and know in your heart that you do not want reality to be as it is; you would love it to change into something even better. So do not let other people—who often have other, smaller, or no dreams—diminish or stop you.

Communication and Immediate Surroundings

As an Aquarian, you are quite direct and no-nonsense in your way of speaking. Sometimes your communication can become somewhat primitive and lead to places you do not really want to go. You easily speak before you think and often act before you are ready to or aware of the consequences of your actions. Just waiting and being silent is not so easy for you. Your mind is quite impatient, and even if you often come about with great force, you can be quite insecure and unsure about your ability to express what you really think and mean. Because of this insecurity, you might seem overly confident, pushy, and inflexible in discussions. It can also be said that few enjoy a good debate as much as you. What you enjoy most is pushing out in force and then withdrawing to observe. In that way, you can enjoy the havoc and see deeper into what is really going on with others. Sometimes it works like throwing a torch into flammable material and then watching as everyone else fights with the flames.

Aquarians enjoy activity and meeting new and interesting people in their day-to-day lives. Often, Aquarians understand a lot about others, but do not have a clue about what kind of impression they give off. They are mostly unaware of the intensity, pushiness, and self-absorption that can be part of their communication. Learning the noble art of really listening is a great challenge for Aquarians. As an Aquarian, you are mostly occupied with your thoughts and all that you want to share and give to others. The minimum you require for listening is that others tell you something new—something that you have not heard about innumerable times before. You are really bored by other people's repetitions of their own and each other's views and meanings.

If an Aquarian is always polite, only mentions balanced viewpoints, and behaves as they are supposed to, be sure it is a facade and that you are not very important in that person's life—another possibility is that they really don't like you. They are never so friendly and polite as to the people they detest and despise. Aquarians are as described as impatient, and when they let go of the reins, they have a tendency to try to run before they have learned how to crawl. If an Aquarian lets their natural self take the lead, they are quite spontaneous and often a bit childish. This impulsiveness, coupled with a lack of understanding of their limitations often leads them into funny and unexpected situations. But just as easily, they might end up in embarrassing, strange, and complicated situations.

Aquarians rarely talk about feelings. They prefer to talk about viewpoints, ideas, what they have done, or what they are going to do. They prefer doing things without talking and it is their actions, not their words, that show how they really experience things on a personal level. If you want to know their ideals and visions, talk to them. If you want to know what they think about you and their life, look at what they do and eventually what you do with them. If you want to get to know an Aquarian, it is good to seek experiences and explore with them. You can talk with them until your face turns blue, but you will not get really close to them through words. Inner safety, intimacy, and heartfelt closeness with an Aquarian come through joined experiences, joined actions, and often the experience of "fighting" for a cause together.

Home and Family

Aquarians seem to like intensity and challenges in their close environments. They have a tendency to challenge and provoke others with their verbal communication, but hidden behind the freedom fighter is a longing for safety and security. Once they settle down and take responsibility for real life, they become almost like immovable pillars you can trust and rely on. When they have waved goodbye to their freedom and childish play, they become very grown-up and reliable and will defend their chosen safety with all available means. They will fight for their loved ones, their home, and their family to their last breath. The loyalty and willingness to protect their nearest and dearest is just as limitless as their quest for freedom. Strangely enough, Aquarians in a responsible mood are very concerned with everybody they care for being warm, full, and satisfied.

In a way, Aquarians have so much restless energy inside that they need safe and stable roots in the home. This can lead to challenging consequences, like one part of them clinging to safety and refusing to let go, while the other part stretches for freedom, unwilling to let go of their dreams. On one hand, Aquarians may stay in relationships and jobs that they should have left a long time ago because they do not want the hassle of setting up all the practical and financial things that moving on requires. On the other hand, they can be extremely jealous and cling to another person by all available means. They can feel that they own not only their partner but also their children and their parents and so on. They want freedom and opportunities for the world at large, but nobody can come and mess with their family, security, or possessions. Aquarians need a foundation of solidity and safety so they can be grounded in reality as they move toward their dreams. They like beauty and aesthetics, but it is far more important to them that their home—their base—is practical and functions properly. Bedrooms are for sleeping, kitchens for cooking, and so on. Home is a place where the family should be able to thrive and enjoy peace and quiet without being disturbed. It is a big strain for Aquarians when that foundation is in a process of resolution or change. They prefer these things to be as they have always been and do not have any need to change their routines or habits in this area. They want everybody to be happy and smiling and safe so that no trouble will happen. In fact, they can be a bit addicted to keeping their family and children safe. This is kind of a paradox for them—they can really go to great trouble to avoid problems at home, and at the same time, do just the opposite in their relationship with the rest of the world. And by the way, living out a paradox is the nature and joy of every Aquarian.

Economically, the Aquarius prefers lots and lots of safety. They want to know that the material foundation of their life is rock solid and that it can be trusted to withstand all kinds of hardships. It is recommended that Aquarians have a financial reserve stashed away somewhere that will make it so much easier for them to play with their experiments and freedom and generally enjoy life. Another way to counteract uncertainty and fear is to take a walk in nature or do some work in the garden. Nature is always great for grounding and stabilizing Aquarians. Most Aquarians love to have their house and home filled with plants and flowers. Dragging nature into the house is a great thing to do for them.

Creativity and Leisure

Everything new is exciting for Aquarians. In fact, everything new and unexplored has a tendency to be almost irresistibly attractive. As an Aquarian, you have an almost unlimited curiosity. You want to smell every flower and peek around every corner and into every nook and cranny of the world. Mostly, you are happy with a glance and a short examination. You just wanted to see what it was and are satisfied that it holds no further interest for you. You enjoy it immensely, and after having seen it, you become able to compare it to other, similar things and tell others about the experience.

Aquarians love playing around and flirting. They can adapt to almost any situation as long as they find it exciting and interesting. They are as flexible and adaptive under nice circumstances as they are fixated and unmovable when life is boring or miserable. And a playful flirtation is just a playful flirtation—nothing more than that. There is no hidden agenda or deeper longing than what has been shown. Aquarians enjoy just playing and do not necessarily want to get anywhere. In fact, they mostly enjoy keeping things superficial and almost impersonal. They are very vulnerable to criticism from those they have let under their skin. They can joke and be unserious with the rest of us, but from those who are emotionally important, they want admiration and respect. You can easily believe that Aquarians are so light and relaxed, but behind that outer flimsiness is a deep layer of seriousness and self-importance. They play and laugh and joke about most things, but as soon as they move from the world of amateurs into the world of professionals, a very different side emerges. Aquarians are very superficial when they want to be and very deep when they have crossed the line between play and seriousness.

As children, Aquarians are talkative, curious, social, and quite easygoing. They are kind of unpredictable, so you can never be completely sure about what that little runner is up to. As adults, they are quite relaxed in their relationships with their children. They are good playmates and friends for their children, but not always present as emotional grown-ups when that is what the child needs. They are more into conversations and togetherness than feelings. An Aquarian parent is guaranteed to help their children explore the world and become self-sufficient.

Since Aquarians likes changes, they often have many different hobbies and like to do a variety of things. Spare time should be entertaining and contain some surprises. It is of great importance that Aquarians do not just float on the top of social communications but rather learn to go deeper and really take an interest in other people. An immature Aquarian just uses other people to spread their own opinions or to entertain themselves. They need to really get beneath the layers of talk and conversation and be present with their heart if they want to have fulfilling relationships. Aquarians might know a lot of people and easily get to know new ones but still have a lack of real friends. At their best, Aquarians make time spent together exciting and vivid for their friends. This comes from the fact that they are always interested, always open to their heart , and always on the way to new insights and expanded understanding. Aquarians are lousy at doing nothing, even when they have spare time and nothing to do. They enjoy being on the move all the time and feel happy with having an endless series of tasks that they can do.

Health, Order, and the Necessary

Order is not very important for this star sign as long as there is enough food in the house and the refrigerator looks presentable. Their ability to take care of the necessities of everyday life is very closely connected to their emotional state. If an Aquarian feels good and satisfied, even the most humdrum and boring of things are done with joy and happiness. But if their emotional state dips into resistance or despair, it seems almost impossible for them to get anything done at all. Well...things will be done if it is completely and absolutely necessary, but they will be done slowly and with great suffering and pain. Aquarians can build resistance to certain chores over time. When they reach the limit, they just can't stand it anymore. They experience less resistance to dull and boring tasks if they do said tasks for other people. But when something is nice, Aquarians can repeat the action endlessly.

Their emotional state is very important for the unfolding of their day-to-day activities. If the emotional surplus is absent, any action feels forced or demanding and difficult to do. When the heart is harmonious and balanced, nothing is demanding or challenging, and time seems to fly as if life were a joyful ride through oceans of interesting things. Because of this emotional influence, routines and fixed systems can be difficult to follow for Aquarians. They "hate" doing things because it is right and love doing things when they themselves feel like it. Others may be troubled by this if they are waiting for the Aquarian to get something done or fixed. If it does not feel right for the Aquarian, it is seldom helpful to try to push them into hurrying. Doing so seems to have the opposite effect. The more force and pressure you use to get them to speed up, the slower it goes.

The health of this star sign is very connected with their emotional state. If they feel like getting some attention by becoming ill, they will soon become ill. There are few who know how to suffer in silence, so everybody sees it when Aquarians experience illness. Their only rival of the signs of the zodiac might be Leos. The most important thing an Aquarian must do to stay healthy is to take their emotions seriously. They have to listen to their feelings and heart instead of their brains and ideas. They need to do things that show that they appreciate themselves and make them feel valued. They easily become ill if they feel unloved and uncared for. One solution is for Aquarians to take care of themselves in different ways.

This sign is good at taking care of others' feelings in work situations, but on the other hand, they can be so possessed by their own emotions that they lose the ability to see what goes on in the inner worlds of others. Their emotions run deep and strong in work situations and the professional arena. To the rest of us, they might also seem a little strange in this area of life. They can be so emotionally relaxed and take it easy in personal relationships, and then become so vulnerable and uptight in the professional sphere. Sometimes it seems like they care more about the people that are far away and insignificant than they care for the people closest to them. This is not the case—it just seems that way because deep love, for Aquarians, means freedom and not having to care so much about all your petty emotions.

As an Aquarian, it is important for you to show compassion and care, not only for yourself and your own needs but also for the people you meet in your everyday life. Love is not just shown in grand gestures, but also—and even more so—in the small acts of attention and care we give to each other. To create close, intimate, and satisfying relationships in your daily life means everything for your ability to feel at home in this world and enjoy living.

One-on-One Relationships

Finding a partner that they feel equal to is both an issue and a challenge for Aquarians. They have a tendency to find a partner that they either greatly admire or find almost intolerably selfish. Sometimes it is a bit of both. Relationships seem to become a struggle around who is more important and who is going to get their preferences met and needs respected today. Aquarians want a partner with strong self-confidence whom they can feel proud to be seen with. In fact, Aquarians have a tendency to project their own need for approval onto their partner. Of course, what Aquarians really want is respect for their own values, and they do not want to always be second in the relationship. In fact, they want to be first at the same time as they want equality and mutual respect. The only way for the Aquarius to solve this dilemma is to have just as much respect and admiration for themselves as for their partner. What easily can happen, especially for unconscious and inexperienced Aquarians, is that they end up having just as little respect for themselves as they have for their partners. Maybe it is not so strange that this sign, who intends to be loyal and steady, often ends up as a serial monogamist.

Aquarians do not let go of their partners easily. They have invested very much of their identity and feelings of value in such relationships. It is clear that, as an Aquarian, it is important whom you get into long-term relationships with. Choose well before you leave the marina and sail out into the open ocean. You might be caught in an unsuitable relationship for a very long time, and if you have really been betrayed and let down by someone you trusted, it may take a lot of work and a good amount of time to get back on the horse. Some Aquarians have a tendency to seek out significant others that have authority and power over them. They easily end up in some kind of parental relationship instead of really being partners. Other Aquarians have a tendency to play the knight in shining armor and then become caught up in games they find unpleasant and limiting because they feel that they always have to try to live up to the ideal they started out with. This can be very tiresome, and it often ends up with them acting out of the opposite scenario: they end up as the bastard just to demonstrate that they are a human and not a shining knight.

All Aquarians need strong partners who know what they like and what they want. Aquarians need to be loved and validated as unique and special. They need to be reassured that they are wanted and loved quite often. If they feel unwanted, demons start to stir in the depths of their emotions and soon pop their ugly heads out into the daylight. As an Aquarian, you need to find a partner who is willing to give you a lot of slack and freedom, one you can trust, but also one who knows what the limits are regarding how much you can be trusted. You both need to have a clear feeling that everything is possible and be aware of the cost and the price if one of you uses that freedom to do things that the other sees as deceitful or disrespectful. So, the person you can really trust is the one that gives you full freedom but also knows what the limits are when it comes to that power you give them. As an Aquarian, you are especially addicted to daily confirmations of your value to your loved ones and you need to share and give this love to them at least once a day.

Beneath the Surface—Sex and Taboos

This lover of freedom can be quite careful and skeptical of all that is hidden in the deep, dark layers of the psyche. If there is one thing that gives Aquarians a creepy feeling of uncertainty and insecurity, it is this hidden inner world of feelings and taboos. Oh, it is not the sex that makes them feel afraid. It is all the personal feelings that come with deep intimacy. Aquarians do not enjoy experimenting with these feelings, even if they are very eager to experiment with everything that is in the outer world. Because of this, they sometimes do not see that their outer world is the inner world of others. On the level of intimacy, they want to feel safe and know what they have, and they also want it to work. If they have found a method that gives them satisfaction, why bother with going through all the other difficult feelings?

Strangely enough, this sign is really looking for inner purity. They want to be good, admirable, and nice people, so they have big problems with confronting their deep and dark monsters and not-so-nice shadows. They just want everything to be right and beautiful for everyone, so it becomes easy for them to see the flaws in others but not the flaws in themselves. They can seem very secure, but the truth is that as far as relationships go, they never feel completely safe. They carry an inner insecurity that makes them feel that if anything goes wrong, somehow, they are to blame. One monster they have to wrestle with is the good old Christian ogre of guilt.

They want an ideal world where everybody does what they like, and everybody is kind and considerate to one another. As an Aquarian, you might be surprised by how often what you thought was reality is a castle of air that suddenly crashes to the ground. What life tries to tell you is that if you really want to create a better world, you have to go deep into your own psyche and understand your own fears and the powers that drive you. In fact, it is very simple for this sign: if they really want to make the world a better place, they must begin with themselves. Psychological insight is of great benefit to all Aquarians. They have to analyze and understand their own motivations and workings. They have to see how they are put together and then see how they can take out their different parts, clean them, fix them, and then put them back together again.

Aquarians like the childish and the innocent, the sensitive and the dreamy. They want to have an inner world of clarity, romance, and beauty. In their hearts, they all long to be poets, but very few of them are called to that. For them, sex is in fact not primarily a sensual or even a sexual experience. It is a sublime search after an experience that will lift them to a higher level of existence. In fact, they have no taste for that which has lost its mystery. On this level, the body is really a temple for them, and the sexual participants are the priests and priestesses of the temple. They are always searching for something perfect—and also the perfect partner. In fact, they are so idealistic that nobody, not even themselves, can live up to these ideals.

As another sign, it is good to remember that what is taboo for others might not be so for the Aquarian. What for them constitutes a taboo might be something very strange or very normal for the rest of us. What is hidden at the very depth of the Aquarian is their romantic vulnerability, their naive goodness, and that they are more sensitive and needy than they ever show. They like to present themselves as logical and rational beings of common sense, but those who get to know them better become aware that hidden behind that cerebral front is a pink Bambi heart.

Education, Adventure, and Life Philosophy

Aquarians love places with interesting people and cultures. They are more into humans and meetings than nature. They also have a great adoration for the exquisite and beautiful. That goes for art and buildings as well as for humans (especially the kind they are erotically interested in). Aquarians love to explore the world but are not so fond of doing so by themselves. They want company, and if they start out by themselves, they are attracted to traveling companions like moths to a light. More than half the fun comes from having somebody to share the experience and adventure with.

Aquarians can feel intimacy and togetherness with others very quickly—in fact, it is easier for them to feel intimacy with someone they have just met than with those they see almost every day. Their great need for freedom can lead them to withdraw when people get so close that they start to become emotionally dependent on them. The primary reason that Aquarians travel is to meet new people. They learn about countries and cultures by meeting people from those places. Many of them feel little need to travel at all—they prefer to let the world travel to them. On the other hand, Aquarians have a great love for and openness to other cultures, so they might travel just to let the world know that they are neither scared nor closed-minded about other ways to live and think. They have a tendency to find life partners that either come from a different culture or are just very different from themselves.

They enjoy learning new skills with others. They are not great students by themselves, but they thrive in an inspiring environment created by people they like. They like amiable, idealistic, and easygoing togetherness. Justice is highly prioritized by most Aquarians. Naturally, they easily end up in idealistic vocations or places connected with education and/or justice. Another possibility for those more into the "pure mind" thing is having a love affair with their work...or with the computer they work on. They love going to cafés and like to talk about this and that. Aquarians have a lot of thoughts about how the world should be and love to share them. This sign also has a tendency to take all kinds of injustice personally, and they can have trouble grasping that justice is not always the same as equality. They are often good at creating togetherness and unity among people that normally don't have anything in common, but they are also masters of creating divisions and turbulence in situations where everything seemed to be peaceful and quiet. They have a tendency to add a quality that is in opposition to the one that is already present.

As an Aquarian, you will benefit from respecting those who are different from you. You enjoy luxury and quality and will get a lot more of that when you accept the rules others follow when they play the game of life. When you really do your best and want to use your skills and abilities to the best, you are not just very talented but also surprisingly diplomatic. Then you can get almost anybody to feel good in your presence...and that is maybe your greatest gift to the world...to make others feel good in your presence. In case you don't know: the rewards for the person that makes another feel loved and liked are huge and very satisfying.

Goals, Profession, and Career

Work and social standing are important for the Aquarius. They are very determined about their chosen path and work with intensity and great willingness. That is, if they feel deeply about the work they do. If this is not the case, the work seems rather pointless, and they will probably leave within a short period of time. They very much need to do something that they experience as creative and future-oriented. Aquarians have no fear of going into difficult and demanding situations—that is, when they burn for the project. Often, it seems like the bigger the challenges, the more the Aquarian enjoys striving toward them. This is not the sign chosen by those souls who want an easy and fluffy ride through life. If they lose faith and hope in their work, they might become cynical and unhappy manipulators who will do anything just to win the game.

They hit rock bottom when even winning gives them no pleasure and they just feel caught in the cynical and pointless games of others. Then they become sucked into the dark depths of their feelings and really have to fight with all their power just to get some breaths of fresh air every now and then. What kind of work they do and where they do it is of prime importance for this star sign. When it comes down to it, they just have to follow their visions. Nothing else will give them satisfaction. To follow those visions can be unbearable, demanding, and taxing; or inspiring, creative, and satisfying. However, whatever it is and however it goes, it is the most exciting and only meaningful thing they can do. They get their fuel for doing this from the high level of emotional intensity their vision creates in them.

Aquarians have the gift of bringing hope where there was none before. They can bring peace where there was war and solutions where things seemed forever hopeless, but to be successful, they need to be aware of their own intensity and emotional power. If they overlook this dimension of themselves, though their intention may be to bring cooperation, the result may only be more strife and differences. As an Aquarian, you need to find a profession where your assets—engagement, intensity, and strong emotions—are seen as valuable and have a natural place in things. You have the ability to be a grounder but remember that you enjoy doing things with others so much more than doing them alone. Be aware: cooperation takes great willingness to be intimate and vulnerable for Aquarians. It is, in fact, one of the places they experience the strongest intimacy. That comes from the simple fact that nothing is closer to the Aquarian heart than their vision and dreams for the future.

If you are an Aquarian, you must be aware of your own idealism. Sometimes you trust others too much and end up in financial and social disasters because you believed what people said instead of seeing what they did. You must also beware of becoming so skeptical from the tough lessons of life that you lose your trust in humanity. Trust is something that is natural for the heart, but something achieved through time in the human world. As long as you are alert, awake, and engaged, you can work with absolutely anyone and anything, but you will always prefer something that is deeper and that has the potential to be part of a better future for individuals and/or humanity. Simply put, you are not happy with having a career or vocation—you are happy with having a vision and a life quest.

Friends, Future, and Ideals

In this area, Aquarians are like Winnie the Pooh: "Yes, both!" Aquarians love friends—the more the merrier. The same goes for visions for the future. Aquarians only go for sentimentality in areas like partnerships and family businesses. As far as the rest goes, it is the possibility, hope, and great exploration of the unknown that counts. They are more occupied with how things are going to be than how they are. What is known and manifested tends to be a bit boring, and all the work the Aquarian does with such intensity is about creating an even better and greater future. Development and progress are the motivating powers that drive the Aquarian engine on its unending quest for that which is yet to be.

And what is this ideal society Aquarians dream about? It is a future of endless possibilities where all people can open up freely without restrictions, and therefore do all the things they really want to do. It is a society of abundance; the word "lack" will be taken out of the language, and empathy and sharing are the words of the day. It is a society based on real justice, so no one will be condemned or misjudged. Everyone will be tolerant, open-minded, loving, and accepting…in other words…Utopia.

It is self-evident that the great test for Aquarians is to live in accordance with their own standards without losing their visions and faith in themselves and humanity. One of their great challenges is to keep their childish naivety, optimism, and good intentions as the many small and great difficulties and setbacks of human life fall down on their heads. More important than accomplishing their dreams is in fact keeping their faith in the seemingly impossible. To have moved the world one little step toward their dream is their true vocation—not to do the whole job for humanity single-handedly.

Giving others the same belief that it is possible to create a better future is one of their greatest gifts to us all. Life teaches them irrevocably that we create the future together and all each of us has to contribute is our own little piece of the puzzle. They learn through life to balance the needs of the individual with the needs of the community and learn to see that the right balance differs from situation to situation. As mentioned, Aquarians need to keep their faith and belief in their dreams and visions.

On the other hand, they need to change both methods and visions as the world changes—and to make all this work, they need friends. Aquarians need friends like a fish needs water. Without good friends that challenge them, Aquarians will stiffen and get stuck in old and blocked patterns of thoughts and behaviors. They need to always be open to new ideas, inspiration, and views. They need friends to really understand that the road to the future always is changing and under construction, because the place you stand and the place from which the future is created, the *now*, always is changing and moving. Wanting something for the future together with friends is of great importance. Something you can believe in or hope for together. Enthusiasm, shared visions, and a common search for new horizons are the most important ingredients in friendship for Aquarians.

Seeking and the Spiritual

Aquarians are a bit odd here as well. In spite of their openness and curiosity, they are generally quite skeptical and do not easily believe in anything. They do not exclude any possibilities, but since anything is possible, how does one separate fantasy, superstition, and imagination from the real thing? In the area of faith and belief, Aquarians often become the most old-fashioned and pigheaded of the lot. When they lack security, they often return to the old and well-trodden roads and methods and accepted scientific ideas. For lack of something better, they start to believe in the collective truth, which is the belief accepted by most beings in the moment. The need to perform a reliable test before anything is taken for granted often blocks Aquarians from moving ahead in their spiritual development. Their religious and spiritual attitude will be based on serious examinations or just their personal experience. The exception is when they subject themselves to a spiritual authority and stop using their capacity for independent thought.

When this sign loses the ability to be open and curious, they can be severely bigoted, brainwashed fundamentalists. Because it is such a big leap to becoming a fanatic, when they do get lost in that way, they leap further and more intensely than others. When they blindly trust others' ideas or their own fanatic beliefs, that is the last thing they will admit. They believe that they are just seeing and following the truth, as should be obvious to everybody. It is very difficult for them to see through their own false beliefs and acceptance of false authorities. They seldom exclude God as a possibility but want absolute proof before they accept that such a being exists. Once they have accepted it, however, there is often no more doubt, either of God's existence or that of their own version of the supreme force. The truth of personal experience is a narrow road that they must walk to the spiritual, but it is at the same time the only road for them. There is no way to find the answers they want through their normal, open-minded way of seeking. They have to accept what they cannot understand in order to find that which they so dearly want to know—a paradox, like most things with this sign. They have to explore the spiritual universe in order to get the experiences that make them want to explore the spiritual dimension further. As you can see, it can be difficult to get started. Since they are not certain about there being any spiritual dimension to explore, why waste the time trying? If they are caught in the idea that there is no spiritual reality, they have a tendency to get more and more stuck. The same goes if they think they have found the eternal truth.

Aquarians need a gentle kick, either from the universe or from some good friends, so that they can open their eyes. That can mean beginning to explore the fantastic scenery that exists in the inner spiritual dimensions, or it can mean opening their eyes to other possible spiritual realities besides the one they are fanatically clinging to. As they start to explore their inner spiritual world, they experience—to their own astonishment—that the world that always has been the most real to them is this inner dimension. In fact, they have always experienced the outer world as quite absurd—sometimes humorous, sometimes tragic. In fact, the outer material world does not really make any sense to them until they get a hold of their inner world and the spiritual dimension of existence. It is a revelation for them when they begin to understand that what most of us call "reality" is in fact an illusion, and that what most of us call illusions and fantasy is the real thing.

For Aquarians, this makes life so much clearer, more understandable, and more meaningful. This quest might be the single greatest challenge for those born with the Sun in Aquarius. There are few who get greater joy from finding the spiritual path to wisdom and unity—and few who have a more difficult road to walk before they find it.

Pisces

February 19th—March 20th

Element: Water
Quality: Mutable
Ruling Planet: Neptune

How to Present Yourself

Showing others your true self is easier said than done for Pisces. How can you show others your true self when you are a bit insecure about who that might be? There are a lot of candidates, and who you are is not a constant pillar of existence but an ever-moving ocean of identity. You can change from moment to moment. As a Piscean, you can handle this situation in two basic ways: you can either simply be as changeable as you naturally are or create one fixed and stable picture of yourself that you cling to as you present it as your identity to the world. Some

Pisceans have a serial monogamous relationship to their own changing personality. This image of identity can be the victim, the victorious, the insecure, the listener, the dreamer, the strong, the weak, and so on.

Pisceans have just as many possible personalities as there are fish in the ocean. Some chose the shark rather than the pink kisser fish. The other strategy is to not have any personality at all—to become like a fish, slippery enough that no one can ever grab or hold you. This variety of Pisces slips through your fingers as you try to hold them. They do not accept being classified or thrown into some stupid aquarium. The Pisces has a great inner need to show their feelings. They need to touch and be touched by the hearts of others. Something that often confuses both Pisceans and their fellow travelers is that the feelings of a Pisces do not need to be personal. Even they do not always know if it is the content of the feeling that has some meaning or if it is enough just to have it. It is like love. To love is maybe more important than who and how you love. As a Piscean, it is important to show your true sensitivity to others. You have a need for others to understand your vulnerability at the same time you have to show and be respected for your strength.

When necessary, you can be quite tough and cut the crap with blades of steel. That is your professional side—as a private being, you are more on the open and vulnerable side. In some ways, as an individual, you give responsibility for you not being exploited and used over to others. You can change your looks based on your mood and how the wind is blowing that day. You are often like a chameleon and can change the way you look to flow with your surroundings. Seen from the outside, it is easy to believe that you have no core and no real substance behind that soft and gracious presentation. You can be more like a beautiful jellyfish that just glides on by in the water of life: not possible to grab, but beautiful to behold as it glides in and out of view. You might have problems with seeing and understanding so clearly that outer presentations are just an endless flow of masquerades. As you grow, you understand that it is not what you do that matters at all, nor who you are—it is how you are and how you do what you do! You have a great need to give to the world from your cornucopia of creativity. Sometimes, you can be so engulfed in the emotions, dreams, and problems of others that you totally forget your own. It is important for you to use your abilities to sift through the material—not only the material you receive from others but also what you give out. In some ways, you are the one giving form and identity to yourself! You are to choose who you are and what you show—if you do not do this job, you can easily be formed by the dreams others carry for you. This might be seen as the one all-important task for a person born in Pisces: to build and create a clear, beautiful, and coherent experience of identity that works in the outer world.

How to Get the Best from Your Talents and Resources

The Pisces is at their best when they concentrate on one thing at a time. It often gets a bit chaotic and confusing when there are too many options available. The Pisces need to be inspired to use their full potential. It can be very destructive for them if they really want something but stop themselves from doing it because they are insecure or think it is too demanding and taxing. Hesitation leads to a place of idleness, or to a Pisces, a feeling like they just do what others tell them to do. They need to take direct and spontaneous action on their impulses if they want to use their talents creatively. There is no way around throwing themselves into the unknown. They will never get a prefilled contract that says things will work out as they wanted them to. They are here to learn to use their will, courage, and initiative to create something new. Resistance—their own as well as that of others—and the dangerous voyage into unknown territory are part of the package.

As a Piscean, you must learn to stand on your own two feet in order to create your own material and financial foundation for your life and development. The only one who can really help you develop your resources and talents is *you*. Others can tell you about your opportunities, they can even follow you to them. But you are the one that has to grab them, use them, and hone them into something even greater. You have to throw yourself out into the deep end and then learn to stand by yourself. It is important for Pisceans to go through this process of learning to trust themselves and acquire an identity. Pisceans manage best when they are not practically dependent on others.

The Piscean values others who have created things with their personal will and talents. They adore those who have shown courage and conquered their dreams. So to adore and respect themselves, the Pisces needs to do what challenges them and find what gives them a true sense of value and satisfaction. Feeling their own value is especially important for a Piscean—otherwise, they will allow others to treat them as if they were without value, and will become a victim that is totally dependent on the compassion and understanding of others. It is not good for them to sacrifice their own sense of worth and value to be kind and help others.

As a Piscean, your greatest talent and resources are, in fact, your courage and ability to take action when it is demanded. It is the ability both to throw yourself into the deep water and then to swim like the fish you are. Your greatest talent is to stay sensitive and still stand in the conflict and take the pressure of life. You can handle so much pressure when you trust yourself and really want to be and do what you are. The halfhearted and so-so is nothing for a Pisces. There is no trying, only doing, as some masters put it. Taking initiative and direct action is best, and remember to play with all your cards open and visible. Try to yield too much and you will lose your own standing. Be courageous and you will grow strong-hearted and even braver.

Communication and Immediate Surroundings

Being safe in the daily environment that they move through is maybe the most important factor in getting a Pisces to feel security. It can be the working environment, the place they live, or their relationship to friends that gives them the necessary dose of stability and predictability. Since it is so changeable within itself, this sign has a hard time handling an outer environment that is too fluid and changeable. When their inner feeling of themselves is fluid, it becomes very important to have some solid rocks of reality to hold onto in the outer world.

Habits are a delicious luxury and sense of safety for Pisceans. Of course, there is the danger that they will become so enslaved by their habits and their surroundings that they get stuck as solidly as if their emotional feet have been planted in concrete. It does feel difficult to move on if your feet are stuck in a slab of concrete made up of obligations and addictions to people and situations that do not hold great personal importance to you. Pisceans may be so caught up in the routines of daily life that they lose their ability for intimacy. They become like fish that are caught in small ponds, almost without water, and have forgotten about the ocean.

Pisceans are better off with a few close friends than knowing everybody and not really being close to anybody. They enjoy talking but can also get very tired of it. Their tendency is to talk quite a lot and then say nothing at all. They are very good at talking about things in a concrete and practical way, so they may be confusing, because when it comes to doing those things, they might be very unpractical. Where the words end, their body language begins. It is easier for them to show their emotions through the way they touch you or through what they do for you than through words. In reality, the Pisces finds words quite inaccurate and unreliable. The only thing that can really convey their heart is their action. They love words but are, paradoxically enough, very skeptical of them. Their mind enjoys simple and clear-cut areas like data, mathematics, and other technical and practical areas. The reason they need so many words is because they try to describe that which cannot be put into words! In some sense, all Pisceans are poets. Sometimes they give in to despair and become lost for words. They feel lonely and like nobody will ever understand them; they do not even understand themselves. This place of no more words can give room for a silent acceptance of the depth and space that is behind them, a space where reality can be shared instead of the thoughts or descriptions of it.

As a Piscean, you need to know that you can seem quite substantial and fixed in your opinions. The more you feel insecure on the inside, the more you will feel the need to seem secure in your presentation. This strange mixture of something very real and concrete and something abstract and fluid in the way you communicate might easily lead to misunderstandings. To avoid this, you need to use language that is very clear and concrete when you want to share and communicate practical things to others. Choose language that is poetic and full of metaphors and nuances when it is the inner world that you want to communicate.

Home and Family

Pisceans often feel like they have more than one home. They have their birth family, but they may also adopt the family of a friend, or they become adopted by the family of their partner. Maybe they feel like part of the family of someone from a different country that they met on a vacation. Pisceans easily get to know new people—if they are open to getting to know anybody at all. They can be very close to almost everybody, and at the same time, they might miss the whole thing with this closeness. That comes from the fact that it is so natural for them that they do not really see the significance. There is a problem with limits, though, since they can shift their emotional baggage very quickly. One moment they are very close and intimate with you, and in the next, they are waving goodbye and seem like a coldblooded fish. They do not easily feel the difference between one kind of love and another. For them, love is love, and the limits society puts around love are not their inner limits. Pisceans know how to entertain themselves.

They have a rich inner universe. In fact, they have a diverse variety and multitude of creations in the inner universe. Because of this, they are seldom bored, but do need to get in contact with others to really feel that they are real and have bodies. The home of a Piscean is not for relaxation and rest, but a place to study, read, listen to music, and to have company— to stimulate and be stimulated. They are seldom silent and still when they are alone. They are running around in the house or apartment in whirling activity—except for the times when they are totally engulfed by the whirling activity of their inner world. Home is first and foremost a place to develop, learn, and explore. There will most often be a lot of entertaining things like books, computers, films, and so on in their home. They are not especially interested in order but are often phenomenal at knowing where things are located in what others experience as pure chaos. They enjoy getting unexpected visitors—except for when they are just too exhausted from all the activities and hobbies that fill most of the moments in their lives.

They enjoy sitting on the couch and talking for hours, whether with in-person visitors or on the phone or through the internet. Mostly, they love to have contact with other human beings when they are in their own little den. Home is not a place to withdraw, but a foundation for reaching out to the world.

Pisceans have a tendency to overfill their homes with a multitude of gadgets and things. You would think that they are sentimental, but that is not the case for most of them. The exception is children and their own childhood. The Pisces just likes to fill their space with things they find interesting and entertaining. One task they have to work on learning throughout life is choosing between what to throw away and what to keep. For them, home is not a place where they can think and that they can use as a communication center in their life. A telephone-addicted Piscean would feel as if they lost their hold on the world and their home and foundation if they lost their mobile phone, with all the numbers and names in it. In some ways, they also need the home to be a place where they can mentally digest all the thoughts and impressions they have received during the day. This digestion happens through the mind—they digest by thinking through everything with all the different parts of the brain. Almost like how cows digest grass in all their stomachs. As a Piscean, be aware that you need this time to digest all the thoughts and ideas that you have experienced during the day. You have to remind yourself of the fact that you need some time for peace and quiet and give yourself the space you need to develop your consciousness and find your inner wisdom.

Creativity and Leisure

When it comes to expressing themselves creatively, Pisceans are very vulnerable and take things very seriously and personally. As children, they were often a bit dependent on their parents. Becoming emotionally and practically independent takes a long time for the Piscean being. Grown-ups of this sign easily revert to behaving like children, desperately searching for somebody to love them unconditionally. They are romantics that easily project their longing for emotional safety and sustainment onto others.

Pisceans enjoy using their leisure time to do something that is connected with emotions and intimacy. They might enjoy gardening, cooking, or holding small gatherings for their friends. Their experience of themselves and the meaning of having freedom are closely knitted to their emotional states. Sometimes they just feel empty, but more often, they want to really get everything out of every minute and go at a speed of 110 mph. Sometimes they just love to flirt and seduce and feel intimacy, love, and joy with almost anyone. At other times, they feel shut out, alone, and misunderstood. Their feelings are seldom calm and in the middle. They are strong and rather heavily lean toward one side or the other, and Pisceans just *love* to display all their feelings. As children, they enjoyed playing games that stimulated their feelings or gave them a sense of stability and belonging.

It is often well hidden, but Pisceans are shy beings. They want you to understand what they feel and sense who they are without them having to show it, tell it, or demonstrate it. The exception is when they really want something from the depths of their heart. Then they are very direct and leave no doubt about their wishes. Activity with a Piscean can be just sitting and feeling together. Pisceans easily believe that the person that is most attentive and understanding when they try to seduce you is the kindest one, and they often get disappointed, because being the most eager does not necessarily mean that you are the kindest. Because of this, Pisceans are not always good at choosing what they want, but easily become seduced by those who want them the most. They must learn that loving somebody and wanting to spend your life with them are two different things.

As for love, the Pisces need to see that the deepest love is not always so wild and romantic, but rather it is full of compassion and willingness to be there when it counts. They need to get a deep understanding of the difference between love as an open-ended ocean and something that is deeply personal. Their expectation that others will feel them and know what they want without them having to say it is the source of much grief and disappointment. As a Pisces, you need to understand the magic worked by being able to express and communicate your need and longings. You must learn to tell others what you want, when you want it, and how you want it. Show the world what you wish, and you might be surprised…you will start to get it!

Health, Order, and the Necessary

You can trust in this sign to do what is necessary. They like to feel that what they do is extraordinary and special, so they can take on tasks that are too much for others and do them with great energy. As far as their capacity for working goes, they are either working like hell or lazy lumps. It is like this: if they feel that the work they do is meaningless and unappreciated, they become very lazy and lose their interest. If they feel they are respected and enjoy themselves and what they are doing, they can just go on working and working and working...and then work even more. As long as they have some interest in it, they put their honor into doing a great job. The Pisces does not like professional carelessness—not taking things so seriously is left for their personal life. They like to be prepared and have warning so they can tidy up before they get visitors. They want to make a good impression because they think that the way you perform says something about who you are. This is also a clue about how to learn about Pisceans: look at how they accomplish their work and tasks. This observation will tell you more about their true nature than anything else.

Pisceans like to learn and explore themselves by seeing what they can manage and create through their work. Work is not something they do; it is an expression of who they are—they love to excel. If somebody beams when they are chosen as the worker of the month, it is Pisces. Unselfishness and humility in the professional area are not natural traits with these beings. They want so much praise, acknowledgment, and recognition that it can become too much and lead in the wrong direction. One danger is that others will praise and respect them, but they will not respect or enjoy themselves. It is best for Pisceans to find work and do things where they can experience pleasure and be of use to others. This feeling of giving to others provides them with a sense of self-respect. The joy of giving is especially joyful for this sign. Work is very important for Pisceans because it is so important for their experience of their life being worthy and having a deeper meaning.

The health issues of Pisceans are quite simple. If they feel good, their health is excellent. When they feel bad, disrespected, and not of value, all that goes into the body. Almost all health issues stem from lack of self-respect and lack of inner feelings of worth. As long as they enjoy life and thrive with themselves, their health seems to be made of iron. As a Piscean with health issues, you should treat yourself with as much care, attention, luxury, and acknowledgment as you can manage. You so much love to feel chosen, and the joy of that begins with choosing yourself.

As a Pisces, you like to be a leader and can be really great at it, but you can also be a very good employee and thrive in any position in a hierarchy as long as you feel respected and somehow chosen. You very much enjoy knowing that it is only you that can do the work that you do and knowing that others are dependent on you for things going right and working out. You do not enjoy being taken for granted, and when that happens, you easily become ill and/or depressed. So do and be what you respect yourself for doing and being, and others will tag along and begin to respect you for what you are and what you do.

One-on-One Relationships

As far as relationships go, love doesn't fall on just anybody for this sign. Even if Pisceans feel love toward humankind in general, their preferences for a partner can be very specific and detailed. One of them is that they want to be of service to their partner, so needing them to save, rescue, or help you is one effective method to seduce a Pisces. But remember, while they are very picky as far as partners go, that doesn't mean that you need to be just as picky. They often fall for those who are the easiest to love. They do not want to be loved a little, but to be the most loved by a partner with a great heart. The road to their heart can go through strange details connected with the way they look , walk, or talk. Pisceans take their choice of personal friends and partners very seriously. They can be very critical and hold high ideals for their close ones, but they are also very loyal toward them.

Pisceans often believe the best of others but fear the worst. They can easily feel hurt or intimidated by their partners. They can be extremely vulnerable to rejection and criticism. Pisceans may be stuck with humans and relationships that no longer fulfill their needs and longings. In their hearts, they are dreamers, while in their brains, they are morc practical and codependent. They are one of the most romantic signs and dream about the one love that is the partner of their soul and the one chosen for eternity. Perfect and everlasting love is how they feel it should be. It might not be necessary to mention that Pisceans often get disappointed in love. Sometimes it stems from the fact that their dreams and longings are so unrealistic and full of pink fantasy illusions. At other times, they seek a partner that really is difficult and demanding and not so nice to be around; but if the Pisceans get a hang of how to have a relationship and it starts to work, you won't find a being with a greater ability to show affection and generosity and to love without craving something in return. The Pisces is rarely jealous and likes to grant their partner great freedom. They really do not want to be loved because their partner doesn't have any choice. Pisces often gives a partner all the possibilities they long for. Pisces will often go on loving their partner even if their partner hurts them deeply.

A Piscean knows how to appreciate the small things and gestures—those that show that you love them in unexpected situations and ways. Of course, the grand displays of romance also go deep into the heart and soul of a Pisces. In fact, they have a great ability to appreciate any sign of love from those that they love. If you really have found the way into the soul of the heart of a Pisces, you know that love between two humans is something holy and unimaginably beautiful for them. It is this sense of the sacred and unblemished that they seek in relationships, and their greatest joy is to experience the sensation of this beauty in their hearts. If you really want to stay with a Piscean, it is quite "easy." All you have to do is love them without regret or remorse and look at the relationship as a unique gift.

Beneath the Surface—Sex and Taboos

Pisceans are not trying to break taboos. They are not even interested in crossing lines or breaking out of limitations—at least not just for the fun of it. If they should set out for such a journey, they want to do it together with another person. Their reason for delving into the depths of the human mind and soul is to find the deepest truth of the heart, and Pisceans need to delve to the depths with others to find out the truth about themselves. This is a strange dilemma for many Pisceans: the closer they get to someone, the more they feel the distance and that which still divides. They can feel so close to people that are unknown to them, but the closer they get, the more the differences become visible. At the same time, real intimacy comes to Pisces through really understanding and seeing that others are different and something other than themselves. Having two different people that can meet and share things is a deeper and scarier side of intimacy for Pisces than crawling under the skin of another person and feeling the unity.

The strongest and deepest relationships for Pisces develop when they are able to totally surrender to the relationship and at the same time fully accept the distance from their partner. They benefit greatly from understanding that it is the distance that creates the possibility for true meetings and a very special and valuable intimacy. So, in some ways, they have to cross all the borders and taboos and still live within their own limits. It is after this transformation through true meetings that they can understand that equality is something very different from equanimity. This is shown as an unlimited understanding and respect for their own and others' unique, individual personalities. This understanding is connected to simple rights like freedom, equality, and justice for all. When this understanding is not theoretical but embedded in the Piscean heart and soul, it can never be lost again. They enjoy secret romantic affairs and have a taste for everything that smells of luxury, style, and high class.

As a lover, Pisces wants to be exclusive and to have a style and standard that is special and exquisite. They have the ability to be incredibly thoughtful and elegant, and they often get satisfaction and peace from giving their partner satisfaction and peace. If you seek refined elegance rather than carnal lust when it comes to sexuality, Pisces might be the partner for you—and they know how to play most erotic games. Whatever they go into, they will do it with a certain amount of unique style and class.

Education, Adventure, and Life Philosophy

Even if this sign is very open to every possibility, they delve in deep before they really commit and believe in some of the possibilities. They know how easily they can become enthusiastic, so how can they really trust in what feels so great and promising? Many Pisceans grab hold of a truth that makes them feel comfortable and secure. It can be either to not believe in anything or to have one specific philosophy and spiritual view that they cling to with all their might. At the same time, they will always know in the depths of their inner space that nothing is absolutely certain, and everything is possible.

Pisceans can hesitate for a long time before they choose an education and set off on a road through life. They have trouble with finding what they really want to do. On the other hand, they are persistent and get an education that gives them opportunities to create a safe and stable life. They are not so much after money as they are after something that is emotionally safe and gives them opportunities to live through, and with, their feelings. When a Piscean knows what they really want to do, they follow their destiny and goal with a firmness and persistence that helps them use their abilities and opportunities to the fullest. They have the stamina to do almost anything they feel strongly about once the decision is made, and trouble and challenges are no hindrance. They are expected and welcomed as part of the road.

They enjoy it when there exists a little resistance, so they have to mobilize a little more. This goes for education as well as journeys and traveling. They like challenges, tests, and anything that gives them the ability to discover their true nature and strength. They do not seek out places to find rest and niceties. They seek out places to find challenges and new experiences. If nothing interesting happens, they will create the entertainment and challenges themselves. They are known to start scandals or have dangerous liaisons and shady affairs just to get something to happen. They like to visit the same country many times and really delve deeply into the language and culture. The same goes for education—they always want to go deeper and learn more and grow in skills and wisdom. They often like to dig down deep and then look at all they have dug up to see if something is usable.

As for justice and judgment, they can have strong opinions. They are into moral righteousness and punishment. Justice is a sensitive topic for Pisceans. Even though they have—or maybe because they have—this great capacity for love, they can fully understand the need for revenge and punishment. One of the things that really fascinates them is the human mind and its inner workings. They love to explore the unknown inner scenery, the ugly as well as the beautiful. Pisceans love to delve to the bottom of the human psyche, and this fact has a very important influence on their choice of both education and journeys.

Goals, Profession, and Career

Pisceans want to know! That is their main goal in life: to know how things work and the meanings behind them. They have an inner drive that makes them always long for expanded horizons and a greater understanding of all areas of life. They also have a great need to share their insights, opinions, and ideals with the rest of humanity. They love to communicate what they perceive as the truth, and they long to do something important and great, so they have to start with finding out what they think is of great importance to them.

In so many ways, the life of this Fish is to swim around in the great ocean of feelings, searching for meaning and food for their heart and mind. However much they have seen and discovered, there is always something more and unexplored in the endless ocean. One of the cruelest things a Pisces can do to themselves is to stop seeking expansion and meaning. A Pisces needs a job they can believe in and a job with a vision. They also need to have horizons so that they see something to reach for. They need to feel that life can always be better and even more exciting. They have the ability to grab something very small, hold it, and see the possibilities in that tiny little thing, then help it to grow and expand into something great.

This sign needs to be in contact with things that are in growth and movement. They would bore themselves to death if their purpose in life was to make sure that the status quo stayed unchanged. They have a unique talent for spreading enthusiasm and eagerness to their coworkers. Because of this, they might get a bit burned out from giving so much of their fire to others. Others do not see this tiredness in the early stages. It is only people close to them, like family and really good friends, that will be shown the despair before it blooms. As a Piscean, you have to be sure that you have a job you really enjoy, and at the same time, you have to learn to know your limits. You are not there to give meaning to everybody around you or to lift and uphold the heart and courage of everyone. You have to be sure that you get enough nourishment yourself before you so generously start to give to others. Further education, taking classes in new topics, and learning new skills are ways to nourish yourself. You also need to be aware of the line between professional support and care and the personal. At work, you cannot be responsible for the personal feelings and welfare of everyone around you. Also, be aware of the differences between personal and professional intimacy for others. You might step over their boundaries without knowing it. Caught up in your own enthusiasm and intensity, you might send signals that can be misunderstood or get involved in things that are really none of your business. Your unstoppable, go-ahead spirit and belief that everything is possible is one of your greatest resources, but do not use this to push others into places where they are uncomfortable and insecure. In many ways, you often have just what it takes to make the seemingly impossible possible—if you just remember to breathe deeply and take good aim before you let the arrow fly toward the future. To do this, you need a job with a lot of exchange of ideas and information at the same time as it is goal oriented and stimulating.

Friends, Future, and Ideals

This is a serious area for the fish, perhaps the most serious area of them all. Family is, in a way, something you are born into. Lovers come and go. Partners might last for life, but you can never be completely sure of that, and there are so many facets of life with a partner where there is also so much struggle, and where deep stuff that rises to the surface must be dealt with. Friends, on the other hand, are a choice, and people you will stick with for life. Some Pisceans have a few friends that they made early on and stick with until they die. Others float around without really connecting deeply with anyone. It is like they are unaware of the qualities that are found in friendship before they start to get a bit up there in the years, but the friends that are found in the mature years will be highly valued and have great significance for the Pisces. Some Pisceans may misunderstand and believe that acquaintances are the same as friends. They feel that they have lots and lots of close friends and are curious about how lonely they still feel beneath the surface. When this sign really has understood the significance and worth of friendship, there are few who respect, honor, and appreciate their friends more. Those few chosen friends might be the most important humans in the life of this sign; the one element they would be unable to face life without.

Pisceans are addicted to having dreams and hopes for the future. At the same time, they are very occupied with what is possible to manifest here and now. It is like they have one set of dreams for the long run and one set for situations in the here and now. Finding the right balance between the utopian dream of a paradisiacal future and the short-term dreams of what is the best to do in a given circumstance is important work for Pisceans. They need to avoid the neither-nor and get into the either-or. They can become unsatisfied visionaries with impossible goals, or unsatisfied pragmatists that never reach for the stars. The trick is to not become enslaved by existing realities or by distant dreams. It is rather to, in a pragmatic way, see how they can move the world closer to paradise.

The Pisces must be aware that they aren't taking too much responsibility for their friends. They have to trust others to be capable enough to handle their own affairs and they have to show their friends trust and respect in this way by believing in their capabilities. At the same time, a mature Fish is a friend you can trust. They come for help when asked, not because they do not trust you to handle the situation by yourself. The Fish will be there whatever the reason and whatever it takes if they are your real friend and you have asked for their support. As they develop, Pisceans really understand that one of the most important parts of being human is being there for each other when it is really needed.

Seeking and the Spiritual

For this sign, the spiritual is a universe that might or might not be explored. They know that it exists and is real in one sense of the word or another, but it is not always something they want to spend time and energy exploring. Sometimes, the mystery of human life and emotions is so great that it simply fills their need for mystery and the unknown. In some ways, the inner spiritual world is always present for Pisceans, even if they might call it something different. You could say that for them, they already live in a world that is full of spirit, and so they can forget all about spirit and think that this is all that is. Really exploring the spiritual as a unique dimension requires a decision and choice from the Fish. Why choose to explore the ocean when you live in the sea and all you do every day is explore the ocean anyway?

Some Pisceans are very spiritual and religious from early childhood; others lose their faith easily or have never had any. One thing they have in common is that it takes effort to conquer their own spiritual understanding and faith. They have a tendency to just carry on the tradition they were born into. As a Fish, you may easily just glide along with the current and choose the path of least resistance. The Piscean that really wants to find their own spiritual truth has to do so like the salmon. They have to go against the current and swim up the river to find where the stream and they themselves came from. They have to take a very personal and individual journey and delve into what religion and spirituality are to them. Not what it is in a collective sense, but what it means in a very personal way.

Most other signs go the other way around. When they get a sense of the collective and impersonal spiritual force, God, essence, the absolute, or whatever it is named, they understand their own spirituality and find the meaning of their life. Pisceans have, as mentioned, natural contact with this Source. They have to find their own personal spiritual identity and find the meaning and significance within their personal existence to really get a hold of that which we call spiritual truth. The great question for this sign is not if the universe has any meaning, but if their personal existence inside the universe has a meaning. Sometimes they stop searching because they know that if they find the answers, they have to take full responsibility for living out these truths in their daily life. As long as they just float around, they can avoid this responsibility, but they also avoid finding any significant meaning for their own existence.

Pisceans know in their hearts that the most important thing in life is the spiritual truth and that we are spirits just traveling through this Earthly life. This responsibility can seem quite demanding and tremendous before it is taken. Afterward, it feels like the one thing that is most natural and in tune with who they really are. In some ways, the realization of the spiritual truth has the consequence that one has to change both their inner and their outer life. The Pisces often has to stop living the life they have lived until now and begin a new one. Spiritually, Pisceans fall into one of two categories. They can be spiritually indecisive, hard to pinpoint, and avoid taking a stand. They flow with the stream and avoid the unpleasant. They do not live out the passions of their hearts but try to be as nice and lovable as possible. The other category is where they have taken a stand and seen everything, including God or their spiritual view, as a very personal matter. Where they stand and what they think and feel around this will be crystal clear, and no one will misunderstand what they think. They can be very persuasive priests or atheists. When they really have taken it in, they have filled their heart with the essence of love, both the personal and the impersonal. Even if they do not always have the words, they know in their hearts that we are one, that the universe is whole and inseparable and filled with love. The magic in some sense of the word is no longer magical, but completely natural…and, of course, still unfathomably magical.

About the Author

Per Henrik has been teaching, giving private consultations, and coaching in astrology and tarot for his entire adult life. A graduate of the University of Oslo, he has a master's degree in theater studies with honors as well as a major in Religious History with a focus on Norse Mythology and Mysticism. In addition to these accomplishments, he is also a trained firewalking instructor. Per Henrik started the Nordic School of Astrology in 1992 and has many storied years of experience in teaching, consultations, coaching and lectures. He is also an ardent theater lover and has participated with many independent theater groups as an actor, director and playwright.

Over the years, Per has written 20 books on astrology, several books on tarot, philosophy, reincarnation, mythology and the spiritual history of mankind, as well as a series of children's books in Norway. Many of his works have been translated into Danish, and several are considered classics in tarot and astrology.

Per Henrik Gullfoss has worked with alternative consciousness since 1980. He was the initiator of the Nordic School of Astrology, which began to train astrologers in 1992. Today, he trains astrologers and beginners who want to work with spiritual astrology and take a closer look at the soul's intention to incarnate on this planet. He is also co-editor and writer for the magazines Harmoni and Orakel. He entered the international market with "The Complete Book of Spiritual Astrology", which was published by the American publisher Llewellyn in 2009 with its latest edition being published by Chicago-based publisher, Crossed Crow Books.

In addition to being a creative astrologer and spiritual inspirer, Per Henrik is an eminent lecturer and is known for having a lively, entertaining and professionally inspiring way of conveying his messages. In addition to countless lectures in Norway, Sweden and Denmark, he has given a series of lectures in England and the USA.

More from Crossed Crow

Available Titles

The Complete Book of Spiritual Astrology by Per Henrik Gullfoss
Icelandic Plant Magic by Albert Bjorn
Flight of the Firebird by Kenneth Johnson
The Black Book of Johnathan Knotbristle by Chris Allaun
A Witch's Book of Terribles by Wycke Malliway
In the Shadow of Thirteen Moons by Kimberly Sherman-Cook
Merlin: Master of Magick by Gordon Strong
The Way of Four by Deborah Lipp
Celtic Tree Mysteries by Steve Blamires
Star Magic by Sandra Kynes
A Spirit Work Primer by Naag Loki Shivanaath
A Witch's Shadow Magick Compendium by Raven Digitalis
Witchcraft and the Shamanic Journey by Kenneth Johnson
Travels Through Middle Earth by Alaric Albertsson
Craft of the Hedge Witch by Geraldine Smythe
Be Careful What You Wish For by Laetitia Latham-Jones
Death's Head by Blake Malliway
The Wildwood Way by Cliff Seruntine

Forthcoming Titles

Magic of the Elements by Deborah Lipp
Witches' Sabbats and Esbats by Sandra Kynes
Dance of the Sun Goddess by Kenneth Johnson
Witchcraft Unchained by Craig Spencer
Tarot Unveiled by Gordon Strong
King Arthur: The Wasteland and the New Age by Gordon Strong
Sun God and Moon Maiden by Gordon Strong
Aislings by Jeremy Schewe
Wiccan Magick by Raven Grimassi
Wiccan Mysteries by Raven Grimassi
Cauldron of Memory by Raven Grimassi

Learn more at
www.CrossedCrowBooks.com